LITERATURE ITS PRINCIPLES AND PROBLEMS

LITERATURE ITS PRINCIPLES AND PROBLEMS

THEODORE W. HUNT

GYAN

Published by

Gyan Publishing House
5, Ansari Road
Daryaganj, New Delhi-110002
Phone: 011-47034999, 9811692060
E-mail: books@gyanbooks.com

Distribution Network
gyanbooks.com
India, USA, Canada, UK, Australia

ISBN: 978-93-7447-066-4 (PB)

First Published, 1888

2nd Impression 2026

Printed at: Gyan Press, Delhi.

LITERATURE ITS PRINCIPLES AND PROBLEMS
Author: THEODORE W. HUNT

LITERATURE

ITS

PRINCIPLES AND PROBLEMS

LITERATURE

ITS PRINCIPLES AND PROBLEMS

THEODORE W. HUNT, PH.D., LITT.D.

Professor of English in Princeton University, Author of "English Prose and Prose Writers," "Ethical Teachings in Old English Literature," etc.

FUNK & WAGNALLS COMPANY

NEW YORK AND LONDON

1906

TO

THE STUDENTS

OF OUR

LITERARY INSTITUTIONS

CONTENTS

Part First

CHAPTER ONE

PAGE

GUIDING PRINCIPLES IN THE INTERPRETATION OF LITERATURE 3

1. Proper Point of View. More than one possible. External and Internal. Dominance of the subjective.
2. True Relation of the Primary and Secondary. Illustrations—Allen, etc. The microscopic method.
3. The Importance of Beginnings. Value of the Primitive Folk-Lore. Examples.
4. The Notice and Use of Genuine Contrasts (*a–d*). Need of balance and catholicity.
5. Recognition of the Unknown Quantity in Literature. Examples—Complexity, etc. *a–c*). The Law of Exceptions. Evils of dogmatism.
6. The Absence of Pre-Judgments. Examples (*a–b*).
7. Constructive and Positive Criticism.
8. Emphasis of the Inner Spirit of Literature. The difficulty, interest and benefits of the study.

CHAPTER TWO

A DEFINITION OF LITERATURE 20

Difficulty of clear definition. History of opinion. Posnett's four causes of such diversity. Views of Worcester, Hallam, Brooke, Jebb, etc. Emphasis of Posnett's and Bascom's views. Suggestions as to such definitions (1–3). Statement of correct definition. Involves certain elements (1–4). Consequent

PAGE

suggestions: (*a*) A test of productions, as literary or not. (*b*) A test as to degrees of literary quality. (*c*) Unity and diversity of literary forms. (*d*) Union of all elements required. Evil effects of their separation. Literature more than words. Need of this higher conception.

CHAPTER THREE

METHODS OF LITERARY STUDY 36

The question of methods an open one.

1. Literary rather than linguistic. The linguistic element subordinate. Shakespeare. What the literary method involves.
2. Suggestive and Comprehensive. Philosophic. What it involves. A protest against undue minuteness.
3. Logical unity and sequence in English Literature. Literary periods overlap each other.
4. Comparative. England and the Continent. Influence of Italy, France and Germany.
5. Historical. Golden ages reveal it. So, in ages of decline.
6. Independent and Impartial. Authors of the first and second order. Counter Tendencies. The Method and the Man.

CHAPTER FOUR

THE SCOPE OF LITERATURE—LITERATURE AND SCIENCE. 52

Seen in light of definition given. Vinet, etc. Seen in classification of types. Ancient, etc. Posnett's classification of literature.

1. Local or Sectional. 2. National. Developed by guiding minds. 3. The World Literature. Isothermal lines. Goethe's conception. Greek Literature. Literary reciprocity. One of the tests of literature found here.

Discussion of relations of Literature.

PAGE

I. Literature and Science. A priori, little affinity. Pater, Coleridge, etc. Tendency to discover and exalt a relation. Lanier and Devey.

1. A Scientific Method in Literature. Observation, etc. Induction. A science of literature.
2. Scientific Forms in Literature. Prose, philosophic and didactic. Literary criticism. Seen in certain kinds of fiction. Didactic verse.
3. Furnishing of literary material. The scientific imagination. Contributions from Nature. Shairp. Seen in the vastness of the universe. Elements of poetic sublimity. Coleridge, Byron, etc. Kepler, Humboldt, etc. Seen in the highest minds. Lyell, Herschel, etc. Science in Literary form. Pater. Richness of English here. Chaucer, etc.

This relationship essential to right study. Huxley.
Science and Literature have their respective fields.
Differences exist. Error of Huxley.
Science is to be kept within its limits.

CHAPTER FIVE

LITERATURE AND PHILOSOPHY 69

An important question. Herbert Spencer. Use of the word, philosophy.

1. Science of Thought and its Expression. Error of excluding the mental. Plato, etc. Emerson's view. Vinet.
2. A Philosophic Method in Literature. Introspective. Essential in authorship and criticism. Schlegel. The intellectual style. Schopenhauer.
3. Mutual Interaction and Indebtedness of Philosophy and Literature. Greek literature and philosophy. Ueberweg, etc. Leibnitz and Hegel. So, in France, in the eighteenth century. So, in England, in Augustan Age. Pope, etc. Historic School of Hume. Highest type of each tends to the other. Burt, etc.

PAGE

4. Presence of Imaginatien in each. Philosophic Imagination. Wayland. Illustrated in Dante. Idealistic Philosophy. Berkeley. Plato. Examples. Each to be restricted to its area. Present need of pressing the relationship. German and French philosophers. Kant, etc. So, in Northern Europe. Danger in the line of the abstruse. Pope, Browning. English literary history shows it. The Mystical, Metaphysical and Transcendental Schools. Influence of Edwin Arnold. Middle ground. Leslie Stephen, etc. Rightful primacy of philosophy in literature.

CHAPTER SIX

LITERATURE AND POLITICS 85

The word, Politics, A priori, etc.

A. Grounds of Influence.

1. Civic Questions to be discussed. Political Literature.
2. Literary and Political Environment often the same.
3. Authors and Statesmen in same personality.

B. Specific Forms of Political Literature. Mainly, prose, Reasons.

1. Political History. Examples. Descriptive. (*a*) History of Political Reconstruction. History of Politics, of Government. History of Parties—unpartisan. (*b*) History of Political Revolution. Action and Reaction. French Revolution. History of Parties—partisan. (*c*) History of Political Reformation, Church and State.
2. Political Biography.
3. Political Miscellany. (*a*) The Political Essay. (*b*) The Political Oration—Written and Oral Discourse. (*c*) Political Fiction.
4. Political Poetry. Satire. Inferences (*a*–*e*). Literature and Life.

PAGE

CHAPTER SEVEN

LITERATURE AND LANGUAGE 106

Earle's view. Opposed by others. Agitated by Collins in England.

1. Literary study, in a sense, linguistic. Language a medium of literature. Ways in which language enters. Authors should be students of language. Good English. Alford, etc. Authors thus classified. Professors as teachers of language and authors.
2. Dangerous extreme of the linguistic. (*a*) In Literary Criticism, as a study of words. (*b*) In Literary Manuals. Rolfe. Due, in part, to Old English study. "Anatomists of Literature." Moulton's view. Influence of Germany. French school. Flourishes in times of decline. Milton, Addison. Eliminates the differentia of literature. Language to be taught in the light of literature. Exceptional cases. Discussion as to classics explained. The Knickerbocker School. Language one thing; literature, another. Disciplinary value of literature.

CHAPTER EIGHT

LITERATURE AND LITERARY CRITICISM 121

The present, an age of criticism. Bibliography. Not studied abstractly. Meaning of the term criticism. Literary criticism illustrated. Different species of criticism. Definition of Literary Criticism. Its radical elements. Constructive criticism. Its present status.

I. Primary Purpose. Arnold, Brunetiere, Lowell. Interpretation and Decision. Qualities needed in the critic.
II. Methods. Various views. (*a*) Historical. Hallam, Sismondi, etc. (*b*) Textual. What it involves. (*c*) Esthetic. Application to style. (*d*) Philosophic—its meaning.

PAGE

III. Results. (*a*) Appreciation of Literature. (*b*) Enlargement and Improvement of Literature. (*c*) Education of Public Taste. Problems of interest. Reopening of the Study. Suggestions (*a–b*).

CHAPTER NINE

LITERATURE AND LIFE 139

Language of Courthope and Vinet. The historical view. Change at the Revival of Learning. Literature and Civilization. English literature. Relation of History to Literature. Courthope. An Historical Method in Literature. The Historical Spirit therein. Hallam. Literature more than historical. Taine's threefold theory.

1. Literature and Race, Shemitic and Aryan.
2. Literature and Environment. Lake School.
3. Literature and Epoch. Golden Ages.

Literature and Personality to be added.

Human Life to be studied. Examples. Authorship thus made timely. Piers the Plowman. Literature of the fifteenth century. Permanence of Letters thus conditioned. Literary forms illustrative of this vitality.

1. Fiction as the interpreter of life.
2. Dramatic Verse. National life represented.
3. So, in Lyric Verse.

Danger in the line of the unduly practical. Application to American Literature. Tendency to Commercialism. All true literature real and vital.

CHAPTER TEN

LITERATURE AND ETHICS 156

The word, Ethics. History of opinion. Selkirk, etc. European Literary History. Rome, etc. Meaning of the ethical in literature. Possnett. Literature has always evinced this element.

In History, Poetry, Drama, etc. Its explanation

PAGE

easy. Clerical authors. Brooke. Reasons for this. Theories of Collins, Shairp, Huxley and Arnold.

A. The danger of ultra-moralism in literature. Stedman. Parochial type. Pietism and Puritanism. Taine's rebuke of Addison. So, in the Georgian Era. Thomson. Young. The didacticism of Wordsworth. Arnold of Rugby.

B. Literature and unbelief, as identified. Its causes. Hume and Voltaire. Its forms and periods, varied. So, in Greece, etc. Its harmful results. Remedy found in a new order of philosophy. Modern skeptical literary tendencies. Ward, Arnold, etc. Especially visible in verse, in the form of despondency. Seen in Clough, Goethe, Byrón. Watson more hopeful. A valid connection between Letters and Morals.

CHAPTER ELEVEN

LITERATURE AND THE ARTS 168

A. The Liberal Arts.

Classification of the Arts—Liberal, etc. The liberal professions. Literature, a liberal art. Seen especially in English Literature. Advantages of this.

1. Knowledge gained thereby.
2. Comprehensiveness of mind and view.
3. Scholarship and authorship thus connected. (*a*) Objection as to uneducated authors—Pope, etc. (*b*) Objection as to impeding nature.

Literature and the Liberal Professions. Relation to Divinity. Relation to Law and Medicine. To Journalism and Education. Distinct views, technical and untechnical. Literary Institutions. Authors and Educators—Longfellow, etc.

B. The Fine Arts—Esthetics.

Fine and Useful Arts—Symonds. Literature, an esthetic product. An artistic method in it. Technique. An artistic spirit and purpose—Longinus, etc. Two dangerous extremes.

I. Materialism.

PAGE

2. Formalism. Belles-Lettres. Beneficent work of solid writers—Bacon, etc. The artistic subordinate. Literature as a Fine Art, different in different spheres. Pronounced in poetry. Reasons for undue ornateness. (*a*) An inferior view of literature. (*b*) An inferior view of the arts. Unity of the arts essential. Literature, a comprehensive art, a force.

CHAPTER TWELVE

THE MISSION OF LITERATURE 184

Emerson's "Uses of Great Men." High character of literary work. Prevalence of lower views. Literature an industry. A matter of ambition. Of pleasure. Self-expression the end.

1. Involves the Conception and Interpretation of Great Ideas. Literature tested here. Dante, etc.
2. Interpretation of the Spirit of the Age. General and specific effects sought. Golden ages and Inferior ages reveal it. Literature, a social and civic power. Greece, etc.
3. Interpretation of Human Nature. In drama, fiction, etc.
4. Presentation and enforcement of high Ideals. Involves imagination and sobriety. One of the tests of authorship. Is literature fulfilling these conditions? The poetry of the future. Modern tendencies unliterary. Quantity rather than quality. A World Literature. Federation of Authors.

Part Second

CHAPTER ONE

PAGE

THE AIMS OF LITERARY READING AND STUDY 203

Use of the term, Literary. A form of study now prominent. Reasons.

1. Literary Information, Enlightenment. Function of a Library. Historical Literature. English History on its literary side.
2. Literary Culture. A literary word. Literature a Fine Art. Extreme View. Poetry. Higher rank accorded it.
3. Literary Discipline. Reading and Study accordant. Studious Reading. The disciplinary books in prose and verse.
4. Incentive. Stimulating Literature. Hence, Great Books to be read. Helpful and Wholesome Books. Characteristics of such books (*a–c*). Objectionable Books. *A.* Unmeaning. *B.* Unwholesome. *C.* Unsettling. Responsibilities of Readers.

CHAPTER TWO

THE GENESIS AND GROWTH OF LITERARY FORMS . . 213

Permanent and variable elements in literature. Teutonic type, as distinct from the Latin. Courthope's view. "Conservatism" in Literature. Old and Middle English. The variable Element. Literary Transitions—in Germany, Greece, etc. Proceed by a law. "Movements in Literature." General and special forms. Prose and verse, the most general. Precedence of verse, in time. Reasons. Prose product, variable—Elizabethan, etc.

1. Narrative and Descriptive Prose—Alfred, etc.
2. Forensic Prose, later.
3. Philosophic and Critical Prose, last.

PAGE

Two emphatic forms of prose: *A*. Satire. Combines various elements. Questions as to its origin. *B*. Prose Fiction. Question as to its origin. So, in Verse. Relation of Verse to Prose.

1. Epic verse. Its origin, quality, etc.
2. Dramatic Verse. The Elizabethan Drama. Causes of differing degrees of excellence.
3. Lyric verse. Relation of lyric and dramatic. Inferences.
4. Didactic and Descriptive. *A*. The Naturalness of literature. Chaucer. Age of Elizabeth. Literature, a growth. *B*. A law of Evolution in literature. Symonds. So, in the drama. Literature and Science. *C*. A law of Decadence in literature. Disappearance of schools. General progress. The spirit of literature survives. Literary forms subordinate to life and character.

CHAPTER THREE

PRIMARY POETIC TYPES—GENERAL AND SPECIAL . . . 230

Possible classifications. As varied as style.

A. Devey's threefold division.
1. The Oriental or Biblical.
2. The Greek or South European.
3. The Gothic or Northern.

B. Convertible terms.
1. The Ethical or Subjective. Poetry, truth and faith. Emerson and Goethe, as distinct from Poe.
2. The Classical or Esthetic. The technique of literature. The Alexandrian School.
3. The Romantic or Objective. School of feeling.

C. The Correct Classification.
I. The Creative or Mental. Poetry of ideas. Genius.
II. The Impassioned or Emotional. A prominent element. Seen in creative verse. A spiritual quality.
III. The Critical or Artistic. Augustan. Poetry of Form. Extreme estimate by Gosse. The Place

PAGE

of Imagination in each type. Tests of correctness of classification.

1. In the accepted Definitions of poetry. Defined in terms of each type. Includes the three.
2. In the accepted Kinds of poetry—Epic, etc. Each Kind shows a type. Great poems evince all.
3. In the accepted Purposes of poetry, mental, etc. Each type has its purpose. Great poems have all, in one.
4. In the accepted Sources of poetry—Internal, etc. In great poems, combined.
5. In the accepted Affinities of poetry. Poetry and Prose, and the Fine Arts. In great poems, combined.

Suggestions: (*a*) Exemplification of types in native and foreign verse. (*b*) Poetry, a gift, a passion and an art. Poetic Masterpieces but a partial expression of genius. The poet greater than the poem. Hence, difficulty of interpretation — Faust, etc.

CHAPTER FOUR

PRIMARY PROSE TYPES 246

The word—primary. The word—types. Classification of Types, Periods, Nations, Authors, etc. Specific Types.

I. Historical Prose. Narrative. Methods, chronological and logical. Province. Biography and History Proper. Qualities—Unity, etc.

II. Descriptive Prose, imaginative. Forms, visible and immaterial. Fiction. Poetical Prose. Qualities. Vividness and Vigor.

III. Oratorical Prose, impassioned. Forensic, Judicial, Popular. Suggestions (*a–b*).

IV. Didactic Prose. Educational. Definitions. Philosophic. Forms. Final Effect.

V. Periodical Prose. Characteristics, Variety, Brevity, etc.; best authors use it. Forms—Travels, Journalism, Letters, Essays. Suggestions (1–4).

CHAPTER FIVE

PAGE

THE HISTORICAL DEVELOPMENT OF EPIC VERSE . . . 264

Classification of Forms:

I. Definition of Epic.

II. Origin, ancient and natural. Age of legend. The epica materia. The Epic, a growth. Historical and spontaneous.

III. Forms. Classification (*a–d*).

A. Primary.

1. Popular. Folk Epic. Primitive. Communal. Herder's theory. Grimm's.

2. Courtly. Art Epic. Schlegel, etc. Their combination in theory and history.

B. Secondary.

1. The Allegorical. Epic of Romance.

2. Ballads and Tales.

IV. Characteristics. As to Structure. Unity and Dramatic Element. Scope, etc. (1–5) Hence, difficult and rare. History of English Epic. Suggestions (*a–c*).

CHAPTER SIX

POETRY 281

A discussion, old and ever new—Burke, Courthope, etc. Questions opened. Poetry and Poetics as distinct—content and form.

I. The Essentials of Poetry.

1. Thought. The poet, a thinker, a creator. In what sense poetry shall be intellectual. More prominent in some poetic forms. Thought, to be indirect.

2. Imagination — various forms, philosophic, etc. Views of critics as to prominence. Bacon, Macaulay, etc. Present, in all its functions—constructive, etc. Expression of it varies. Imagination and Fancy. Must keep within the rational.

PAGE

3. Feeling—Wordsworth, Milton, etc. Poetry must be vital, varies in its expression. Its comprehensive scope. Hence its power.
4. Taste, Theories of Taste. Cousin, Burke, etc. Definition—Involves Beauty. Theories of Beauty—Plato, Goethe. Its definition. Esthetics, Sublimity. Agencies of its cultivation (*a–b*). Ways in which it embodies itself. Style. Definition of Poetry. Poetic Personality, The demands of Verse.

II. Characteristics of Poetry.

1. Scope. The Imagination gives it range. Freedom of the poet, limits conceded. Sanity essential.
2. Rhythmic Quality. Poe, Gummere, Schlegel, etc. Meaning of the term. Poetry and Music. A test of poetic excellence.

III. Uses of Poetry.

1. A Revealing Agent. An Interpreter. Shairp, etc. Seen in all forms—Epic, etc.
2. Elevating and Refining Influence. Longinus, etc. The language of the ideal. Devey, Moral Sublimity. Presence of Taste, as refining. Culture. The functions of the stage and of song. Unworthy poets. Explanation.
3. Pleasure, defies analysis. Has a wide field. The unpoetic soul. The Poetic Spirit. Relation to the Literary Spirit. Varies in authors, people and periods. Their coexistence.

CHAPTER SEVEN

POETICS 300

Previous discussion. The importance of Form in Poetry. Structural Beauty. The Component Parts of Poetic Structure.

I. Verbal Structure. Characteristics.

PAGE

1. Figurative Words. Imagination involved. Suggestive Terms are symbolic. Etymological meanings thus in place. Biblical Verse, symbolic. So, dramatic and descriptive verse.

2. Antique and Novel Words. A poetic element in age. A partial obscurity allowable. Language seen at its sources. Old English. Native words thus preferable. Dialect Poetry.

II. Textual Structure. The use of the sentence.

Flexibility, or Variety, its main feature. Poetic License. Hence, inversion, paraphrase, etc. The danger of an extreme. Browning. Old English. A test of excellence. Longfellow.

III. Metrical Structure.

Definition of Terms—Verse, Versification, Rhythm, Meter. Critical opinion as to its necessity. Sidney, Shelley, Johnson *vs.* Goethe, Poe, etc. Rhyme. Blank Verse, Alliteration, Assonance. Foot, etc. Structure and Content not to be sharply divided. Their union effected through Rhythm and the Poetic Spirit. Poets classified at this point, as superior or inferior. The use of meters by the poets. The meters of Milton, in his epics and lyrics. Blank Verse or Couplet, etc. Variation of feet, line, etc. The discussion as to Shakespeare. Moulton, etc. Schools and Theories of Poetry here classified. Wordsworth, etc. The Romantic and the Classical Schools. Genius unifies and fuses.

Suggestions: 1. Relation of Poetry to Esthetics. Current view. Dependent on definition of Beauty. Evils attendant upon error here. The correct view. 2. Poetic Composition and Criticism. A literary exercise *vs.* linguistic or educational. Benefits accruing to the student. 3. The Poetic Outlook. Questions involved. Arnold. Law of Periodicity in Literature. Possible advance in one direction. 4. Duty of liberally educated men as to Poetic Interests.

PAGE

CHAPTER EIGHT

PROSE FICTION AS A FORM OF LITERATURE. 318

Prevalence of Fiction—Causes.

I. Origin and Progress—Natural.

Also Historical, following social development. Beginnings unknown—Scandinavian, etc. Probably medieval. Historical Development of English Novel —Malory, etc.

II. Characteristics.

1. Idealism. The work of the imagination. Synonymous terms, fable, etc.
2. Realism.
3. Pleasure, primary. Allied to poetry. Question as to the instructive element.

III. Variety of Type. Romance and Novel.

Historical, Descriptive, etc. Other forms. Political, etc. Relation to other literary forms—Poetry. To Narrative and Descriptive Prose.

Suggestions: 1. Essentials to success (*a–c*), Imagination. The Ideal Novel. 2. Probable permanence of its present status.

CHAPTER NINE

OPEN QUESTIONS IN LITERATURE—I. 335

Stable and variable elements. New questions a sign of life.

I. The Relation of Prose and Verse.

Differences and Resemblances. Poetical Prose, Prose Poetry, Prose Fiction. Freely mingled in authors and periods. Shakespeare.

II. Relative Rank of Epic, Dramatic and Lyric Verse.

Re-opened, Unsoundness of the old view. Comparison as to age. Scope, etc. Emphasis of the dramatic. Reasons.

III. The Drama and the Stage.

The word, drama. View of Irving. Literature and the Drama normally related. Authors and Actors

PAGE

IV. The Drama and the Novel.
A priori view. Common definition of each. Macready, etc. Romantic dramas and Dramatic Novels. Historically related. The dramatization of novels. Dramatist and novelist in one. Literary unity.

V. Generalization and Specialization.
Literature thus related to Science and Philosophy. The terms, deductive and inductive. The dominant method dependent on conditions. Union of methods. Error of Moulton's theory. Tendency to undue specialization.

VI. Literary Standards.
The standard—what? An area of freedom of opinion. Tendency to lower standard. Literary Fashions. Maintenance of the standard, a duty.

CHAPTER TEN

OPEN QUESTIONS IN LITERATURE—II. 351

I. Relations of Literature as a Written Form to its Oral Presentation.
Some differences—Literature a written form. Literary ability, one thing; ability, another. Different methods and aims. Matthews and Jebb. The oratorical quality is important. The Forms of Literature, Prose, and Verse, thus classified. Discussion of Oratorical Literary Forms.

1. The Oration in manuscript form, popular, argumentive, etc. Written for delivery. Webster. All vigorous, impressive Literature, oratorical.
2. The Play, Dramatic verse, adapted to delivery. Closet Dramas, Plays that fail. Successful Plays must be dramatic and theatric. The literary quality may be subordinate. Shakespeare, etc. Applicable in the critic of the play. The actor himself, an important element. Subordinate Oral Forms—the Novel, Song, Literature Recitals.

II. Relation of Literature and Style—the product and the Form.

PAGE

Twofold theory—External and Internal. The Esthetic Critics. Blair, Macaulay, etc. The Intellectual Critics. De Quincey, Spenser, etc. Correctness of the latter view. Union of the two theories in Personality. What it involves. Literature and Style, a unit. Best confirmed among best authors. Literature thus allied to other departments. Style involves: Vocabulary and Structure.

III. The Literary Spirit.

1. Elements or Characteristics. Spirit *versus* Technique. The Spirit and the Letter. In periods of literary decline, the letter dominant. Test of true critic here. Educational Literature at fault here. The temptation of the teacher of literature. "Analytics of Literature." Spontaneity, the main feature. Literary License. Involves scope.
2. Special Expressions of it, dependent on conditions. Authors, Peoples and Periods differ. Literary Institutions.
3. Methods of securing it. Literary Activity and Association. Largely, a gift.
4. Its value. Literature and Life. Literary Spirit and Literary Taste.

CHAPTER ELEVEN

HEBRAISM AND HELLENISM IN LITERATURE 367

Statement of Matthew Arnold's theory. Interpretation of terms. Contrasts. Poe's theory. Unsoundness of theory. Raises vain questions. Mental narrowness of the critic. True theory. Fusion of the two views. Endorsed by Keats, Ruskin, etc. Illustrations of partial theory. Seen in Schools of English Verse. Oriental, etc. In Literary Periods. Puritan, Taine's view of Puritans. In English Authors. Milton and Bunyan. Illustrations of true theory. Seen in schools, periods and authors. Arnold's inconsistency.

PAGE

Suggestions: (*a*) Every important literature involves each element. (*b*) Hebraism and Hellenism not the whole of literature. (*c*) Higher view of Literature.

CHAPTER TWELVE

THE PLACE OF LITERATURE IN LIBERAL EDUCATION . 387

Room for independent judgment. A vital question remaining, Educational Literature. Reasons for increasing interest in it. Agitation in England. Collins. Prior Questions. What is Literature? Its disciplinary value. Moulton, etc. Its final purpose. What is Liberal Education—its province, etc.? Hence, the place of Literature, prominent. View of Scholars. Such prominence involves—(*a*) The readjustment of the curriculum. Past area limited by other interests. (*b*) The more systematic teaching of Literature. Past neglect. Low views of Literature. Schools of Literature. Advantages (*a–c*). A Literary Laboratory.

Suggestions: (*a*) The Literary Outlook. (*b*) Existing Needs. (*c*) Place of Literature in Technical Schools. (*d*) Place of English Literature.

PREFACE

The most interesting and instructive literary study is Literature itself—its foundations and sources; its problems and principles; its scope and spirit; its types and tendencies, aims and affinities. As difficult a study as it is recompensing, it becomes, at the outset, a mental exercise of a high and healthful order, and, as it is conscientiously pursued, begets an increasing desire to pursue it further. Thus interpreted, Literature takes its place among the disciplinary studies, and it is primarily from this point of view that the present discussion is conducted. In the wide variety of topics suggested by such a theme, we shall discuss a few of those that seem to us most fundamental, trusting that others may be induced to extend the survey into equally inviting fields. It is especially hoped that literary students in our higher institutions of learning will find the volume stimulating and healthful.

PRINCETON, N. J.,
February, 1906.

PART FIRST

CHAPTER ONE

GUIDING PRINCIPLES IN THE INTERPRETATION OF LITERATURE

At the very outset of our discussions emphasis is needed of the fact that there is a Science of Interpretation, applicable, as such, in all the great departments of human knowledge, in philosophy, history, language and economics. There is a body of laws or principles arranged in systematic order and applicable, as a system, for the guidance of the student in the examination of these respective departments, essential to the securing of the best results, and without which, indeed, no satisfactory progress can be made. So, when we approach the study of Literature, with primary reference to its interpretation, we are, at once, confronted with the necessity of the scientific method, with the fact that there is a Science of Literature, and of The Interpretation of Literature, an order of discussion based on the presence of well-established literary laws. Such critics as Knight, Shairp, Spencer and Bascom prefer to call it, The Philosophy of Literature. Lewes calls it, The Principles of Literature. Huxley and Dowden accept the term, Science of Literature. Cranshaw and Mabie prefer the phrase—The Interpretation of Literature, as best conveying the desired meaning, while such a critic as Schopenhauer, under the title, The Art of Literature, practically unfolds its character as a Science. Whatever the specific terms, however, the essential fact of the scientific character and aim of Literature is conceded, and students are urged to approach and investigate it from this only rational point of view. This is all the more important in that the counter theory finds far too much sanction among the people at large and even in literary circles themselves. Literature, we are plausibly told, is its own best reason for existing; has its own place independent of all related provinces; is a law unto itself, and lives, in its best expressions, quite above the domain of the scientific. Especially in poetry, as the product of the imagination and emotions, it is urged that authorship is literary just to the degree in which it is unscientific or non-scientific, the principle of poetic license removing it from the restrictions of ordinary mental procedure and giving it all the scope and freedom it desires. Such a current view, it will be seen, is based on a total misconception of the term, scientific, accepting it in its narrowest purport as applied to the study of physical phenomena only, rather than in its comprehensive sense as that which in any sphere is founded on correct principles, is developed by orderly procedure and, as such, is as far removed from the influence of mere caprice as it is from all that is purely technical. Literature, thus approached, is a scientific investigation, and we are now prepared to discover and discuss the principles that govern it.

1. The Proper Point or Points of View are to be secured from which literature may best be seen as to just what it is and what its relations are to all that lies adjacent to it and conditions it. As an object in space to be clearly seen and described by an observer must be examined from the proper view-point, from what we call a

commanding eminence or outlook, as a city or landscape is thus seen and studied, so must a literature conceived of as a substantive something existing in the world of thought and life be similarly examined. The supposition is, that there is some one point of view, some vantage-ground, as we suggestively style it, from which the literary horizon may best be scanned and the safest conclusions drawn. Moreover, it is not to be forgotten, as indicated, that ere the observer has finished his survey, other points of view, even tho less commanding, may of necessity be taken, in order to secure an absolutely comprehensive survey. Thus Rome, as a city, is studied from each one of her seven hills. Thus may a landscape be examined from a variety of outlooks, each one affording, perchance, some new revelation of natural beauty. Indeed, it may be said, that the more complex and diversified the phenomena are, the more essential will such a variety of view be seen to be, such a world-embracing department as literature demanding of the student the utilization of every agency by which he may come to the fullest knowledge of its meaning. If it be asked, more specifically, just what these View-Points are, as essential to Literary Interpretation, we answer, that they must be both External and Internal, so that the student shall stand both outside the literature and inside of it. Taking his own observation from each position, he will reach his desired results by their comparison and combination. The tendency in literary study, at present, is strongly toward the subjective as the dominant method, becoming, at times, the exclusive method, and, as such, leading to grave and ever increasing error. We may stand at the center of a city or a landscape and secure, to some degree, the results of observation we are seeking, but, at best, they will be but approximate, limited and local.

No literature can be comprehensively viewed from within itself only, a literature's environment, as Taine suggests, being an essentially determining factor in reaching the sum total of its qualities and influence. The doctrine of Relativity is as applicable in Letters as it is in Philosophy. It is true that there exist in literature, as in the verse of Browning, what are known as Closet Dramas, not designed for public presentation or adapted to it. There is, it is true, a species of Private Literary Interpretation, when the critic enters into the deepest interior of the literature, and closing his eyes to all external literary phenomena, proceeds to theorize and speculate at will. Literary Insight is essential in its place, but Literary Outlook is equally essential, it being invariably true that when the examination is introspective only the resulting judgments are abnormal and misleading. Hence, such a critic as Coleridge is safer than Carlyle, and our American Lowell safer than Poe.

2. The True Relation of the Primary and the Secondary must be sustained, so that neither shall be allowed to usurp the place of the other, and all conclusions be thereby impaired. It is here that a high degree of discrimination is needed to draw safe and sound distinctions between things that may be confused as superior and inferior, essential and non-essential. There is needed in literature as in life itself what the economist calls, a Knowledge of values, of literary estimates, the ability to rate things at their real worth. Such a faculty of selection and elimination is especially difficult of exercise where causes and qualities are involved rather than vis-

ible commercial commodities and interests. Some of the violations of this principle may be cited. We are told that the Celtic element in English Letters is the controlling one; that the English Drama in the days of Elizabeth was mainly dependent on Classical and Continental models; that the indebtedness of Shakespeare to un-English sources was so pronounced that it impaired his originality as a dramatist; that such authors as Carew and Lovelace and Waller and Denham rank among the poetic leaders of our literature; that Doctor Johnson is the best example of standard English Prose; that the American poet Whitman belongs to the first order of authors; that American literature is too young and local to be called national. In all these instances, the interpretation is defective and misleading by reason of the confounding of primary and secondary elements in the mind of the investigator. Nothing is gained by an order of study that thus reverses the natural and logical sequence of things. One of the most pronounced examples of the violation of this sequence is given us in what is currently known as the Microscopic Method, applied especially in poetry, whereby the most minute details of structure are exalted to the rank of principles, and all distinctions between the vital and the incidental are ignored. In the light of such a procedure, the date of the composition of a poem or of its first appearance is made the all-important point; diction, meter, the order of clauses, the punctuation of the text and kindred data are made the controlling subject of study to the subordination of the sense and spirit of the work and those generic elements that underlie and vitalize it. Modern European Criticism, and chiefly in German Universities, is gravely at fault in this particular, so as to make it a question of serious moment whether a student of literature does not lose more than he gains by thus controverting a prearranged order and unduly emphasizing the irrelevant.

3. The Importance of Beginnings in Literature is to be acknowledged, what Elton would call, The Origins of Literature. The inquiry here is, when and just how it first takes concrete, independent form as a literature, as distinct from those various immature and unorganized expressions that it assumes prior to its separate, national type and life.

Literature in embryonic form is, still, literature, germinal, genetic and present in essence, pronounced and vital enough to be determinative of future qualities, and, therefore, not to be ignored by the interpreter of literary conditions. Herein is seen the importance of what, by way of allowable contradiction, may be called, the Oral Literature of a people, its songs and proverbs and legends and traditions, its unrecorded saga, the Folk-lore and Folk-speech of a nation or a race, such a body of uncollected material being abundant and valuable, in proportion to the length of a people's primitive life, the richness of its early history, the intrinsic character of the stock, and the closeness of its relation to other peoples farther advanced in civilization and culture. The old Celtic Literature of Britain existing long before the island was invaded by Continental tribes is rich in these pre-historic data. The Scandinavian countries as a class are notable for such a wealth of literary material lying on the surface of the people's life, the suggestive sagas of the North out of which such epics as Beowulf were constructed. Those Medieval epics of which Bayard

Taylor writes found their occasion and subject-matter in such tales and traditions of the primitive Gothic nations, the "lost lays," of the old Teutonic divinities, legends full of interest to English students in that they have contributed of their romantic stores to such works as Tennyson's "Idylls of the King," Arnold's "Tristram and Iseult," Morris' "Lovers of Gudrun," and Longfellow's "Golden Legend." Of this semi-historical material, France and Switzerland and the Orient have their full share, while Old English Literature prior to the Conquest and on to the days of Chaucer was as much mythical as it was historical, and reads, even yet, like a romance. The so-called histories of William of Malmesbury and Geoffrey of Monmouth are histories but in name. Chaucer's "Roman de La Rose" and "Legend of Good Women" and More's "Utopia" carry us directly back to the region of romance, while "The Travels" of Sir John Mandeville are a fitting illustration of the legendary lore of the Orient. Even The "Faerie Queene" of Spencer and The "Arcadia" of Sidney continue this romantic narrative down to the middle of the sixteenth century and the opening of Modern English, while, on through the developing literature, it appears and reappears on to the days of Moore in the mystic pages of "Lalla Rookh," in which the Orient is again in view and the East and West unite. Hence, the necessity of tracing literature to its crudest origins; of studying the true relations of the realistic to the romantic; of the nineteenth century of Victoria to the ninth century of Alfred, if so be the law of historic sequence may be observed.

4. The Use of Genuine Contrasts in Literature. One

of these contrasts is expressed in the terms Realism and Romanticism, and we are bound by literary law to accept and apply it. Literature, we are aware, expresses often, prevailingly the one or the other of these tendencies and ideals. Especially may any one separate literature, as the English or French, be thus approached and studied, it being more or less evident that the English is realistic and the French, romantic, as determined by their respective antecedents and national character. Thus, Romanticism is Oriental or Asiatic, and Realism is Occidental; Greek Literature is romantic, and Roman, realistic; while modern Russian Letters must now be mainly viewed as an expression of the romantic type. So, we are to examine literature as an embodiment of Thought or as an expression of Structure, and the Contrast is that of Subject-Matter and Style. Periods are studied and authors are classified on this principle. Here again, German Letters are substantial, developed on the intellectual side, while Gallic Literature is structural and ornate, developed on the esthetic side, it being conceded that Literature as a whole may be viewed under the one or the other of these aspects.

An equally evident contrast is given us in De Quincey's favorite distinction—the Literature of Knowledge and the Literature of Power. On this conception, the student is urged to examine literature as a storehouse of facts, on its historical side, or as a collection of principles, on its Philosophical side, the line of division being definitely drawn. So, is there a pronounced contrast between Representative and Average Authorship, and we are expected, in our studies, to recognize the difference between the literature of Goethe, Racine and Shakespeare, and that of Herder, Fontenelle and Goldsmith. We are, in a word, to view literary development as an expression of genius, or of talent only.

Such contrasts there are and they must be accepted and examined, the word of caution to the literary interpreter being, that, after all, they exist but in a modified form and measure, often as a matter of convenience and educational method rather than as indispensable factors or features of literature itself. It is not so much Realism or Romanticism, Content or Structure, Knowledge or Power but each in turn and in unison by which a resultant is reached that will meet the test of truth. The literary student is not so much a student of antitheses, making it his main object to exalt the differences among schools and types and movements and authors, as he is a student of relations and resemblances and elements of coordination, if so be that literature, the world over, may be presented as a unified world-product, developed, in all great nations, on the same great lines and contemplating the same great ends. Hence, the need of mental balance and catholicity in criticism, so that all lines of convergence may be detected, all focal forces given due place and influence, and what Bacon calls, the "intuition of unity," become the end of humane letters as well as of philosophy.

5. The candid recognition of the Unknown Quantity in Literature is another Guiding Principle. In literature, as in mathematics, most of the factors needed in the solution of questions are at hand or accessible. In both departments, however, some of these factors are unknown and unknowable. This is especially true in Letters. Literature, in the main, is an open field for free investigation or, to change the figure, an open mine for free exploration, and most of the treasures from field

or mine may be discovered and gathered by ordinary observation and industry. As a department of study, Literature can not be said to be intricate and involved, defying analysis and synthesis, obstructing, at frequent intervals, the advance of the student, as if it were akin to astronomical physics or quaternions or the chemical separation of elements. This is not to say, however, that there is not a region of complexity within its enclosure taxing the utmost acumen of the inquirer, defying, at times, his most sedulous efforts to compass and comprehend it, in any satisfactory manner. If it be asked, more definitely, what these indeterminate elements or factors are, it may be answered that, first of all, Complexity itself is difficult of interpretation. As we approach, with such a scholar as Possnett, the examination of universal literature, what a vast expanse and profound we find—how diversified in its features and elements, how characterized by the play of primary and secondary forces, of direct and indirect causes! What a net-work of interacting agencies is here! For the time being, how both reason and imagination are appalled at the outlook! Then there is, in literature, an element of Secrecy or Mystery, that is often baffling. There are provinces that forbid an entrance, problems that will give us no clue to their unfolding, so that we probe and probe in vain. What is literature, its specific province and quality; just when is the date and where is the place of its origin; just how are certain of its developments evolved; to what extent precisely is it an index of a people's character and life, and what are its underlying laws—these and questions such as these take us at once, into the region of the obscure, and the best results are problematical.

Still again, explain it as we may, there is in literature, as in language, the appearance of Caprice, the conspicuous absence, for the time, of anything like law or method or principle. Irregularity is the only thing visible. All precedents on which we have depended are nullified ; all literary history is ignored; and we sit in the presence of a panorama that is moving before us, apparently without any causal agency behind it,—autonomous and unique. Hence, we have genius, in its highest form, in a dark and unpromising age, as we have the reign of literary mediocrity in an era of general excellence. We have not yet fully accounted for the composition of "Caedmon" and "Beowulf" in the seventh century, or of "Paradise Lost" in the sensuous days of the seventeenth, nor for the presence of Shakespeare in the sixteenth, nor for the conspicuous lack of epic and dramatic ability in the eighteenth and nineteenth, nor for the high literary achievements of the Celtic mind, nor for the low estate of English Poetry, since the death of Browning and Tennyson. In fine, the principle of exceptions is applicable in literature as elsewhere and equally difficult of exposition. Even where something like definite results are reached, the student is wisest who regards them as, at best, approximate, preparing the way for fuller outcome as the literature develops and unknown facts are brought to light. Hence, the evil of dogmatism in literature, of literary arrogance and bold assertion on the part of the critic, or of any other spirit than that of modesty in the presence of the mysterious. Literature is, indeed, a science, but not necessarily final in all its issues; a science, as all others, partly tentative, forced, at times, to discard all accepted data and to accept that which has hitherto been ignored. Literary Interpretation, just because it is scientific, freely admits the existence of the unknown, even while it is earnestly seeking to reduce its area.

6. An Unbiassed Mind is an essential in literary inquiry,—the absence of Pre-Judgments. Questions, as they arise, are to be examined on their merits. Nor does this, in the least, contravene the desirability of independence of judgment in the examination of literary problems. Without such independence, literary criticism is robbed of its most essential element and reduced to a level on which no right-minded student should be asked to stand. The contention is simply this—that independence shall not degenerate into bigotry; that the wisest of men is subject to the necessary limitations of human knowledge; that there is such a power as Public Opinion in the world of letters.

Some of the most harmful of these Prejudices may be noted. One of them is found in an Unduly Exalted Estimate of one's own literature as compared with that of less favored peoples. Attention has been called to the necessity of assuming, at the outset, the right Point or Points of View, such Points of Observation being outside the literature as well as within it. The Pre-Judgment now before us violates, at once, this initial principle of procedure, confines the observer to the area of his own vernacular, and thus prevents him from making wide and truthful generalizations. His assumption, that his own literature is central and commanding, is fundamentally wrong, and confirms him, at the outset, in a state of mind under the influence of which neither his own literature nor literature in general can be impartially examined. Nor is there any proof of disloyalty in this refusal to open the discussion after this biassed manner. What is demanded, as fair and just, is, that literature shall be viewed in its entirety and separate factors as a something standing on its own merits and so to be examined apart from all prepossession. To the student interested, his own literature may be without a peer or an approximate rival. On patriotic and logical grounds, he may be convinced of its decided superiority. This is not to say, however, that when he comes to the work of literary interpretation he has the undoubted right to press this preference and conviction and reason out therefrom as a point of departure in argument. He must, on the contrary, approach the subject as a new one, while there is a sense in which, in case of doubt, he is to give the benefit of the doubt to other literatures than his own. Courtesy, modesty and justice alike require it.

Another Pre-Judgment may arise in the form of Inherited or Derived Opinion. There are what may be called, Traditional Views of Literature in general or of this or that literature, which have been accepted without question or have been the product of education and environment. However secured, they have our unqualified endorsement and we allow no counter-opinion seriously to conflict with them. Just as a man's political and economic opinions may be a part of his dowry as much as his patrimony is, or be the result of special training and environment and accepted by him as final, so a man's literary opinions may be purely of the nature of a patrimony or the product of mere imitation, and so fixed in his beliefs that he always opens every literary discussion with the pre-supposition of their validity. Not inclined to learn new facts, he is unwilling to unlearn old ones, and accepts conclusions only to the degree in which they may be adjusted to what he has been taught to believe is true. This is Inherited Opinion. Certainly it is not in any sense original, or even acquired by personal observation and study. Thus did Gibbon write his "Decline and Fall of the Roman Empire," with a presupposition of the invalidity of Christianity. Thus did Buckle write the "History of Civilization," accepting the needlessness of Christianity as a vital factor in human progress. Thus did Taine enter upon the interpretation of English Literature so as to produce a history as brilliant as it is often misleading. It is here that Hume and, to some extent, Froude fails as an English historian; that the Edinburgh Reviewers, at the opening of the last century, overreached themselves in their malicious criticism of contemporary British Letters. Herein lies the special weakness of Matthew Arnold as a critic as, also, of Poe. Here Voltaire erred, in his study of Shakespeare; and Macaulay, in his estimate of the Puritans; and Carlyle, in his strictures on American institutions. An interpreter, as the word signifies, is a mediator. He is to view all sides, hear all claims, and reach conclusions which are demanded by the facts and conditions.

7. Literary Interpretation should be Constructive and Positive, ever seeking definite results whereby the interests of literature may best be subserved and ever higher vantage-ground be secured for those who succeed. There is such a thing as destructive and negative exposition, having, apparantly, no other purpose than to undermine existing beliefs and prove by labored argument that this or that ought not to be. It is an order of

investigation that rejoices in the detection of error; exposes to conspicuous view the worst side of literary life and work; magnifies the forces unfriendly to literature, and is ever prophesying the speedy approach of literary decadence. These are the Pessimists of literature, and, as such, have no valid place in literary circles. Literary Interpretation is the search for the best things in literature, a specifically organizing and upbuilding function, aiming to discuss and emphasize that which makes literature what it is in the general economy of things; a positive, healthful and recompensing study, "a criticism of life" in its highest capabilities and ideals.

8. We note, as a final law of Literary Exposition, the aim to reach and express The Inner Spirit of Literature as quite distinct from anything external and conventional. The whole truth is not stated when we say, that Literature is a something expressed in written form; that a mere collection of books in a library is literature; or that it is this or that offered to the reader for his instruction and pleasure. Literature is more than printed matter, more by far than the books that contain it. It is, as Carlyle states it, "the thought of thinking souls"; it is the expression of mind and heart and will and conscience and taste; of the sum total of a man's being; the embodiment in language of the life of the world; an aspiration and an inspiration; the last product of the centuries; the approximate realization of the highest human ideals. Above all, it is a living thing, instinct with the presence of knowledge and power; a vital and vitalizing product; the manifestation of human experience in its breadth and depth; a life-sized portraiture of the loves and hates, the joys and sorrows, the ambi-

tions and actions of men. We call it, The Spirit of Literature; its animus, its personality, its inspiring principle, its genius—all that gives validity and value to its external forms. Thus, the Greek and Roman and German and English Literatures have their respective personalities, while literature as a whole may be said to have its own governing instincts and ideals. What is now known as The World's Best Literature, best expresses this innermost literary spirit which through the progress of the centuries, since the dawn of letters, has been gathering strength and charm. To find and reveal this spirit to men so that they may fully see and receive it is the primal and final function of the literary interpreter. Without it, all else is found in vain, and with it all else is practically present. Here, as nowhere else, all schools and theories of literary exposition may be successfully tested in that they succeed or fail in their search for that spirit of life which lies at the basis of literary art and makes it what it is of worth to men. "All the influences of the century," writes a recent critic, "have passed into the being of poets." All these influences, we may add, have passed into the province of letters, in one form or another, and these influences in their diversity are to be studied.

Hence, the difficulties and the recompenses of such a study, ever baffling the diligent inquirer and ever inciting him to renewed endeavor. It is the Quest of the Holy Grail applied to letters, full of high inducement and promise, and making it impossible for the seeker ever to cease his quest, as long as new discoveries of truth yet remain.

Such are some of the Guiding Laws and Principles of Literary Interpretation; a procedure based, throughout, on a stable, scientific method, and, yet, affording to the candid and patient student all the area that a free human spirit could desire.

It is of literature that Mr. Lowell is speaking when he says—"I venture to claim for it an influence more desirable and more widely operative than that exerted by any other form in which human genius has found expression."

CHAPTER TWO

A DEFINITION OF LITERATURE

CLEAR and concise conceptions are rare, and especially so in those departments of thought that are the most important, and which, as such, suffer the most from any degree of vagueness.

Definition, from its very etymology, means, to set the limits of the truth or topic defined—to separate it, in its complexity, from anything similar to it with which it might be confounded. The large variety of conception possible in any high domain of mental work, and the infrequency with which we select any one of these conceptions as manifestly superior to all others, will reveal, on the one hand, the many-sidedness of such topics, and, also, the serious difficulty involved in the attempt to correctly bound or define them. In no province of intellectual work is this effort more baffling than in Literature—a province including so much in itself, and touching, as it does, on all sides, and at every point, some kindred province of study. In common with such generic and comprehensive terms as Philosophy, Science and Art, the best that can be done is, to approximate as closely as possible to an ideal conception of the subject—all inclusive and yet all exclusive, embracing what the old writers called, its substance and its accidents.

One of the best methods of securing this result is, first of all, to survey The History of Opinion on this subject—to select and emphasize, from the numerous conceptions or definitions, those that carry with them the most weight and bring us the nearest to the end we are seeking.

If asked, at the outset, why the term Literature should be so capable of diverse interpretation, and why so obscure, Mr. Possnett suggests four distinct causes, as follows:

(*a*) The Source from which it has reached us.

(*b*) The Unhistorical Ideas about it, by learned and unlearned.

(*c*) The Subtle Changes in the Means of Literary Workmanship.

(*d*) The Subtle Changes in the Ends of Literary Workmanship.

Of these, we may note that the third and fourth are especially potent, and will occasion, in every succeeding age, wide divergence of view among critics and scholars. Some of these Historical Opinions may be cited.

According to Worcester, we mean by literature, "The results of learning, knowledge and imagination, preserved in writing," in which definition the words, imagination and writing, are the emphatic ones.

Mr. Hallam, the historian of literature, tersely speaks of it as, "Knowledge imparted through books," a definition singularly defective, as failing to differentiate the knowledge called literary from any other form of knowledge. It is, also, singularly redundant, as including in literature all kinds of knowledge imparted through books.

According to Brooke, "By Literature, we mean the written thoughts and feelings of intelligent men and women, arranged in a way which will give pleasure to the reader," in which language he means to emphasize the term pleasure, or esthetic enjoyment, as marking the prime purpose of the author. It is precisely this that he means when he adds, "Prose is not literature unless it have style and character, and be written with curious care." By "character," he means artistic character, and by "curious care," that painstaking devotion to technique which characterized such a prose writer as Matthew Arnold and such a poet as Keats.

When Jebb tells us that "Literature implies fixed form," he insists not only that it must be written as distinct from being oral, but that it must have a well-developed style or esthetic quality—must be, as we say, in good form.

"Literature," says Vinet, the French critic, "embraces all those writings in which man reveals himself synthetically to man"—a statement in which the meaning turns on the critic's use of the word, synthetic. By it, Vinet probably meant that, as synthesis, in logic, embraces the sum total of a proposition in compact and practicable form, so literature expresses the sum total of human knowledge in condensed and adjustable form. It is but another way of saying that literature is embodied thought or truth, expressed in a manner germane to the nature of man.

Literature, writes another French author (Gauckler), is "*L'art de la Parole*, the art of the word, expressing itself as—*La Poesie*, *La Prose ecrite*, and *L'art oratoire.*"

So cultured a critic as Matthew Arnold writes: "Literature is a large word. It may mean everything written with letters or printed in a book, as Euclid's Elements, or Newton's Principia," embracing, as Cicero argued, all learning. Professor Huxley makes it synonymous with Belles-Lettres. Saunders, in his Preface to

Schopenhauer's "Art of Literature," writes: "Literature can be taken to mean a process as well as a result of mental activity. It is an Art. . . . The problem of this art is the discovery of those qualities of style and treatment which entitle any work to be called good literature."

Among additional definitions that might be cited, there are two of special interest. "Literature," writes Possnett, "consists of works which, whether in prose or verse, are the handicraft of imagination rather than reflection; aim at the pleasure of the greatest possible number of the nation rather than at instruction and practical effects, and appeal to general as against specialized knowledge.

So Bascom, of our own country—"The Literature of a nation is the embodiment of that which is most artistic and complete in its intellectual and literary life. No work is a part of national literature until it is possessed of such merit of execution as to give it permanent value. Thought alone can not save a work to literature. It is some completeness, symmetry, excellence of form that gives identity and ownership to a product. In proportion as the excellence of the form transcends the value of the matter does the literary work gain perpetuity. Literature is essentially of an artistic character."

With regard to these definitions as thus stated, one or two suggestions may be offered.

1. Most of them illustrate the subject—Literature—rather than defining it. They are descriptions rather than definitions, dealing with facts or truths about Literature, rather than with Literature itself in its essential nature and spirit.

2. Further, it may be noted, that, in the main, they cover but a portion of the ground that is to be included in a full definition; express but partial truth, and thus fail to satisfy the student in his desire to reach a complete idea and survey of the subject. When, as Professor Jebb tells us, Literature implies "fixed form," this is true as far as it goes. Such so-called definitions lack one of the essential features of definition—viz., completeness or comprehensiveness.

3. A notable additional feature and fault of these definitions is found in the fact, that, as a rule, they state and defend extreme positions. As they are expressed, they seem to inculcate the idea that Literature either is coincident with all learning, or that it is reducible to the mere art of pleasing, and brings into play only the artistic or executive faculty in the line of verbal finish.

As an approximately safe and satisfactory definition, we submit the following: Literature is the Written Expression of Thought, through the Imagination, Feelings and Taste, in such an untechnical form as to make it intelligible and interesting to the general mind. English Literature, consequently, is such an expression of English thought to the general English mind.

In this definition certain fundamental facts are included.

1. That Literature involves, in its very idea, authorship in written form—the Litteræ of the study. The Literateur is precisely what Emerson would call, "the Writer." Oratory or Oral Discourse, however excellent or adapted to its ends, is not Literature, and can not become such until it is reduced to manuscript

form. The orations of Cicero and of Burke did not enter into Latin and English Letters until presented in "fixed form." Those that have not been so embodied finished their function when delivered, and share the common fate of all that is transient. It is thus that the French critic already quoted, (Gauckler), is wrong when he speaks of Literature as "*L'art de la Parole*" including "*L'art oratoire*" as well as "*La Prose ecrite.*" Whatever may be the mutual relations of the Orator and the Writer, the voice and the pen, the difference between them is so marked as to make them mutually exclusive when Literature is to be sharply defined.

2. Further, Literature, in its very nature and ultimate ideal, is Untechnical. It has little to do with specialties, or with what Possnett calls, "specialized knowledge." The truths that it embodies and expresses must be of a more general and comprehensive type; if we may so state it, more human and catholic, and, as such, the most likely to find their way, awaken a common response, and subserve their specific purpose. In this sense, History, when it takes the form of Annals, or Chronicles, or Compends, or Manuals of Instruction, is not Literature, as Biography is not, when presented only as Memoirs, or as collections of data as to the life in question. Text-books, as we understand that term, are not properly classified among literary books. Analysis, Statistics, Dates, and Formulæ are not Literature. They are too specialized in form and aim to be such.

So, in the whole sphere of the Scientific, as we shall see, there is a place for Literature, but science, as such, in its technical and abstract character, physical, mental or moral, is not Literature, but takes its place within a separate and well-defined area. When Goethe wrote his "Faust," he wrote as an author within literary lines; when he wrote on "Optics," he wrote as a Scientist and for other ends than literary ends. Dr. Johnson's "Rambler" is literary; his "Dictionary of the English Language," or Carlyle's "Translation of Legendre's Geometry," is not. It is thus that Literature is addressed to the General Mind—to the people as such, to the great middle classes of society as distinct from either extreme. In this respect, Literature may be said to be popular in its purpose as in its form, and is so in the one because so in the other. It seeks to interpret truth to the common understanding; to deal with generic and comprehensive ideas; to avoid the narrow, pedantic and professional.

When Lord Bacon wrote his "Essays" and "History of Henry VII.," he wrote on literary ground and for the general English mind; when he wrote his "Novum Organum," he wrote for English scholars and for the schools. It is here an open question whether such a book as Hooker's "Ecclesiastical Polity" or such pamphlets as Milton's on "Divorce" and the "Church" are not excluded, on this principle, from that category which includes the "Paradise Lost" and "Comus."

Edmund Burke's "Philosophical Inquiry into the Origin of our Ideas of the Sublime and Beautiful" is addressed to one section of the English Public, and to this extent is not literary, as his Speech on "Hastings' Impeachment" is. One need not be illiterate to be unliterary.

3. Still further, Literature is an expression of Thought. Nor is it meant by this that the man of letters is the man of learning in any scholastic and formal sense. The lan-

guage used by Pater, that "the literary artist is of necessity a scholar," might be modified to read, that he is of necessity a thinker. Hence, the error of statement made by Bascom when he writes—"In proportion as the excellence of the form transcends the value of the matter does the literary work gain perpetuity." This would be to place a premium on the absence of thought in letters as, also, to hold the unphilosophical view, that literature as an art could have any true basis or safe expression apart from its intellectual character. When we say, therefore, that Literature is the expression of thought, each extreme is avoided—that of making literature unduly scholastic and abstruse, and that of making it unduly artistic and ornamental.

What is insisted on is this—that Literature shall be, in the best meaning, sensible; that it shall be the expression of mind to mind ; and that it thus shall be saved from becoming the mere record of words for the words' sake, or from subserving any other ends than those that are high and worthy. Literature may have, and does have, pleasure as one of its ends, and, yet, that pleasure must be of an exalted character and need not be frivolous and enervating. Prose and verse should be made attractive in the method and process of their presentation, and, yet, this is not to say that they should be unintellectual. It can not be too strongly urged in seeking a true conception of literature, that it is not and ought not to be shallow and superficial. A recent critic, in commenting on Modern Authorship, remarks, "that, as there may be in literature substance without style, so, there may be style without substance—the perfection of manner and the minimum of material." This is true, indeed, as a literary possibility, and, yet, such a collection of words is in no sense deserving of the name of literature. All genuine authorship has some degree of educational or educating value. Even the lightest forms of what is called light literature need not thereby be devoid of mental tone and quality. The best poetry and fiction and descriptive miscellany, tho written mainly with the intent to interest and please, has a substratum of good sense, and is out of place when classified among the trivial and trashy effusions of the day. Even wit and humor, as every well-informed critic knows, must have an intellectual type and temper in them to meet their highest ends. In this spirit writes Vinet, the French critic, "The art of writing (literature) implies so universal, so varied, so delicate an application of all the faculties of the understanding that it is hardly possible to imagine a course of gymnastics more profitable to those faculties. It is almost the art of thinking. It is the art of thinking applied to the expression of our own thoughts. All great thinkers have not been great writers, but where is the great writer who has been in other respects a commonplace man."

When Emerson tells us that "Literature is a record of the best thoughts," or when Matthew Arnold speaks of it as the embodiment "of the best that has been known and thought in the world," this mental and disciplinary element in all good authorship is emphasized as opposed to the current view of its character as a mere accomplishment or secondary issue.

So, in a very suggestive paragraph by John Morley, as he writes—"Literature consists of all the books . . . where moral truth and human passion are touched with a certain largeness, sanity and attraction of form." By "largeness and sanity," the English critic refers to the vigorous mind that lives and moves in the center of all genuine written expression, making it what it is and coordinating it with all other kinds of high human activity.

4. The important place of the Ideal, Impassioned, and Artistic in Literature is to be noted. Essential as thought is to Literature, Bascom is right when he says that "thought alone can not save a work to Literature." There must be a certain medium or manner through and by which the thought is expressed so as to make its expression literary rather than something else, be it what it may. These media are Imagination, Feeling, and Taste, by the presence or absence of which we are enabled to classify all written expression as literary or unliterary. These elements will repay a special examination and are substantially one.

Literature, we say, is the expression of thought in Ideal, Impassioned, and Artistic forms. The thought itself, however important, must be mediated through these three channels in order to constitute it Literature as distinct from any other form of the expression of thought, philosophic or scientific, with which it might be confounded. Hence, as we have seen, Literature has been called "the handicraft of the imagination." So Pater, "Literature is the representation of fact connected with soul"—*i.e.*, there must be in literature that which awakens a personal response from him who reads or hears it. As Mr. Arnold would say, it must be "interesting."

So as to the artistic, there must be the "merit of execution," a cast and style about the product not expected outside of the specifically literary province. Whenever thought is embodied in forms that appeal to our ideals, our sensibilities and our tastes, rather than in those which appeal merely or mainly to the speculative reason or the logical faculty or to solely utilitarian ends, literature may be said to exist.

Those books which best express these elements are the most literary. Those authors in whose personality they are the most potent factors are the most literary, while any book or writer conspicuously or essentially devoid of them, may be this or that, may serve this or that purpose, but is not literary in the truest meaning of that word.

Men may have ideas numerous and valuable. They have not written literature, nor can they write it apart from the presence of ideals. Men may write that which is entitled to the praise of being sensible. Unless it have within it the element of sensibility, it is not literature. So, also, talent may exist in most pronounced forms. Its best embodiment can not be called literature, save as it is vitally connected with taste.

With this interpretation of Literature before us, some suggestions are in place relative to it.

(*a*) We find herein a true test or principle of classification of the different embodiments of human thought, viz., whether or not such thought is expressed through these three agencies as media. If so, it is, to a greater or less degree, literary. If not, it must be relegated to other spheres and subserve other ends. Hence, we say, and say correctly, of such a work as Newton's "Principia" that it belongs to the unliterary or non-literary province of mental activity or expression in writing. It belongs to the unliterary department of Mathematics and Physical Science. Whewell's "Philosophy of The Inductive Sciences," or Mill's "Logic," or Kant's "Critique" are not literary books, but come within the realm of Metaphysics or Mental Science, as Edwards' "Treatise on The Will" falls under Ethical Science, and Adam Smith's "Wealth of Nations," under Economic or Political Science. So, as to Blackstone's "Commentaries," Quintilian's "Institutes," Aristotle's "Poetic" and Milton's "De Doctrina Christiana," and Kames' "Elements of Criticism." Whatever these books are or are not, they are not literature or literary in the meaning already given, and, mainly, because they are too unimaginative, unimpassioned, and unartistic. Characterized as they are by their wealth of thought, the thought is embodied in technical and practical forms for technical and practical ends, and is literary only in that subordinate and indirect sense in which any written embodiment of ideas may be said to be such. Imagination, sentiment and art however present are not sufficiently present to give to these productions literary character and weight. They are too matter-of-fact to possess them.

(*b*) Herein, also, is found a test by which the different forms of Literature itself may be classified as more or less literary by way of comparison. Hence, we say that Epic, Dramatic and Lyric Verse are unquestionably literary as forms of verse, while it is an open question whether didactic verse, so called, is such, by reason of its want of imagination and sympathy. Pope's "Essay on Criticism" and "Essay on Man" are too unimaginative and dispassionate to be literary in the sense in which "Paradise Lost" and "Hamlet" and Gray's "Elegy" are such, and this is true even tho they may possess a good degree of esthetic skill. So as to Tupper's "Proverbial Philosophy" and much of Whitman's so-called poetry. If these works and such as these are called Poetry, it must be so with a certain amount of mental reservation and with the clear understanding that they are not such in the sense in which Shakespeare's Plays are such.

Precisely so as to the various forms of Prose. Historical Portraiture of events and men ; the graphic Description of great scenes in life and nature; the emotional utterances of great orators reduced to writing; and the varied delineations of the novelist, are literature and literary, and so understood to be, while to what degree, if, indeed, to any high degree, the textual criticism of authors is such, or what is called philosophic prose is such, is an open question. Prescott's "Conquest of Mexico," Wallace's "Vesuvius," the recorded deliverances of Burke and Webster, and the novels of Hawthorne and Charlotte Bronté are literary books, in a truer sense, perchance, than are such accredited literary books as Bacon's "Advancement of Learning," Hooker's "Ecclesiastical Polity," Schlegel's "Philosophy of History," and much of that literature that passes under the name of Critical Miscellany, the very phrase Literary Criticism seeming almost to imply a contradiction.

(*c*) On the basis of this view of Literature, we see the real unity as well as the diversity of Literary Forms and, most especially, of Poetry and Prose. Poetry alike with Prose is the expression of thought, while Prose alike with Poetry expresses thought through imagination, feeling and taste, while each involves the element of pleasure or interest among its final purposes. The difference lies only in the fact that, apart from the metric form of the one and the unmetrical form of the other, Poetry seeks to emphasize more fully than Prose the elements of imagination and taste, and to seek more directly the pleasure of the reader. In all essential elements, however, they are one, and seek, each in its own way, to secure what all literature seeks to secure, the interpretation of truth to the human mind, the revelation of man to himself, and the elevation, thereby, of the thought and purpose of the race.

(*d*) We further note that Literary Genius lies in the Union of all these elements in symmetrical and effective activity. If Professor Dowden is right in calling Literature an "interpretation of external nature and of the nature of man" this complex nature of man within the spacious domain of the imagination, taste and sensibilities is to be viewed in its unity and so interpreted to the student of letters.

Any one side of this nature developed by the writer to the exclusion or partial neglect of the others would be abnormal in itself and lead to injurious results. The ideal would develop into the visionary, the artistic into art for art's sake, and feeling into superficial and vapid sentiment. The Great Writers, as Robertson calls them in his invaluable series, are great representatives of literature largely because they are exponents of this unity and give to each its proper place in the comprehensive study of man.

It has thus been especially easy, by the abuse of a good principle, to reduce Literature to Belles-Lettres or Polite Learning; to exalt Poetry unduly over Prose; to magnify the value of the Novel, the Sketch and Story; to follow Arnold rather than Emerson; to give to Literature no place outside the province of the Fine Arts, and, by making it mainly an exercise of taste, to reduce it to the level of the esthetic. So strong is this tendency that it reappears in every age and makes it difficult for those who insist upon the union of taste, imagination and feeling to find a favorable hearing.

One of the most dangerous features of modern literary development, so called, is the reducing of the ideal and the sympathetic to a minimum and the exalting unduly what is called the Practical and the Real. The Experimental Novel has thus been fruitful of untold evil in hastening that decay of sentiment and faith and hope and outlook which goes on quite rapidly enough by the force of its own inherent energy. Realism in Fiction and general literature has been pushed to such an extreme as to make literature itself in the eyes of many a cold, heartless and often a revolting exposition of life, devoid of sweetness and cheer and promise; of inspiration and aspiration; and possessed of no more essential vitality than the blind forces of nature or the mechanical appliances that obey the will of man.

And here we come in our definition and conception of Literature to the sum and substance of it all, viz., to the fact that Literature, after all, is a something more than words arranged in such and such a way and supposed to subserve such and such a purpose. It is, as Dowden finely expresses it, "a revelation of the enduring possibilities of human life, of finer modes of feeling, of dawning hopes, of new horizons of thought, of a broadening faith and of unimagined ideals."

We sometimes speak of Literature as a Profession and, in these days of material Philosophy and the Bread and Butter Sciences, and the tyranny of Commercialism, it is an easy process to reduce such a form of effort to the level of the mercenary and practical, and, if this is all, then is our occupation gone, and it is better to turn our steps toward some other province where we may have "ample room and verge enough" to express our thought and express ourselves, quite apart from the ever present idea of the specific objective end to be attained.

Literature, it can not be too strongly urged, is the exponent and revealer of the best that is in us in order to accomplish the best possible ends. It is instinct with thought and soul, with imagination and taste and spiritual life, and fails of its high mission when it does not stimulate, enlarge and refine the entire nature of man.

One of the supreme functions of Literature, we may say, is Mental and Moral Enfranchisement. It sets free all human faculties and forces—frees them from prejudice and passion and selfishness and sordidness, and lifts the whole being aloft to that plane of "high thinking" of which Wordsworth so aptly speaks.

That this conception of Literature is not the prevailing one is all the greater reason why it should be pressed and sanctioned until it receives something like a deferential hearing. English and American Letters are in urgent need of this Miltonic conception of authorship, whereby ceasing to view it as either a mere esthetic accomplishment or a means of material livelihood we shall view it as the embodiment of a man's best mental and ethical energies, whereby the thought and life of his time may be purified and widened.

The province of the technical apart, there is no sphere or function in which the author may not exercise his gifts and no worthiest end which he may not hope to secure. Shakespeare and Goethe and Dante and Milton and Vergil and Tennyson and Lowell and Emerson—these are they who understood and magnified their office and for whose successors in ever larger number the modern world of letters is patiently waiting.

CHAPTER THREE

METHODS OF LITERARY STUDY

It is patent to every careful observer of educational progress in modern times that new interest is constantly awakening in all that pertains to language and literature, nor is it possible or necessary to state in which of these two sections of the same general department such interest is the more pronounced. While, as to philology, the student's attention is directed to the rapid increase of books and appliances, careful inspection will mark a similar enthusiasm in distinctively literary work. This healthful zeal is seen in all the branches of such work; in history, fiction, biography, in descriptive, philosophical, and miscellaneous prose, and in poetry. One of the special features of this modern development is found in the large variety of suggestion that is given relative to the best methods on which such a study may be conducted, and how the academic student or the citizen at large can best secure those helpful results which are supposed to follow from diligent attention thereto. Such volumes as the "English Men of Letters" series, edited by Morley, or the "American Men of Letters" series, edited by Warner, are of this special character. They are admirably designed, on the one hand, to give a sufficiently scholarly view of English and American letters to satisfy the critical student, and, on the other, so to simplify and vary the subject discussed as to bring it within the province of the readable and popular. Much of the profit and pleasure arising from such a form of intellectual pursuit depends on the particular method of procedure. No department has suffered more than that of letters, both from the absence of any definite method and from the application of superficial methods. In no department is a well-adjusted order of study more desirable and feasible. It will be the purpose of this chapter briefly to enforce some of those cardinal principles which the student of literature must have in mind in the prosecution of his work. Applicable in substance to all literatures, we shall find it of benefit to apply the teaching more especially to that of English-speaking peoples.

1. *Literary.* The study of literature should, first of all, be a literary study, as distinct from any other possible form. As has been well remarked, "We are to learn language by the study of language, and literature by the study of literature." Literature is one thing, linguistics is another. Hence, those among us who incline to make the study of literature purely, or in the main, philological, are guilty of confounding two lines of study that should be kept clearly distinct. Such an erroneous conception seems to be gaining rather than losing ground in our day, and, unless checked in its progress, will work irreparable harm to the cause it espouses. Let us not be misunderstood. There is a true sense in which literature as a branch of study has to do with language as a study. No one will deny, for example, that in the examination of such an author as Milton or Coleridge close attention must be had to certain linguistic features—as to the vocabulary, in its richness or poverty; as to the use of words in etymological or popular senses; as to correctness of idioms and other mat-

ters mainly philological. There should be enough of this element in all literary work to secure the presence of good diction and propriety of structure, but this is the limit of its presence. When such study of an author becomes, however, as it so often does, mainly a dictionary study of words and forms, then does it overreach itself, and impair to that degree the true function of literary art.

In the sphere of poetry, no author should have suffered less, and none has suffered more, than Shakespeare, at the hands of these "anatomists" of literature. This order of critics is fast succeeding in reducing Shakespearean study to that of diction and structure. Even so excellent a series of English prose and poetry as the "Clarendon Press" series is not without fault at this point. Here, as elsewhere, much of this evil is due to the fact that such so-called literary work is prepared originally for teachers and schools of learning. With the idea of a manual prominently before the author or editor, he is led to follow the class-room method of verbal analysis, rather than that distinctively literary method that is applied more easily in the outside literary world, and should find a larger place in the college itself. Literature must, at times, be studied linguistically, but, when so studied, things are to be called by their right names. Craik's "English of Shakespeare," as illustrated in the play of "Julius Cæsar," is a strictly philological study of the dramatist, and does not claim a place under the head of literary study proper. Morley's "English Writers," on the other hand, is a strictly literary study of English letters. Hudson's "Art and Characters of Shakespeare" is of this order, as is Warner's "Life of Irving," or Lounsbury's "Life of

Cooper." More precisely, the literary method is that by which the study of the author's style is made prominent. In such a study, diction, structure, and idiom will enter, but always subordinately. The great topics will be: the way in which the author embodies his thought, his intellectual cast as a writer, the quality and range of his imagination, the clearness of his poetic conceptions, his narrative skill, and his ability to illustrate the great principles of successful discourse. In fine, the study is one of taste, art, and sensibility. It addresses itself to the sublime and beautiful, to the appropriate and effective in written expression, and ministers as such to the highest forms of mental pleasure. It is, in the best sense of the words, artistic and esthetic, a study of style as related to the thought and personality behind it. There is a valid intellectual element in all true literary art as an esthetic art, and it should never be lowered to that level on which the French school of polite letters has seen fit to place it. The strictly literary method, however, is but one among a number, and reveals the flagrant error of those who have made the study of literature nothing more nor less than a study of style and esthetic criticism. As a method, it should never exist alone. Essential in its true place, that place is subordinate and not primary. It needs that infusion of energy and that special disciplinary value that comes from the presence of those higher modes to which attention is to be called.

2. *Suggestive and Comprehensive.* This is noticeable at once as a higher modus than the one just discussed. While it is a study both of thought and style, the primary reference is to the former. It has mainly

to do with the intellectual character of the authorship examined, and but secondarily with its esthetic and emotive elements. It might fitly be termed the philosophic method, as having to do with causes and effects, laws and agencies in literary life, rather than with any form of detailed inspection. On such a method, the limits of literary eras are determined more by the development of ideas in the national mind than by anything merely chronological. There is now what President Bascom has called, the Philosophy of Literature. There is now an inquiry into the scientific basis of literature as an art; its hidden relations to political, social, and religious life; the great active forces that underlie and determine it,—in a word, the principles that compose it. On such a plan as this, the study is at once uplifted from the level of the technical and formal to a real intellectual gymnastic. It is more than philosophical. It is a psychological study outside of mental science proper, and serves to coordinate literature with all that is far-reaching and thorough. In terming this method a suggestive and comprensive one, the student of literature is guarded against that unduly minute examination of authorship which magnifies the text above the spirit and forestalls any such result as genuine literary stimulus. "The marvel of Shakespeare's diction," says Mr. Whipple, "is its immense suggestiveness—the power of radiating through single expressions a life and meaning which they do not retain in their removal to dictionaries." If this be so, the principle will apply outside of the great dramatist's work, and is so applied by representative minds. The language of our leading authors is indicative rather than exhaustive. There is a potential reserve behind all that is made actual in expression, and "more is meant than meets the ear." Hints and glimpses are given in order to awaken interest and reward research, and the student is to interpret the truth in the same comprehensive manner in which the author has embodied the truth. On the basis of such a method as this, barren and fruitful eras alike yield a rational explanation. We understand the Restoration and Augustan periods. Literature has a soul as well as a visible form. Conscience, intellect, and will are there as well as taste. Despite the strong tendency to the microscopic method, this wider one is fast gaining the practical support of modern critics, and may yet fully obtain among us. Until such an era opens, the best results of literary criticism will be out of reach.

3. *Logical.* This observance of what may be called a logical consecutiveness in literature would seem to be involved in the very word "method." The terms are synonymous, and yet their wide separation is so frequent as to call for special notice. By the logical method in literature is meant the emphasis of its unity and regular sequence all along the line of its different periods of development. Amid the limitless diversity of English letters there is the presence of this unity. Despite all variation and digression there is ever visible a law of continuity, holding everything in place, and enabling the student to relate all that precedes to all that follows. There is nothing of what Coleridge would call "the nonsequacious." All is coordinated and centralized. It is one of the first offices of the literary student to understand and reveal this principle, and the more decidedly he is able to effect this the more recompensing will his labor become. So marked is this principle of logical movement in English letters that there would seem to

have been some one superintending mind presiding over its evolutions, correcting its tendency to deflect from clearly drawn lines of advance, and restraining it within the prescribed bounds originally assigned it. This is done, even while individual forces and authors work with the most pronounced freedom. Tho these lines of sequence may be for a time concealed and apparently obliterated by great political changes, by the presence of marked intellectual lethargy, or by a general tendency to literary lawlessness, a careful scrutiny will detect their unvarying presence, and in due time they will emerge into prominence. No student of literature can venture to ignore for a moment the operation of this law. Providential or not as it may be, it still exists and acts. The literature of any people at all progressive is not a haphazard product of fortuitous combinations, but the normal outgrowth of definite principles, and is always able to give us the best of reasons for the particular type of literary life which it exhibits in any particular era. It is just by reason of this logical closeness of structure and growth that all literary periods have more or less overlapped each other. Such encroachment has been unavoidable and manifest in proportion to the individuality of the era. No critic can afford to be too dogmatic as to the boundaries of such epochs. We speak of Chaucerian and of Elizabethan days ; of the literature of the Commonwealth and of the Restoration ; of Augustan and of Georgian letters. All such distinctions are but relative and conventional. No one can tell us precisely when First English became Middle English, or when English literature as dialectic became fully national. Who can determine exactly the limits of the Augustan age, or when the classical era of Pope as defined by Mr. Gosse passed over into the romantic school of Burns and Cowper? Convenient as such lines may be, they have no existence in the nature of things, and will always mislead him who so interprets them. The logical nexus is beneath the letter and form. "In the literature of any people," says Morley, "we perceive, under all contrasts of form produced by variable social influences, the one national character from first to last." It is in this national character that we find the law of continuity. It is because amid the infinitely diversified unlikenesses of such character there is a substantial likeness and unity that the sequence is apparent. This is signally true of the English mind and soul as expressed in written form. The Englishness is always marked, however flexible its forms. There is behind every author of note both a national and a personal individuality. To say, therefore, that we must proceed after a logical method is simply to say that we must follow the development of the national character in any literature, let it lead us where it may.

4. *Comparative.* There is such a thing as international literature. Such is the local position of the British Isles relative to the other countries of Europe that this method becomes especially essential in our literary study. Speaking geographically and etymologically, it may be said that English literature should not be insulated—confined to the island in which it took national origin. The leading nations of modern Europe on each side of the English Channel are so conjoined in the great movements of civilization, and so interdependent in the sphere of national industries, that the literary life of the one affects that of all, and is affected by it. On the very highways that are opened up for commerce and trade

these higher influences find their avenues of entrance, while, apart from this, scores of unseen agencies are at work to bring adjacent peoples more fraternally together in the interests of general culture. The Continent of Europe may thus be regarded by the literary student as one vast central organism in the world's culture rather than as a collection of independent centers. The Straits of Dover are far too narrow to effect any valid separation of interest and progress. As the student of English applies this comparative method more specifically, he is led to note the threefold influence of Italy, France, and Germany. The first of these countries developed its golden age under Dante and Petrarch just at the time when English poetry was taking on its national form in the pages of Chaucer. Later on, in the days of Henry VIII. and Elizabeth, it exhibited an almost equally vigorous life in the persons of Ariosto and Tasso. Hence, the influence of Italian letters upon English in Chaucer's time, and, especially, in the days of Wyatt and Surrey, Spenser and Sidney, must form an important factor in the study of our authorship. In the seventeenth century, in England, the second of these countries rose into prominence. The effect of the Norman-French in the Middle English times quite apart, a distinctively Gallic school of writers appeared at the Restoration, dating its inception as far back as the founding of the French Academy in the reign of Charles I. Visible, particularly, in the realm of dramatic poetry under Dryden, it permeated the national thought and life, and reappeared in more didactic form in the days of Pope through the agency of Boileau. At the very time when literature at home was inferior and despondent, such French authors as Racine, Molière, Fénelon, LaSage, and Voltaire were in their glory, and England, of course, was under Continental sway. The supremacy was partly for good and mainly for evil. So as to Germany. Quite devoid of influence in England at the invention of printing and the time of Luther, it came to potency in the reign of George II. through the influence of Klopstock and Lessing, and rose to masterly prominence under George III. through the authorship of Schiller and Goethe. It was, in fact, to this invigorating German force as much as to any other one cause that the correct school of English poetry, under Pope, gave way to a more impassioned verse. It may almost be said to have introduced the era of modern English literature. When Southey and Wordsworth are seen tendering their respects to Klopstock, and Coleridge busies himself with the translating of Schiller's dramas, it is evident that international comity exists among authors. Enough has been said to mark the necessity of this comparative method. It is thus that Mr. Sismondi gives us his graphic view of the connected literatures of Southern Europe. It is thus that Schlegel presents a combined account of dramatic writings from Euripides to Shakespeare, while our own historian, Hallam, follows a similar method in his narrative of European literature. In each case the method is the same, and is happily in keeping with that plan of study now obtaining in all the important departments of human thought. In common with the fact that the modern drift is toward specialisms, it is fortunately true that specialists themselves are obliged to apply the comparative method within the domain of their respective specialisms. As the scientific specialist in any one science must be conversant with all forms of physical science, so the man of letters, as a specialist, must aim to compass the general province of letters as it affects the separate section in which he is working. It is impossible to see how, upon such a basis, the student of literature can be narrow-minded—how he can fail to see the truth in all its bearings and so present it. Literary criticism is the last sphere in which bigotry should have sway. How far existing facts correspond with such a theory must be left to the intelligent observer to decide.

5. *Historical.* So vital is the relation of literature to history that the one may be said to be the interpreter of the other, or, rather, the two may be viewed as but different forms of expressing the same fundamental ideas. "In Greek history," says Hare, "there is nothing truer than Herodotus save Homer"; to which we might add, conversely, that in Greek literature there is nothing truer than Homer save Herodotus. This historico-literary law is amply illustrated among all peoples. Why the golden ages of Arabian, Spanish, Greek, Roman, and English literature should have occurred precisely when they did is a question that finds much of its explanation in the political and religious history of the respective nations, shaped as it was in each case by the general providence of God. No intelligent reader can fail to see the close connection between the rich development of Arabian letters in the reign of the caliphs, from the eighteenth century onward, and the political character of the government which they established. Under their benignant rule every capital city was as much a literary as it was a civil metropolis. The successive aspirants to the throne of the Abassides vied with each other to foster the interests of letters, and nothing apparently could have limited that development then begun save what actually did

arrest it—a speedy return to the evils of Mohammedanism. The Periclean and Augustan ages of the older empires came just in the fulness of time, as designated by historic life. If the golden age of our letters is coincident with the reign of Queen Elizabeth, it is so largely by reason of the political character of the time, and the special historical relations of the epoch to the Protestant Reformation. Such an element as this is no less emphatic in days of literary decline, as in the fifteenth and seventeenth centuries in England. We have but to open contemporary records in each of these periods to find sufficient explanation of such results. So true is this historic relation that, were the civil records lost, much of their substantial meaning could be gathered up from the literature. In the writings of Chaucer a large part of Middle English records could be restored. If Guizot and Clarendon had not written on the English Revolution, we might resort to the Puritan authors of that century for the facts. If, later on, we are startled by the rise of a skeptical school in literature in the persons of Hume and Gibbon, the very literature is historical. It is history itself. In aiming to account for the peculiar type of our letters at the close of the eighteenth century, we must study with care the history of Germany and that of the revolutions in France and America. The older students were right, in motive, at least, when they insisted on dividing literary periods into successive centuries, if so be the progress of national civil life might exactly correspond to that of national culture. Their error lay, as we have seen, in pushing this division to the extreme of mechanism. Decided improvement is manifest in modern times in the application of a higher method. Such authors as Morley, Arnold, Azarias,

Coppee, and Tyler have worked in obedience to it. Historical literature, or literary history, is coming into favor. One of the best results of this method is the addition of a new interest to the department. The study is made attractive. To a narrative and descriptive element, already present, it unites the special feature of historical narration and description. To a distinctively personal element already present in the lives of authors, it adds the personality of great historic personages and peoples. Events themselves assume personality. When we deem it essential to read Masson's "Life and Times of Milton" before reading Milton himself, we acknowledge this natural bond between the historic and the literary. In such a method we derive the double benefit of understanding more clearly the meaning of the author and enjoying more fully that graphic effect which history lends to literature.

6. *Independent and Impartial.* It is yet an open question in literature as to what the precise relation is between what are traditionally termed standard authors and those next in rank : whether the latter are in every sense subordinate, and whether, after all, the dependence may not be mutual. This is fitly suggested by Hazlitt, in speaking of the relative position of Shakespeare to the other dramatists of his time, as he says : "These writers are the scale by which we can best ascend to the high table-land of literary prominence which Shakespeare occupied." Tho not upon the table-land themselves, they make the approach to it possible, even for those who may be termed their superiors. Reciprocal indebtedness must always exist between the higher and the lower. The one can never look with disdain upon the other.

Shakespeare himself acknowledged such indebtedness, "desiring this man's wit and that man's scope." Had it not been for Wiclif and Tyndale, the English Reformers of later date might have failed. Long before Bacon compacted those principles by which men should better know how to apply philosophy to practical ends, Telesio, Bernard, Campanella, and others, had opened up the way along a similar line of inquiry. The "Novum Organum" was not so new, after all. There has never been any great awakening in church or state that has not thus been heralded and hastened by some John the Baptist. This is preeminently so in literature and in English literature, and the point we are pressing is, that in the estimate of these authors and agencies criticism must be independent and scrupulously just. Traditional opinions as to first, second, and third class writers must be reexamined in the light of newly revealed facts, and the student must insist upon an intelligent freedom of view. Here, as everywhere else, men must know what they believe, and why they believe it, nor is such a state of mind in any sense devoid of deference to the history of opinion and rightful precedent. We are convinced that the tendency has been far too strong to study so-called representative authors exclusively, quite disconnected from any lesser names. It is still reserved for some discriminating and kindly pen to write the record of English letters with this thought in mind: to give to Cæsar the things that are Cæsar's; to show what second-rate authors have done for first-rate authors; or, perchance, to show that the accepted classification of our authors should be readjusted on more independent principles. The quaint and keen Sir Thomas Browne wrote thus in "The Urn Burial": "Who knows whether the best of men be known or whether there be not more remarkable persons forgot than any that stand remembered in the account of time!" The exclamation is a timely one. Who knows, we may add, why in English prose we have traditionally limited the best of standard authors, from Bacon to Carlyle, to about a score of names! Why should Addison and Lamb rank above Steele and Goldsmith! Where is the true place of Charles Kingsley in prose fiction; of Coleridge, in philosophical prose; of Dryden, in critical prose; of Wordsworth, in poetry? In our poetry, as in no other department of our literature, is a more impartial spirit needed. Nowhere is the traditional classification so arbitrary. Should not Shakespeare stand absolutely by himself? Who with Milton are to form the second group? Is Mr. Gosse at all consistent in ranking Gray as high as he does? What valid claim has such a modern poet as Swinburne to the position critically assigned him? Why should Keats occupy so exalted a place among the classical poets of English, and where, after all, are we to place the poet laureate? Unbiassed literary criticism must look at these authors anew, and test them by the best criteria at command, quite apart from what has or has not been agreed concerning them. Much of the good work that Mr. Hazlitt has done for English letters has been in this sphere of independent opinion. Despite the hostility which he naturally provoked, many of his positions are as yet unassailed. "Very little of me would be left," says the great Goethe, "if I could but say what I owe to my predecessors and contemporaries." It is part of the duty of modern criticism to discover and express such indebtedness, and to examine a vast number of similar questions now arising for settlement. This spirit of literary servility should certainly decrease with the growth of general culture ; and there are some signs of promise in this direction. The protest in New England against Mr. Arnold's estimate of Emerson was a healthful one, in the line of personal independence at the very shrine of the Delphian oracle. Mr. Froude's attitude relative to Carlyle in the face of English opinion has been similarly courageous, while it may be said that in literature, as elsewhere, the principle is spreading, that if men are to give reasons for the character of their beliefs they must first of all examine the grounds of their beliefs. No method in literature is more needful, and none will yield more helpful results. Here, as in higher spheres, it is the truth that makes free.

Such, as we conceive them, are some of the leading methods applicable to the study of literature. Being, first of all, a literary method, it must be, also, suggestive, logical, comparative, historical, and impartial. On such a basis the study becomes one of the highest order as to knowledge, discipline, and culture, and is just as recompensing as the student himself is pleased to make it. It is at once a study of mind, of character, and of esthetic art, while, in addition to what it is in itself, it stands as one of the most helpful media through which national life is to express itself and be transmitted to future generations. Let it, moreover, be especially emphasized that there is one thing more important than the best possible method can be, and that is the living agent behind it, giving it direction and effect. The student of literature, as the author or the critic, must, first of all, be a man whose literary personality pervades and quickens all his work. Back of English letters as a product are English men of letters as a creative cause and an inspiring principle.

CHAPTER FOUR

THE SCOPE OF LITERATURE—LITERATURE AND SCIENCE

FROM our investigations hitherto as to the meaning and content of Literature, it is not difficult to see what must be the breadth and width of its domain.

As expressed by Vinet, "That to which men have agreed to give the special name of Literature . . . comes into contact with everything else. Other disciplines have a more definite area. It is not so much a science apart as it is the common bond, the mutual interpreter of all sciences. It will always be the meeting-place of all those thoughts that are very broadly human, free from too special application and too immediate utilities."

Just as the old writers regarded Philosophy as the content and end of all studies—the scientia scientiarum, the ars artium, so, in this sense, Literature might be viewed as the best expression of truth in written form—what Bacon would call "the haven and port" of the seeker after truth.

"I love the sciences," said Napoleon. "Each one of them is a beautiful partial application of the human spirit, but Letters are the Human Spirit itself—they are the education of the soul."

This spaciousness of scope may best be seen by attempting a classification of the various types of literary expression. We may speak of them as Ancient, Medieval and Modern; as Asiatic and European; as Hebraic and Hellenistic; as Oriental and Occidental; as North European and South European; as Pagan and Christian; as Foreign and Native; as English and Continental.

Posnett, in his "Comparative Literature," gives a classification that may claim attention, for a moment. There is, first, Local or Sectional Literature, including that of the Clan and the City, the first being illustrated in such as the Provencal, the Gaelic or the Low Scotch; and the latter, in such as that of Athens, Florence, Edinburgh and London.

Following this, is The National, as a broader and higher type, as illustrated in any representative literary people—as France, England and Spain, these three, according to Possnett, being the only nations in which "we find truly national groups."

A Literature, as we know, takes on national form and function under the guidance of an author of genius, some organizing and inspiring mind, as Goethe, among the Germans; or Petrarch, in Italy; or Calderon, in Spain; or Lope de Vega, in Portugal; or Chaucer, in England. We learn that after Luther translated the Bible into German in the early part of the sixteenth century, almost contemporaneously with Tyndale's version into English, the German Language became classical, and the explanation is partly found in the fact that Luther was able by his comprehensive and fusing mind to make it so. Gower and Langlande were contemporary with Chaucer, but neither had the ability to do what Chaucer did—to transform local or provincial English into the great Midland speech of the fourteenth century—the national speech of Elizabethan England.

Then, there is The World Literature, racial and international literature, cosmopolitan and universal—literature proper, unrestricted by local or national bounds, and finding its home wherever truth is recorded in forms of imagination and taste for general ends. What we call Comparative Literature is but another name for this, wherever there exists that unity of idea, spirit and aim that reduces all differences to a minimum and magnifies the essential elements found in all.

We speak of Isothermal Lines in the study of the world's Meteorology—lines of similar temperature in countries widely separated in space and time. There are isothermal lines in the literary world—lines of mental similarity as visible in the literary product of different peoples, so as to bring the most distant authors into nearness and sympathy.

In that invaluable work entitled, Eckerman's "Conversations with Goethe" (Gespräche mit Goethe), we read—"The epoch of World Literature is at hand, and each one must do what he can to hasten its approach." Goethe himself was a notable example of a world-author, as distinct from a local or even a national author. He was more than German. He was a man of the race, penning the thoughts of the people and for the people. So Dante and Shakespeare and Milton and Cervantes and Aristotle and Plato and Emerson. These writers are above the limits of community and nation, and find their constituency out among the people for whom they labor. They are, in an eminent sense, writers at large, having to do with those generic and germinal ideas that represent the best thought of the world and compass the most comprehensive ends.

Greek Literature, truly national as it was, and, in a

sense, boastful of its specific character and type, was in its prime a world literature, and is so still, in the fact that it embodies the genius and essential principle of all literature. We are living in the days of Literary Reciprocity. Nations are affecting each other in literature as never before; touching one another at all possible points of contact, just as they are doing in commerce and politics and the various industrial activities. Demogeot, in his "History of French Literature," has shown at length this influence as applied to the relations of Italy, Spain and England to France, while English Literature evinces, in a marked degree, as does English Civilization, this interaction of authors and authorship.

Just here, indeed, lies one of the tests of the rank and potency of any separate national literature—viz., in the presence in it or absence from it of these universal and universalizing qualities. Certain Literatures, as certain Languages, seem to be the common property of the world and the media for the interchange of general truth. Such was the Greek among the older literatures, and such has been the French on the Continent of Europe, while the German and the English in more recent years have taken on more and more of this universal form.

Mental action, spiritual movement and literary expression are based on the same fundamental laws in all nations, and that author or separate literature that best discusses, interprets and reveals these impulses and ideas, approximates the nearest to the type of universality. The comparison in English Letters of such authors as Shakespeare and Sidney or Tennyson and Tupper will reveal the difference between universality in literature and local range and art. "We are to search in Literature," says one, "for the conceptions which have proved themselves vital and to study the expressions given to these whenever they have assumed final and adequate form. It is to follow in peoples the growth of expressions needing expression and to endeavor to make out that in literature which constitutes the catholic faith."

There is, we may say, a relativity of literature as well as of knowledge in general, and he secures the largest result and profit who, as a student of letters, discusses the various features and forms of this relativity and succeeds in revealing them to others. The study of what a recent American critic calls "The Border Land of Literature" is quite as important as the study of literature itself. In fact, the study of the one involves that of the other.

We are now prepared for a more extended and specific discussion of these varied relations and affinities of literature. Such a discussion may be best conducted by noting in what way Literature touches and is affected by the other great departments of human thought and effort.

LITERATURE AND SCIENCE

A priori, there would seem to be little or no connection between these two branches of study, while the history of opinion goes far to confirm such a presupposition. If we revert to the definition already given of Literature, it would appear that there are certain terms and elements included apparently at variance with our traditional idea of the nature and end of science. Such terms as taste, imagination and sensibility are of this character. The province of literature as untechnical would seem to involve a feature of difference as, also, its ultimate purpose to interest and impress rather than to instruct, and to reach the average or general mind rather than the professional or even the scholarly classes. There is here an apparent contrariety of content, method, outlook and aim ; enough, at least, to form a valid explanation of that idea of the mutual exclusion of Science and Literature which still so largely obtains. Thus, Pater writes, "In Science, we have a literary domain where the imagination may be thought to be always an intruder" in which language the critic, while speaking of the imagination as an "intruder," also calls the domain into which it intrudes "literary." So Coleridge, "A poem is a species of composition opposed to Science as having intellectual pleasure for its ends," the thought of our critic being that the two departments differ radically in their ultimate purpose—that of Science being intellectual discipline and profit rather than pleasure. So Matthew Arnold, in his noteworthy paper, on "Literature and Science," is at special pains to teach that Literature as especially exemplified in classical culture is essentially different from and superior to what is known as Science.

So Cardinal Newman states it by a series of contrasts —"Science has to do with things; literature with thoughts; science uses words as symbols, but literature uses language in its full compass." The old discussion as to Nominalism and Realism was simply this spirited controversy as to the comparative value of Words and Things, of the Humanities and Utilities, of Literature and Science. When Principal Shairp suggestingly asks, "Will Science Put Out Poetry," altho he is careful to answer it in the negative, he evinces by the very question the current view as to the mutual antagonism of the two.

Hence, it is interesting, in the light of this a priori variance and the historical confirmation of it, to note a tendency in later critical opinion to magnify the elements of relationship. Lanier, in his "Development of the English Novel," emphasizes the fact that Science, in one of its forms, at least, that is, Music, and the Novel, "took their rise at the same time," while he quaintly calls "Science the quartermaster and commissary of Poetry," furnishing rich stores of material, as he would say, for the imagination to appropriate and transmute into literary form. So careful a critic as Devey goes so far as to say that "Shakespeare and his contemporaries preceded, if they did not prepare the way for, those scientific discoveries which culminated in Newton."

An examination of some of these affinities, therefore, will be of interest and all the more striking because of the conceded difference at various points between the literary and the scientific.

1. We note that there is possible and desirable a Scientific Method in Literature,—a method in fact essential to the obtaining of proper results within literary realms. By this it is meant that there is such a thing in literature as the principle of observation and experiment,—the investigation and classification of phenomena, the only difference being that these phenomena are literary rather than scientific, immaterial rather than material and tangible. The method, however, is the same, and applied, to all intents and purposes, in the same way. The great method of induction which Bacon so early applied to English Philosophy, and which is the governing method in Science, is the method that now obtains in Literature—the gathering and grouping of literary

facts and data with the final purpose of reaching through a broad generalization some essential literary laws. What Newton would call Literary Principia are thus reached through Literary Induction. In fact, one of the main forms of literary advance is seen just here in this Novum Organum in Letters—this substitution of principles for precepts, of fundamental laws for facts and data, of induction for mere acquisition and accumulation and statement.

There is, therefore, a Science of Literature as much as there is a Science of Astronomy or Physics. There is not only what has been called a "Scientific Movement and Literature," but a Scientific Movement in Literature, by which the student is enabled to secure, tabulate and utilize his facts for some higher end than the facts themselves. In this respect, and to this extent, the study of literature must be scientific—a sincere, patient and thorough investigation of phenomena, while it must be conceded that Modern Science has been of invaluable benefit to Literature, because insisting that its conceptions, processes and statements shall be more and more definite, as definite as they can consistently be within a province in which the imagination as well as the judgment enters. Literature to be truly scientific must be concise and precise, clear and pronounced, sure of its ground, of its liberty and its limits, and never become unscientific in the sense of being vague and visionary, just because it includes a poetic element and has a wider range than Physical Science.

2. It may be further noted, that some of the Forms of Literature are, in the main, Scientific Forms. If we reduce matters to their last analysis, it may be said of

Prose, as distinguished from Poetry, that it is the scientific form of Literature. Of certain forms of prose, such as the philosophic and critical, this is signally true. The very phrase—literary criticism—involves this truth. Matthew Arnold's "Essays in Criticism" are literature in scientific form, as are De Quincey's philosophic essays. Coleridge is a literary writer in a scientific form. Even his studies of Shakespeare are of this character.

While this feature is not so prominent and should not be in narrative, descriptive and forensic prose—in such writers as Irving and Hawthorne and Burke, all prose, as such, is didactic and, to that degree, scientific in form. Even Fiction, the most unscientific literature in its character, is no exception to this principle, in the domain of the great historical, political, philosophical and ethical novels. The novel of purpose, so-called, is essentially scientific in its form. We speak of science as experimental. Is it not a little striking that the latest form of fiction is the Experimental Novel of the school of Zola! It is reserved for Fiction, the characteristically universal form of literature, to illustrate what is now known as, Realism in Letters, which is simply another name for the scientific in letters.

Even Poetry, in its didactic sense, as in Pope and Horace, Lucretius' "De Rerum Natura" and Vergil's Eclogues, is scientific in form, the drama itself illustrating the principle in the great Historical Plays of Literature. In imaginative discourse, in the great historic debates of Literature, as recorded for us, we have the most fitting example of the literary and the scientific in unison, and so conjoined as to make it impossible to dissever them.

3. Science furnishes to Literature literary material.

There is a Materia Literaria as well as a Materia Medica. A study of the amount and character of such material furnished to Literature by Science will well repay the student, and, if we mistake not, be as surprising as it is repaying.

So true is this relation of indebtedness, that we have the apparently contradictory expression—the Scientific Imagination, as distinct from the Poetic, and, as we shall see in the sequel, distinct from the Philosophical and Historical. The combination is most suggestive, implying the very truth we are aiming to enforce, that there is in Science food for the imagination—a place for the exercise of the distinctly literary function.

The most striking proof of this perhaps is found in the material opened to Literature from the realm of Physical Phenomena—from the World of Nature. Dr. Shairp, in his "Poetic Interpretation of Nature," dwells at length on this indebtedness of letters to the external world, referring to nature as one of the Sources of Poetry; discussing the different ways in which scientific truth and discovery may be said to modify Poetry, and, by way of concrete example, showing how the different poets, such as Lucretius and Vergil and Chaucer and Milton and Burns, have embodied in their verse the literary material gathered from such a source. He speaks of the "noble earth and skies as the storehouse from which imagination furnishes herself with her earliest forms." Professor Dowden, in referring to the same line of thought, definitely indicates three or four particulars in which the natural world feeds the imagination—in the vastness of the universe and of the agencies at work in it; in the idea of law; in the idea of totality, unity in universality, and in that of force as an ultimate principle.

If we reflect for a moment, we shall see, that, in these and kindred external phenomena, poetry especially finds its food—it being noticeable that Scientific or Physical truth would seem to be more closely identified, at this point, with poetry than with prose, so that Coleridge's view as to their mutual exclusiveness must be modified.

The fact is that all the elements of poetic sublimity are thus furnished in these all comprehensive ideas of immensity; of power; of the serene and silent operation of law, and of all the agencies and movements of the universe in unison. There is moral sublimity, here, as well as physical, and that same feeling is induced by them as that to which the philosopher Kant refers when he speaks of the supreme majesty of the heavens on a starry night, and of the moral law. The very essence of poetry is here, as we have it in Coleridge's "Mont Blanc," or "Hymn Before Sunrise in the Vale of Chamouni"; in Byron's "Apostrophe to the Ocean"; in Shelley's "Prometheus Unbound"; in Dante's "Inferno"; in Byron's "Cain"; in Milton's Epics, and, in fine, in all the great masterpieces of literature in prose and verse. If the "undevout astronomer is mad," the unimaginative or unpoetic astronomer is doubly so. The earth is merely his point of view from which to study celestial phenomena. The "Mecanique Celeste" is far more than a Mecanique. It is instinct with force and soul and spiritual life. Kepler at work in the discovery of his great planetary laws was far more than an astronomer. He was a seer and poet as well, and it is not surprising that the feeling induced by the anticipated and realized success of his work was well-nigh overwhelming. The great movements of the heavenly bodies through space are in themselves sublime.

Those great cosmical ideas that Newton and Copernicus and Galileo entertained lie hard by the essential ideas of literature as expressed in poetry. Humboldt's "Cosmos" is a book that required a poetic imagination to write it, as it requires such an imagination to read it, while even the abstruse processes of scientific investigation through which physicists and astronomers go are not sufficient to prevent, however much they may modify and hinder, the free play of the mind. The statement of Shairp, "that it is not possible to combine imaginative contemplation and scientific investigation at the same time and in one mental act" is not theoretically or historically true. Certainly, it is not true in the study of the astronomer, nor even in that of the mathematician, where he is obliged to take the infinities into his calculations, and keep his imagination on the stretch at every point along the line of his inquiry. Newton and Mitchell, as astronomers, thus worked; Michael Faraday, as a chemist, thus worked; Hugh Miller, as a geologist, thus worked; Linnæus, Linacre and Cuvier, as botanists, thus worked. Of Faraday, Burke writes—"that Nature and her contemplation produced in him a kind of spiritual exaltation, and, like the poet, he continuously reached that point of emotion which produces poetic creation." In scientists of inferior mind and narrow reach there is undoubtedly this irreconcilable conflict between scientific power of analysis and synthesis and anything like literary ideal and work, but not so in those master men where all the powers of the mind work in harmony, and truth and the world are viewed in their unity and totality.

There is a dry-as-dust science as there is a dry-as-dust philosophy, and it goes without saying that in those who represent it imagination has no place or function. "I do not know," writes Vinet, "how it would be possible to be scientific and yet unlettered. We shall not find that any man and, especially, of the first rank in science, has been absolutely in this condition, while we often find scientific celebrities adorned by great literary superiority."

In addition to the names already cited in proof of this, there might be mentioned those of Lyell, Sir William Herschel, Audubon, and the more modern names of Tyndall, Huxley, Sir Robert Ball and our American Hardy, the Mathematician, Poet and Novelist. Mr. Pater enunciates a very important principle at this point when he says: "The functions of literature reduce themselves in Science to the transcribing of fact. Yet here the writer's *sense* of fact will take the place of fact: just as the writer's (scientist's) aim comes to be the transcribing not of mere fact but of his *sense* of it, he becomes an artist." So we may say that matter-of-fact, technical scientists stop with the fact; literary scientists give us, also, their sense or their interpretation of the fact. Prof. Guyot, in such a work as "The Earth and Man," writes not only as a geologist but as an author, giving us geological facts in their relation to man, and, thus, vitalizing them. Prof. Drummond has written as a scientist and an author in his "Natural Law in the Spiritual World." There is Natural Law in the Literary world, and it is one of the prime functions of the student of letters to interpret and apply it.

"One of the characteristics of World Literature," says Possnett, "is the rise of new esthetic appreciations of physical nature and its relations to man. Popular life and the life of nature are the only two fountains of literary inspiration." Here we see the close connection of the scientist or naturalist and the author, and the possibility of so interpreting each that they shall not be made to exclude but to explain and exalt one another.

Literature, and, especially, English literature, is notably rich on this naturalistic side, not only in such scientific poems as Darwin's "Botanic Garden," and Fletcher's "Purple Island," but, especially, in those great descriptive writers who have written in a literary way on topics more or less within the region of physical phenomena—as Chaucer and Milton and Thomson and Burns and Collins and Gray and Goldsmith and Cowper and Wordsworth and Whittier, while even such authors as Shakespeare and Spenser and Browning and Tennyson are by no means devoid of it. It is thus that Bryant fittingly sings:

> "To him who in the love of nature
> Holds communion with her visible forms
> She speaks a various language."

That language has been interpreted from the days of Chaucer down, beginning before Science began, and utilizing the facts of Science when appearing so as to awaken new interest and life. There is what may be called the Natural Method in Literature—that of determination and classification, as expressed in history, fiction and poetry. It is of high importance, as we view it, to press this relationship of Literature and Science, partly, to secure a correct study of each, and, also, to exhibit the unity of truth.

These two great fields of human activity can not be divorced, as some have divorced them, without irreparable harm to each. Mr. Huxley is right, for example, when he tells us that literary men or the classicists so called can not claim a monopoly of the Revival of Learning in the fifteenth and sixteenth centuries; that there was a revival of science as well as of classicism; of the Utilities as well as of the Divinities and Humanities; and he might have added, that, from the Elizabethan era down to our day, what Draper calls, "The Intellectual Development of Europe" has been both scientific and literary, and these, more or less in unison. All this is true, while it is, also, true that Science and Literature do not cover precisely the same territory. Each has its own province and its own purpose in the world of mind. The one deals, mainly, with visible phenomena, and the other, with invisible; the one has, mainly, in view the material and industrial progress of the race through the media of discovery and invention and the better understanding of the external universe; the other, has, mainly, before it the interpretation of national thought and taste; the method of the one is more analytic and formal than that of the other, and decided ability in the one is possible quite apart from a commensurate talent in the other. These are differences of province, function and purpose and are valid differences. Prof. Huxley is, in this respect, wrong when he states, "that for the purpose of obtaining real culture an exclusively scientific education is at least as effectual as an exclusively literary education." This is wrong in theory and fact, save as we give to the word, culture, an entirely different sense from that in which it is commonly used by literary critics, and this is precisely what Mr. Huxley does, in a sense, begging the question by defining culture, at the outset, in terms of science. Still, it is to be urged, that, in so far as there is relationship between these two departments and provinces, such relationship is to be acknowledged and emphasized for the good of each, just as later on we shall see that the relation of Literature to Philosophy and Life is to be enforced.

When Milton says that Poetry is "sensuous" he means that it has to do in part with the senses, the sensible, tangible, visible, physical world, and fails of its mission if it ignore this side of its vocation in exclusive attention to the unseen and spiritual.

The special caution of which the writer stands in need is, that the scientific should not be allowed to have anything more than its normal influence in literary style and should not be allowed to trespass where there should be no admission.

This caution may be included in the word, Technicality. Literature, as a form or method, as our definition insists, is untechnical, as seeking to reach the general mind. The formal processes of physical science, if allowed to have place in letters as in science proper, would go far to rid it of its spirituality and to defeat its ultimate aim. There may be a scientific method in literature, as we have seen, in the sense of gathering literary phenomena and inducing from them literary laws, and in the further sense of securing definiteness to literary conceptions and statements, but not in the sense of a bald, analytic process, or of invariable formulæ mathematically applied. This would reduce all Poetry to Prose, and all Prose to the level of the pedantic and textual. Keats was exasperated with Newton for reducing the colors of the rainbow to a prism—that is, for reducing poetry to fact.

Poetry and fact, Literature and Science may coexist and interact without provoking any such hostile comment, when each is allowed to be supreme in its own sphere, and to affect each other only in that large middle ground to which each has access and where they may meet and modify each other.

An English critic has told us that if Byron's poetic genius could be fused with Faraday's scientific genius, the result would be a poem "for which the world waits," which is as much as to say, that the present relations of Literature and Science are but approximate, and that when such relations are fully realized, Literature will take on a new form and a higher function, and another Golden Age of English Letters be ushered in.

CHAPTER FIVE

LITERATURE AND PHILOSOPHY

WE enter here upon a field of inquiry full of fertile suggestion, and one which, as yet, has been but partially traversed by the students either of philosophy or literature. While increasing attention is given to each of these departments in its separate area and function, by no means the latest word has, as yet, been said upon the equally important topic of their relations and mutual dependence.

One of the earliest writers of Modern England to call special attention thereto was Mr. Herbert Spencer, in his "Philosophy of Style," his opinions and conclusions being especially valuable in that he stands as an acknowledged representative in each of these spheres of effort. So, Shairp and Symonds and Stephens and Knight and Dowden, in England, have done similar work, as, also, Schlegel, in Germany, and Vinet, in France, have done, while President Bascom, of our own country, has attempted a corresponding form of literary discussion in his "Philosophy of Literature." In the view that we shall take of these two related departments we shall not use the term, Philosophy, in its most scholastic and formal sense, as a "metaphysical technique," but rather in the well-understood and more general and equally valid sense, of a study of the human mind—of the faculties which it involves—the laws which govern mental movements, and the methods and processes most apparent in all normal mental action. Philosophy, in this sense, is nothing more nor less than the study of any and everything that is characteristically intellectual—the study of mentality wherever it expresses itself—in philosophy proper, in science or art or literature. Here, we come to the first and most important point of contact between the two departments.

1. As Philosophy is what Max Müller would call, The Science of Thought, Literature, at this point, is The Science of the Expression of Thought—or, more definitely, that thought itself in expressed and visible form.

Hence, we see, that, in the last analysis of each, we come to Thought as the fundamental factor, the essence of each. If we say Philosophy is a study of Mind and Mental action, so is Literature, whatever may be the different emphasis which they respectively place upon the special processes or modes of such study.

Irreparable harm has already been done to Letters by insisting that the intellectual principle is not present in them in any vital and active sense—not even in Prose Literature—while not found, we are told, in poetry by the necessary laws that obtain in each. Even Plato saw no possible compatibility between Poetry and Philosophy, and, therefore, excluded it from his Ideal Republic. Nor is such exclusion or undervaluation confined to Plato, but finds far too much endorsement among authors themselves and nations and peoples who are accepted as true exponents of literature.

It is with this thought in mind that Mr. Emerson criticizes English Literature as being local in type rather than spacious—that is, philosophical. "The English shrink," he says, "from a generalization," and he quotes against them Bacon's famous declaration that, "they do not look abroad into universality," which is to say, that they do not philosophize as authors but particularize as pedants. He condemns Hume and Johnson and Hallam and Macaulay as unphilosophic or non-philosophic; speaks of Dickens and Bulwer and Thackeray as writing "London tracts," while even of Coleridge he adds "the Englishman was too strong for the philosopher." This is plain language and, at times, extreme, but contains far too much of substantive truth to be unnoticed by any one who is aiming to give a true account of literary progress in England and correct its erroneous tendency.

Of light literature there will always be enough, and for some degree of it there will always be a valid place, by way of pastime and mental recreation, but breadth and depth and thoroughness are qualities that do not appear at sight and at call, but are the result of force of thought and force of will, and are as desirable as they are difficult of securing. It is precisely this that Vinet has in mind as he writes—"There is a natural contiguity between Philosophy and Literature. A great literary epoch will always be a thoughtful one. The thought may not always assume a philosophic form, but it will always possess a philosophic substance. A quite literary age can not be anti-philosophical," can not be, we may add, "unphilosophical," and can not be for the good reason given—that thought is dominant in each, even tho in the one it may be more conspicuously so than in the other. One of the highest praises that can be given to Philosophy is, that it is organically connected with all the branches of high learning and, therefore, organically connected with the best Literature.

2. We notice, further, that in all true Literary process there is a Philosophic Method—that of interpretation and discussion, deductively and inductively applied, a study of causes and effects in literary product; of governing principles and great historic tendencies as revealed in letters; of the significance of literature rather than its merely verbal expression; a study of the life and substance of authorship. In a word, the method is introspective and psychological and widely different, at this point, from the merely scientific method in literature, which contents itself with discerning and explaining the phenomena, the external features of literary life. It is what is meant by literary insight, as distinct from mere outlook, possible to him only who has closed his eyes to the world and opened them fully on God and truth and the inward being, and with his head buried in his hands sees what the natural eye could never see. The Philosophic spirit is but another name for this state and process—a profound and sedate inlooking upon what lies below the level of mere appearances, and of which the apparent is the faintest indication and revelation. No one is an author until he has cultivated and opened his inner eye and seen the inner light. Nor can any one interpret such authorship aright save as he has by endowment or discipline developed such a faculty. "No man can be a true critic," says Schlegel, "without universality of mind," without, we may add, mental penetration and inspection. Literary criticism, if of any lasting value, must be thus philosophic in its methods and spirit—a study of mind as revealed in language.

Hence, the fact that what is called, The Philosophic or Intellectual Style is the first in order of value, the style that has substance and body as well as artistic form and beauty, by which the beautiful itself is made more beautiful in the view of all intelligent minds. Bacon's Essays are thus philosophic as specimens of English Prose, and in their type and spirit as much so as any distinctively philosophic treatise that he wrote.

The German author Schopenhauer has uttered, at this point, many truths of permanent value, as he says—"Style is the physiognomy of the mind. It receives its beauty from the thought it expresses. The first rule for a good style is, that the author should have something to say." He mercilessly satirizes those writers, especially among his own countrymen, who insist upon the use of words for the words' sake, and aim to conceal their paucity of thought by sophistry and false ornament and profound verbiage. In other words, he insists that authorship must be philosophical in the sense of being thoughtful—full of thought and expressed with but one ultimate end—to increase the thinking capacity of him who peruses it.

If we turn to that series of "Great Writers" which is now in process of preparation under the editorial eye of Robertson, we shall note that their greatness consists in having truth and thought to communicate, by reason of which they are widely separated from the vast majority of writers of lesser fame—the small writers, who have written either of necessity or for personal ends.

3. It may further be noted that Philosophy and Literature have so vitally affected each other along the lines of the historic development of each that a mutual indebtedness has resulted and the elements of resemblance between the two been emphasized.

The history of Greek Literature, for example, could

not be written apart from the history of Greek Philosophy. There is a true sense in which at and after the time of Plato all Greek Literature was more or less impressed with the Platonic philosophy. The same is true, approximately, of the influence of Aristotle as a philosopher upon all contemporary and subsequent Greek letters; true of Socrates, in his practical teachings; true, in a sense, of the great Stoic and Epicurean schools, and of the celebrated Schoolmen in the Middle Ages, as, conversely, their respective literatures variously affected the growth and history of philosophy itself. Thus Ueberweg, in his "History of Philosophy," writes as to Philosophy—"The efforts of the poetic fancy to represent to itself the nature and development of things divine and human excite to and prepare the way for philosophical inquiry." He refers to the influence of Homer and Hesiod and the "Orphic Poesies" in this direction. The great Greek Tragedians clearly reflect this influence in their dramatic masterpieces which are nothing more nor less than the application of pagan philosophy to the interpretation of human life and destiny.

This principle finds a striking confirmation in Germany, in the philosophy of Leibnitz and his contemporaries, and in the subsequent philosophy of the eighteenth century, while from the time of Kant on through the Modern German School, in the person of Hegel, especially, it is equally apparent. The Hegelian philosophy may be said to penetrate and suffuse the literature of Germany throughout the opening and middle years of the last century, and is still a potent tho a waning influence. In no country is this interaction more visible and vital than in France, especially in the eighteenth century—the age of Voltaire and Rousseau and the Encyclopedists, when the relationship between philosophy and literature was so close that they may be said to have become fused, and philosophers wrote literature and authors philosophized in the same way, on common ground and for a common end—the overthrow of truth and faith. Voltaire, Rousseau, Montesquieu and Buffon were the four great French philosophers and authors of the time, aided by Diderot and D'Alembert and Fontenelle and similar minds. Voltaire, the center and head of the age, author alike of "Henriade" and "The Age of Louis XIII.," of such tragedies as "Mort de Cesar," and of such discussions as "The Philosophie de l'Histoire," is the best representative in the century and in all France of this combination that we are discussing. So, as to the influence of the Deistic Philosophy of the eighteenth century in England upon English letters, signally illustrated in the writings of Pope, of the critics, satirists, novelists and dramatists of the time, as in the specifically philosophical writings of Bolingbroke and Priestly and Taine. No better illustration of the mutual influence of philosophy and letters can be given in this eighteenth century than that which is found in the celebrated Historical School of the period—in the pages of Hume and Robertson and Gibbon. A deistic philosophy begets a deistic literature; a pantheistic philosophy, such as that of Spinoza, a pantheistic literature; a materialistic philosophy, a corresponding literature; a Christian philosophy, such as that of Bacon and the Scottish School, a Christian literature; while it would be difficult to state which of these, in any given age of eminence, has had the larger influence upon the other. There have been eras in England, as on the Continent, distinctively philosophical or distinctively literary. Even these, however, are diminishing as history goes on, and philosophers and writers are working more and more on common ground.

Where these two types of mind, the philosophical and the literary, are found in the same personality, as in Bacon or Hume or Coleridge or Emerson, we have the most fitting exhibition of the natural influence of the one upon the other, or rather of their organic unity.

This much, however, may be said, that the highest literature tends to the philosophic type, as that philosophy is best expressed which commends itself to the good judgment and taste of literary men. Lucretius the critic, acknowledged his indebtedness to Epicurus the philosopher, as Dante did to Aquinas; and Spencer, to Plato; and Pope, to Leibnitz; and Goethe, to Spinoza; and Emerson, to Plato and Plotinus; as philosophers, in turn, have been quick to acknowledge their debt to the representative authors of their day. Burt, in speaking of such a relation, remarks—"that philosophy owes to literature the imaginative and emotive impulse by which philosophic truth is set forth," while, as it might be added, Literature owes to philosophy much of that solid and substantial truth which is to be set forth and applied. As Literature gives to Philosophy ease and flexibility and freedom of movement, and, in this sense, opens the way for the entrance of philosophy more effectively into the minds of men, so does Philosophy give to Letters those more stable and vigorous qualities which, after all, make the truth largely what it is.

4. A further principle of resemblance is seen in the way in which the Imagination is present as a faculty in

each. We speak of the Historic, Scientific and Poetic Imagination, as this mental power is applied in these respective fields of inquiry. So we speak of the Philosophic Imagination, in the sphere of philosophy. It is, however, one and the same faculty which is exercised and one and the same mind which is at work, nor can any too close discrimination be made here as to which of these forms or functions of the Imagination is the superior.

The special point before us is, that the very phrase, The Philosophic Imagination, involves the unity of these departments. According to earlier usage, when it was held that the Poetic Imagination was the only form of it, as illustrated in the outlook of the poet, such a phrase would have implied a verbal and real contradiction, as if there could be any such element as strength and stability in any office of our Imaginative power, while the existing use of the word, Fancy, calls attention to a double function of this same faculty—a higher and a lower, a wider and a narrower.

By the Philosophic Imagination then is meant, the exercise of this power on its more serious side, as the great organic or constructive faculty of the soul, the faculty of correlation and combination, as distinct from the same faculty on its poetic or pictorial side. The eminent American metaphysician, Dr. Wayland, has stated the difference between the poetic and the philosophic imagination in two or three suggestive contrasts, as he writes —"By the poetical imagination we form an indelible picture which may be represented to the senses; by the philosophical, we form an ideal conception of some general truth. By the one, we form images; by the other, we frame hypotheses. In the one case, the conception is addressed to the taste; in the other, we appeal to the understanding. The design of the one is to give us pleasure; of the other, to enlarge our knowledge." It is really the principle of induction applied within the sphere of the ideal; the exercise, in the best sense, of the speculative reason, by which original conceptions and general principles are reached.

If we apply this to Literature, the difference may be readily seen. The Dantean, Shakespearian and Miltonic imagination, as illustrated in the "Divine Comedy," in "Hamlet" and in "Paradise Lost," is philosophic as much as it is poetic. The conception, in each case, of the epic or the play is unique, comprehensive and complex, and, yet, all within the sphere of the imagination—the sphere of the ideal. So, in Browning's, "Ring and The Book," and in Tennyson's "Idylls of the King," and in Goethe's "Faust." In such a philosophic historian as Guizot we see it, or in such a philosophic novelist as George Eliot, as it is also seen, in signal form, in the construction of any great philosophic system, such as that of Descartes or Bacon or Hobbes or Hamilton, where the highest truths are set forth by the philosopher as an author.

If, according to Bacon, "the end of philosophy is the intuition of unity"—that unity is grasped and mastered by the philosophic imagination in its best exercise and thus brought out of the world of unreality into that of reality. We speak of certain forms of Philosophy, as that of Berkely, as Ideal or Idealistie. In the sense in which we are now using language, all Philosophy, as such, is ideal—the result of the action of the Philosophic Imagination—the action of the mind in the realm of the ideal. So the great epics and masterpieces of Literature are the product of the imagination and the rational understanding in joint activity—no masterpiece in Literature being the product of either one of these faculties acting dissevered from the other.

The Platonic Philosophy in its central principle—the dominance of ideas, was really a philosophy of the ideal, inasmuch as no power short of the imagination on its philosophic side could have conceived and grasped such ideas and expressed them in intelligible form.

Mr. Dowden, in his "Studies in Literature," discusses "The Transcendental Movement" as it has affected Literature. This Platonic Philosophy was transcendental and, because such, compassed by the imagination as philosophic just as it was by Emerson and his school in our own country. Shelly evinced some features of it, as did Wordsworth, in the interpretation of nature; so, Browning and Carlyle and Arthur Clough and, so, the recent poetry of Edwin Arnold.

There is such a thing, then, as Philosophy and Literature as related, a literary philosophy and a philosophy of literature. Literature itself may be said to be a philosophy of life, one of the methods of interpreting the human mind to itself, such authors as Lucretius and Cicero and Coleridge and Emerson being examples of philosophical litterateurs, while such as Descartes, Malebranche and Shaftesbury and Berkely and Bacon and Hobbes and Mill may be adduced as examples of literary philosophers, each in his own way seeking to find and explain the truth and lead his fellows to the acceptance and application of it.

All this is true and, yet, Philosophy and Literature are not to be viewed as covering precisely the same ground, as following precisely the same methods, or subserving in the world of thought the same specific ends. Each has its own sphere and does its own work, and each has territory which is not to be invaded with impunity by the other. The one may emphasize some things that the other does not; may reach the same end by a different method, or contemplate some different ends; may study the moral and mental action of the author more than his specific mental product called literature, and yet, in the broader view, each is the adjutant of the other in the cause of truth, so that to Burt's declaration—"that Literature is the best avenue leading to Philosophy," we may consistently add, that Philosophy is the best avenue leading to Literature, each of them leading to a highway wider and larger than either—to the open way of thought and truth.

Special need exists at present, both in philosophy and literature, of pressing this relation to the fullest. While, on the one hand, philosophy in its tendency to extreme discrimination and the discussion of theory for the sake of discussion becomes itself more and more unliterary, so, literature, in its modern emphasis of the lighter forms, in the widely developing sphere of sentimental fiction and miscellany inclines less and less to the philosophical, so that each needs the other for those permanent benefits which as mutual departments they respectively lend to each other.

The German philosophers as a class tend to this unliterary extreme, in their philosophic writings, while, as authors, within the sphere of literature proper, they are philosophic. The French, on the other hand, reverse this condition, and, while, as philosophers, they write in literary form, as authors pure and simple, they tend to the absence of the weighty and philosophic. Kant and his school write philosophy in anything but literary manner, altho the great prose authors of Germany, such as Goethe, Lessing, Herder and the Schlegels write in philosophic form, such an author as Jean Paul Richter finely illustrating the relation of philosophy and literature.

So, in France, such a philosopher as Cousin or Descartes writes philosophy from the literary side, while writing literature from the side of philosophy. North European literature, as such, is, in the main, philosophic, while, in Southern Europe, there is less of the philosophic and more of the literary.

In England, where the North and the South, the Teutonic and the Latin races meet and fuse, we should find what we, in fact, do find, the combination of the philosophic and the poetic—authors like Bacon and Hume writing philosophy in literary form, and such as Coleridge and Emerson writing literature in philosophic form. Wordsworth's "Excursion" is a philosophic poem, tho containing true poetic genius, as is Tennyson's "In Memoriam" and Goethe's "Faust."

In speaking of the relations of Philosophy and Literature, special caution is to be exercised, lest Literature, in aiming to become philosophic in the sense of becoming substantial and forceful, become such on the side of abstruse theorizing. There is such a thing as Speculative Philosophy, legitimate as a form within the province of philosophy. Literature should not be speculative. Literature is a mental product for realization and not a mental problem for curious inspection and solution. It is a mental pleasure as well as a distinctly mental gymnastic—a revelation and an interpretation more than a speculation. Pope's "Essay on Man" is an example in point—so reflecting the speculative philosophy of the day, as discussed by Bolingbroke and others, that, its correct versification apart, it might take its place among the didactic, philosophic treatises of the time. It was simply the way in which Pope preferred to state and apply his philosophy, just as he stated and applied his view of Critical Laws in his "Essay on Criticism."

The "Essay on Man" is as speculative as is Locke's "Essay on Human Understanding"—their only difference being, that one is poetry, and the other is prose in its essential form. Much of the vagueness of Mr. Browning's verse is explained at this point, in that the psychology of the poet's mind is made prominent on the speculative side, and while reading some of his works, we forget, for the time, that we are reading a poet at all. So decided is this tendency in literature that the study of literary history in England and elsewhere is sufficient to evince its presence and its power. We see it in the Neo-Platonic writings of Greece, as applied in philosophy, theology and literature proper.

It is clearly seen in what is known as The Mystical School, as Mr. Selkirk has discussed it in his "Ethics and Æsthetics of Modern Poetry," as, also, developed, on the side of prose, among the Pietists of France. The Metaphysical School of the later Elizabethan era illustrates it, as, also, the prevailing Euphuism of the days of Sidney.

In our own country, the Transcendental School of Alcott and Emerson incorporated its main principles in their attempt to philosophize as authors—to minimize the distance and the differences between Literature and Philosophy so as practically to obliterate such differences and place the speculative reason on the same plane as the taste and esthetic nature of man.

Through the influence of Edwin Arnold and his School, this mystic and ultra psychological method in letters is increasing rather than diminishing. This Asiatic type of literary treatment, which hitherto has been viewed as florid and pictorial, has taken on more and more of the subjective and metaphysical, largely induced by the fact that much of this verse is the interpretation of Brahminic and Buddhistic theology. "The Light of Asia" is nothing more nor less than the impersonation and glorification of Gautama in literature—a mythical, vague and dreamy reverie, wherein the theology and philosphy of the Orient on the pagan side are embodied in verse. The result of all this is neither Poetry nor Philosophy, but an abnormal combination of the two, and when the reader rises from the reading, he is less sure than ever of his ground and is quite at a loss to tell whether he has been studying literature or wrestling with the abstruse vagaries of the East. Here, as elsewhere, the middle ground is the desirable one, where the philosopher and the author, recognizing their respective spheres and aims, seek to magnify all points of resemblance and establish thereby the unity of truth.

Leslie Stephen, in his "History of English Thought," gives fitting place to this relationship, as he is careful to trace the development of English Literature side by side with that of English Philosophy. Draper, in his "Intellectual Development of Europe," emphasizes the literary development as the necessary counterpart of such development. Bascom, in his "Philosophy of English Literature," devotes a separate chapter to the discussion of the great Philosophical systems of England, from Bacon through Hobbes and Hume to Bain and Spenser and the Scottish School, the right conclusion being in these and kindred treatises that the connection between the two spheres is such that no true account of the one can be given without a study of the other.

If, indeed, matters are reduced to their last analysis, the place of prominence should be given to Philosophy as the first of all the secular sciences and the one in the light of which all related and subsidiary sciences should be studied.

The Degree of Doctor of Philosophy in the Universities of Europe significantly includes far more than philosophy proper, and stands for that symmetrical training of which he should be possessed who pretends to be a scholar. It is quite suggestive, following the same precedent, that, in our own country, the old degree of Doctor of Letters is giving place to the broader and higher title of Doctor of Philosophy in Letters. In all such classifications we note the place of philosophy as primal and central, the study of studies, and that without which all others are but partially pursued.

Literature, therefore, as correctly interpreted, presupposes and involves philosophical study as necessary to the interpretation of literature itself. On such wise, the best results are reached both in philosophy and literature, while to literature itself is given that stable and stimulating quality which it especially needs. Hence, the important relation of a liberal education to the developing literature of a nation, so that the colleges and universities of this and other lands may furnish authors disciplined in every faculty and able to embody their best thought in the best external form.

CHAPTER SIX

LITERATURE AND POLITICS

THE term, Politics, is here used in its widest and highest sense, as contrasted with that narrower and lower view current in popular speech. By it we mean, all that is meant by Civic or Political Science, by State-craft or the Life and Rule of the State. In this sense, we speak of the Scholar in Politics, the Author in Politics, Literature and Politics, so that the discussion takes us, at once, out of the region of the mere politician so called or the public demagogue into that of the statesman proper, as a representative and servant of the people at large.

A priori, it might be argued, that such a relationship, if existing at all, is a distant and an indefinable one. We are not accustomed to connect these two great departments of human thought and activity by any necessary or vital law of interaction, assigning them, on the contrary, to different spheres, and noting their contrasts rather than their resemblances and points of contact. In a word, we view them as mutually exclusive, in their nature, methods and expression and ultimate aims, and are willing to concede that they affect each other only in the sense and to the degree in which any one branch of mental activity affects another contiguous to it.

The more we examine the matter, however, disarmed of all prejudice, the more clearly it appears, that a relationship of interest and value exists, so pronounced, indeed, in the sphere both of politics and literature, that no student of either can afford to ignore it, or be said, if ignoring it, to understand aright the one or the other subject.

A. If we inquire as to any actual Grounds or Reasons for such Relation, we note—

1. That Great Civic Questions are to be discussed, outside the province of legislatures and political assemblies, and by other methods than by oral address in the presence of the people as their official representatives. They are to be discussed in writing by the author in his study, so that the pen and the voice may be unified in their expression and contribute to a common end. Indeed, many of the great Civic Deliverances, so called, of ancient and modern times, were never uttered in any legislative hall or in the hearing of the people, but have found their first and only expression in the written form. Some of the Orations of Cicero are proof in point, as, also, of the great debaters of the Modern European and American world. It is an open question, whether or not Gladstone's pen was not as busy and potent as his voice in expounding and defending those great political questions to the study of which his life was devoted.

2. We find a further Reason for such Relation in what may be called—The Common Environment of Authors and Statesmen, finding themselves, as is so often the case, surrounded by the same class of influences, agencies, opportunities and motives, so that the situation, as it presents itself, can not be fully seen or utilized save as it is studied from the twofold point of view, that of

literature and statecraft. The greater the literature and the greater the state, the more decidedly is this Environment one, and any attempt to distinguish it, difficult and unnatural. In the best days of Classical Literature, as in those of English and Continental Literature—the Golden Ages, so called—authors and statesmen were seen to stand on common ground, and seek, in the end, the same great interests, even tho by decided difference of method.

3. Hence, a third Reason is apparent, in that the Author and the Statesman, as a matter of fact, are often found in one and the same personality, as seen in Gladstone, Disraeli and Macaulay, of England; and in Lowell, Irving, Bayard Taylor and Hawthorne and Bancroft, of America. In not a few instances, indeed, so thorough has been the identification with both of these forms of activity that it would be difficult to draw the line of separation, or to decide in which of these arenas the person in question was the more successful. 'Twas so with Gladstone, and is so with John Morley, Justin McCarthy, and Mr. Balfour, now living and working with equal facility and distinction in literature and statecraft. Such a combination, in any marked expression, is, certainly, indicative of genius, creditable alike to literature and politics, and full of promise as to the possible future coordinate development of these two great lines of mental life.

We are thus brought to the second and wider question before us, as we inquire concerning—

B. The Specific Forms of Political Literature, how it exemplifies itself in actual written product, while, in advancing this inquiry, we need scarcely pass beyond the bounds of English Letters to illustrate and confirm the relation.

Nor need we be surprised to find that the department of Prose Expression, as distinct from Verse, is the one in which such a principle is especially applied; sufficient reason for this being found in the fact, that, in the nature of the case, civic ideas find their natural medium in the various forms of prose, while, in literature itself, the sum total of prose expression is far in advance of that of poetic expression and, prospectively, in an ever-increasing ratio.

Noting, then, these Specific Forms, the first that impresses us is—

1. Political History, The History of Political Development, as we have the History of Philology, Language, Art, Literature and Science, such a type of narrative Literature, often, tho not, necessarily, always, being embodied in controversial terms—political polemics, the record of partisan strife. Such a politico-literary series is amply illustrated in "The Story of the Nations," now in process of publication, as, also, in The American Commonwealth Series, wherein the civic life of Nations and States is portrayed with all the minuteness of biographical narrative, and as if these States were possessed of a conscious personality and life. In fact, they are so studied and presented; and so lifelike is the story that the reader forgets, for the time, that he is reading the history of the abstract and impersonal.

Especially is this result obtained, when, to the distinctive narrative element, the descriptive is added, as in Prescott's Conquest of Peru or Mexico, or Macaulay's History of England, or Lecky's History of European

Morals, when great historical facts and scenes and personages appear in such vividness as to make the record real to us. Of Political History Proper, there are, among others, three Forms or Types deserving emphasis—

(*a*) The first, we shall call, The History of Political Construction and Reconstruction, the Building of the State. It is a History of Formations, constructive as it is reconstructive, the principle of synthesis applied to national life. It has to do with what Elton calls, The Origins of a nation. It is an account of Civic Organization from existing materials. It is thus that Hallam and Stubbs and Yonge and Bryce and others have given us The Constitutional History of England and America, which is but another name for the History of Political Reconstruction, its genesis, process, and result.

At times, it takes the form of The History of Politics and The State, as in Von Holst's Constitutional and Political History of the United States, in Draper's Civil Polity of America, in such a volume of The Epoch's of English History as The Settlement of the Constitution —(1688–1788).

At times, it appears in the form of a History of Civil Government, as in the works, respectively, of Harrington and Sidney and Locke and Maine, whatever the form of the government may be—Monarchic, Aristocratic, Democratic or Mixed.

At times, it is seen as Parliamentary History or the History of Political Assemblies in general, or as illustrated in any particular nation, as England or France.

In such a narrative of Construction and Reconstruction, the History of great Political Parties is involved, as representing, respectively, great political principles and policies, that are, as such, deemed essential in the structure of the state. We are treating, here, of Party Politics in the highest and best sense—the Politics of Parties, honestly differing in their conception of the nature, province and purpose of Civil Government, earnestly anxious for the well-being of the state, adhering to their respective convictions and, yet, not unwilling to make concessions for the common good—Party Politics as constructive and not destructive, coming to agreement after full discussion, preferring settlement to dispute. In a word, what is meant here by Constructive Political History, is what Mr. Green means in his instructive volume, The Making of England, in which he aims to set forth those elements and factors which go to the making of a nation out of the raw material which lies at hand, whence they are derived, and how they are adjusted, and what these respective factors are.

(*b*) A further form of Political History, as presented by the author on the literary side as well as the political, is the History of Political Revolution, the destructive side of the subject, analytic or divisive rather than synthetic or constructive, as necessary and frequent a form as the other; in fact, more in consonance with the disintegrating forces of human nature, as embodied in society, government and civilization at large.

Hence, it is that, by a kind of historic and providential law, the law of action and reaction, progress and decline, re-construction and de-construction, organization and disorganization, alternate at somewhat regular intervals in the life of the state. The History of Civilization, so-called, is but the history of such transitions, their causes and processes being, at times, revealed, and, at times, concealed. To give a true account of these

Political Revolutions and Evolutions, in so far as known, is a part of the duty of the literary historian, to trace their origin; their development, as gradual or violent; their manifold consequences in the nation or nations specially affected; and thus to make it possible for succeeding annalists to continue the record as necessity may require.

The French Revolution is as notable an instance as there is of this particular type of national life as affecting literature and being affected by it. Prof. Dowden's recent contribution to this subject under the title "English Literature and The French Revolution," is a fitting illustration of the case in point, as are all those historians of that struggle, as Carlyle, who aim to give a true account of its occasion and results. Indeed, as the history of nations, tho called civil history, is largely a history of national revolutions, the phrase, Revolutionary history, might justly be adopted in lieu of the term civil or descriptive. Thus, the History of the French and English Wars, as of the Wars of The Roses, involves, as a fundamental factor, the History of English Letters in the fifteenth century; as that of the Stuarts, and of the House of Orange involves such a history in the seventeenth and eighteenth centuries. Prof. Tyler, in his recent interesting volume, "The Literary History of The American Revolution," applies this fruitful principle of relationship to American Letters, insomuch that it is seen that the History of that period is nothing more nor less than a History of Political Revolution, and the authors of the period are merely the representative exponents of such developments. So, Gibbon in his Decline and Fall of the Roman Empire; Grote, in his History of Greece; Napier, in his Peninsular War; and

Schiller, in his Thirty Years' War, reveal the close relation of political life on its revolutionary side and literary life proper, here and there, as in the case of Cæsar, and of Æschylus, a soldier at Marathon and Salamis and Platæa, the author appearing as an actual personal participant in the strife of arms. In such volumes as "The Struggle Against Absolute Monarchy" (1603–88), "The Rise of the People" (1216–1485), this is the special topic in hand.

Hence, it may be stated, that, as in the History of Political Reconstruction, the rise and function of Political Parties is a necessary portion of the record, so, in the History of Revolutions, Parties become strictly partisan, organizations beneficent in themselves are degraded and perverted to sectional uses, so that, in the place of salutary constructive work, the entire process is unsettling and disturbing, requiring, however, none the less, the services of the author to observe the phenomena and submit a truthful record of them to his age.

c. Hence, a third and essential form of Political History, as seen in The History of Political and Religious Reformation, the term, Reformation, as a distinctly ethical term, at once transferring the whole subject of politics proper into the domain of moral action and accountability. Here, is evident, at once, the close relation of church and state, and when it is remembered that, in most of the great literatures of the world, such a relation exists and is operative, it will be clearly seen how large is the volume of that politico-ecclesiastical literature which the conscientious reader must take into account. Continental Literature, especially in Protestant Germany, Switzerland, and the Netherlands, is thus ecclesiastically connected, as it is in England herself, as an Anglican nation; the history, also, of the Roman Catholic Church in Europe, being vitally bound up with that of European Letters. The Histories of Lingard and Soames, respectively, defending Romish and Protestant interests, in Early English Literature, illustrate the same great truth. The History of The Great Reformations, as the Lutheran and the English, is but a record of this relation. Such volumes as "Tudors and The Reformation" (1485–1603), "The Puritan Revolution," "The Protestant Revolution," "The Epoch of Reform," and "The Crusaders" illustrate it. D'Aubigne and Burnet as specially church historians of the Reformation are literary historians, as well. So, Froude and Macaulay and Lecky in their respective writings. What have been called, The European Wars of Religion, incited and conducted with reformatory ends in view, must have their historians, wherein the author must appear in the double rôle of narrator and ecclesiastic. Richard Hooker, in his famous work, "The Ecclesiastical Polity," appears so at home in each of these spheres of thought that we can not disconnect him from either. Ecclesiastical History is an essential branch of History proper and, therefore, of Literature.

Such are the three great departments of Literary Narrative as related to Politics, with which the author proper must deal—The History of Political Reconstruction, of Political Revolution, and of Political Reformation, on the ecclesiastical side.

Summed up in a single statement, we have here, both on the political and literary side, nothing less than The History of Civilization, wherein profane and sacred history are alike presented, the complete story of the world given as it stands. In such authors as Guizot and

Buckle, the close connection of literature and politics is seen on every page.

2. Closely connected with the Department of Political History is that of Political Biography, a second form in which this politico-literary principle comes to view, partaking of some of the general features of history proper, and yet having a field and function of its own. There is a sense, indeed, in which it may be said to possess a more definite and vital interest, in that it involves the personal element, by which we see living men as veritable actors on the open stage of the world's manifold life.

Nothing could more clearly evince the increasing interest that is attached to this particular branch of political literature than the rapidity with which such an order of literature is appearing in this and other lands. In England and America alone, no less than ten or twelve distinct series of such publications are already at hand or in the course of preparation—such as: The English Statesmen Series; English Radical Leaders; Forster's British Statesmen; English Men of Action Series; The Queen's Prime Ministers; Thackeray's Four Georges; Strickland's Queens of England; The American Statesmen Series, and The Heroes of the Nations. The sum total of the volumes included in the various Collections runs up into the hundreds, and still new series are anticipated. Whatever the special title, they are alike politico-literary, the biography of great national leaders in peace and war.

If, to these, we add, the list of separate biographies—the lives of men who have taken prominent part in political history as reconstructive, revolutionary and reforming, the number is legion—such as: Carlyle's Cromwell and Frederick The Great; Froude's Cæsar; Abbot's Napoleon; Motley's John of Barnevelde; Hughes' Alfred the Great; Irving's Washington; Prior's Burke; and the lives of Machiavelli, Charlemagne, and Cavour, and Peter The Great, and similar historic characters. In these and kindred volumes, tho the author sits down to his work in a somewhat different attitude from that assumed when Spedding wrote his Life of Bacon; or Forster that of Dickens; or Holmes, that of Emerson; the author is still an author, tho with the civic life of the man or the nation prominently in view, and tho by reason of such a prominence, the literary record may lose something in the line of verbal refinement and esthetic type, it may, also, gain as much in a vigorous and impressive style.

3. A third and interesting form of Political Literature is included in the wide-reaching phrase—Political Prose Miscellany. Here is opened a vast and an inviting field as distinct from Political History and Biography; so spacious, indeed, as a separate province, as in itself to justify the discussion before us, and to prove, beyond all question, the close relation of Literature and Politics. With that special branch of Prose Miscellany which is called Critical, as illustrated in the writings of Dryden, Coleridge, Bayne, Matthew Arnold and Pater, Political Literature, of course, has little, if anything, to do, our attention being directed to that section of Miscellany called Descriptive, not a few of the ablest authors in English and Continental Letters having chosen this particular form of prose as the one best adapted to embody their best endeavors.

Of this Prose Type, there are three distinct divisions that express a specific political feature.

(*a*) The first is the Political Essay, and finds abundant illustration in British and American Literature—beginning as far back as the fifteenth century, in the publication of "The Paston Letters"; the writings of Fortescue, on "Monarchy"; Malory's "King Arthur," and similar treatises on Government and Constitutional Law. Coming to the Elizabethan Age and Modern English Proper, we note among Bacon's Essays, such political titles as "Seditions" and "Troubles," "Empire," "The True Greatness of Kingdoms," and "Faction"; in Jonson's "Discoveries," reflections on "Love of Country," and on "Princes"; in Cowley, Essays on "Liberty" and "The Government of Cromwell"; and, in Milton, "The Tenure of Kings and Magistrates," "A Free Commonwealth," and similar civic discussions, the Prose of the Commonwealth, whether in extended book-form, or in the essay proper being best designated as political prose, necessitated as it was, by the temper of the time. Later in the literary history, as we come to The Augustan Age of Swift and Addison and the so-called Pamphleteers, we note an intense politico-literary type, in Swift's "Letters to the October Club" on "Governmental Reform"; his "Public Spirit of the Whigs"; in the numerous political essays of "The Spectator," and "Guardian," and in the "Freeholder," a purely political periodical on behalf of The House of Hanover; in the "Rambler," and "Idler" of Dr. Johnson, and in his "Rasselas, Prince of Abyssinia"; in Macaulay's civic papers on "Machiavelli," "Mirabeau," "Frederick," "Hampden," "Pitt," "Chatham," and "Hastings"; in De Quincey's papers on, "The Cæsars," "Charlemagne," "The Revolution of Greece," and on "Whiggism in its Relations to Literature"; in Carlyle's

"Lectures on Heroes," his "Latter Day Pamphlets," "Chartism," "Early Kings of Norway," and "Restoration of Modern Europe"; in Arnold's "Culture and Anarchy," and his paper on "Numbers" and, so, on through English Literature and History down to the last decade and the death of Gladstone, himself a brilliant example of the civico-literary essayist. So, in American Letters, as distinct from British, have Irving and Bryant and Hawthorne and Emerson, Longfellow and Whittier, Lowell and Prescott written political miscellany and so, in General and European Literature, have authors thus written, as in Germany, especially in the days of The Sturm and Drang Period (1770–1830), when the greatest authors of the nation, Goethe, Schiller, and Herder aimed to voice the Revolutionary sentiments of the time; as in France, in the Age of Louis XIV., and of Voltaire and in every nation when great civic interests were threatened, and men of letters were obliged to take an active part in the field of political controversy.

(*b*) Closely connected in occasion and purpose with the political Essay is the Political Oration, as a second form of Political Prose Miscellany—the distinctive forensic or parliamentary form, as contrasted with the others that are less outspoken and demonstrative, the most declarative and practical of all, the political essayist and the political forensic writer often being embodied in the same personality.

Nor is the reference here, necessarily, to the oration as pronounced in open assembly, but to it as a literary product, in manuscript, prior to its oral presentation, judged on its own merits as such, and possibly never delivered in public address, as is true of many of the great orations, so called, of ancient and modern times. In

English Literature, the best illustration of this type of prose miscellany is found in the great British and American Orators—as in Edmund Burke's "Speech on American Taxation," on "Conciliation With America" and on "The Impeachment of Hastings"; in the stirring deliverances of William Pitt, and Grattan and O'Connell; and, in America, in Adams, Otis and Webster, wherein the didactic yields to the impassioned; indirect address, to the direct; speculative theory, to practical issues, and the only object of the author is to produce conviction and open the way to immediate action.

Probably, the most effective form of the Political Oration is the Argumentative and, indeed, its most natural and frequent form, wherein the writer, as a prospective orator, assumes the attitude of the disputant; accepts, at once, his position, for or against a proposed policy or principle, and proceeds to defend it against actual or supposed opposition. The great written Debates of Literary History are thus deducible in this connection, having all the advantage of the ordinary, oratorical production with the additional advantage of that pertinence and impressiveness that comes from the discussion of vital topics in the presence of hostile influences.

It is, hence, at this point, that written and oral discourse come into closest connection, it being difficult, at times, to draw the line of difference between them. It is here that the specifically literary quality of prose miscellany as a necessarily written product is least pronounced, and the oratorial quality the most conspicuous, while it is never to be forgotten by the writer and the orator that literature comes to its best expression when possessed of the correctness and refinement of the essay proper as a written product, and of the vigor and impressiveness of the oration as an oral product.

(*c*) A third and prolific form in which Political Prose Miscellany expresses itself is Fiction, the Political Novel having become a distinctive type with special civic and literary ends to subserve. Nor is it at all surprising that Civic Teachings should express themselves in this imaginative form, in that by such an indirect and attractive method they are often better represented and more effectively impressive than by the more direct and didactic methods of ordinary prose. As far back as the reigns of Henry VIII., in the opening years of the sixteenth century, Sir Thomas Moore utilized this principle in his semi-romantic treatise, "Utopia," the burden of whose teaching is political and social, with primary reference to the age in which it was written. Indeed, it may be said, that Malory's "King Arthur," published in 1485, opened up this line of political prose "the best prose romance" of the language, according to Scott. Later in the history, Cowley, in his work entitled, "A Discourse by way of vision concerning the government of Cromwell," adopts the same romantic method. Coming on to the days of Daniel De Foe and the historical genesis of the Modern Novel, so plentiful are the examples of the political novel proper that only representative specimens can be cited—De Foe himself opening such a series, suffering persecution and imprisonment, as he did, by reason of his relation to the politics of the time. We see it in Johnson's "Rasselas, Prince of Abyssinia"; in Jane Porter's "Scottish Chiefs"; in Scott's "Count Robert of Paris," "Kenilworth," and other novels; Bulwer's "Harold"; Disraeli's "Lothair" and "Coningsby"; in Mrs. Stowe's

Anti-Slavery Romance, "Uncle Tom"; in James' "Arabella Stuart," and "The Huguenot," and Cooper's "Spy," and "Lionel Lincoln"; and in such later and living authors as Crawford, and Kipling, and Mrs. Ward; in Louisa Mühlbach's Historical novels, such as "Napoleon and Blucher," "The Empress Josephine," "Frederick the Great and his Court"; in Victor Hugo's "Ninety-three," and Goethe's "Götz von Berlichingen," and in other foreign authors. All these writers utilize the function of romance and symbolic language to specifically political purposes. Of all these examples, Mr. Disraeli is perhaps the most pronounced, whose work as a novelist was prominently political, and who probably did more efficient civic service in this direction than he could have done on the English Hustings.

4. A fourth and final form of political literature is seen in Political Poetry, one of the strangest mediums, at first sight, for the expression of civic truth, and, yet, one of the most frequent and popular. Many of the prose writers whom we have adduced in the sphere of political prose miscellany, the essay, the oration, and the novel, have also, as poets, aimed to secure the same political ends, thus testing, in their own experience as writers, which of these two forms could be made the more effective. At the very opening of national English verse, in the days of Chaucer, John Gower, penned his "Vox Clamantis" in the light of the English Politics of the time; as did Langlande, his "Piers The Plowman"; and Lawrence Minot, his Political Poems in honor of Edward III. and in connection with The French and English Wars. So, in Spenser's "Shepherd's Calendar," and the "Faerie Queene," there runs a distinct

political thread, as, also, in his "Complaints." Shakespeare, in his Historical Plays; Ben Jonson, in his "Sejanus" and "Cataline"; and Marlowe, in his "Tamburlaine" and "Edward the Second," illustrate the decided political bent of the Elizabethan dramatists. So, Byron, in his "Siege of Corinth," "The Two Foscari," "Sardanapolus," "Marino Faliero," it is seen, as in Scott's "Marmion," in Southey's "Nat Tyler" and "Joan of Arc"; in Coleridge's translation of Schiller's "Wallenstein" and, so, on through the series of English Poets, to Tennyson's "Harold," and "Queen Mary" and "Becket," not to speak of the long list of Political Sonnets and National Lyrics, composed by Milton and Wordsworth and Burns and Whittier.

Nor is it to be forgotten that, both in Prose and Verse, Satire forms a vital element in Political writings, such a species of literature, in its terseness and pointedness, being specially adapted to political effect. Thus the "Drapier Letters" and "Gulliver's Travels" by Swift; that portion of Pope's verse, under the name of "Satires"; Dryden's "Absalom and Achitophel" and Butler's "Hudibras," and Lowell's "Biglow Papers" are instances in point of political prose and verse, in satirical dress, poetry especially seeming to offer an inviting field for sarcasm, burlesque, and humor, such deliverances often descending to the level of buffoonery and offensive personality, as in the verse of Pope and his school, produced, as it was, in the bitter controversy of the Augustan Age.

Thus, it is clear, that there is such a distinctive type of Literature, as Civic or Political Literature, expressed chiefly, indeed, in almost every form of Prose and Verse—in History, Biography, in Essay, Oration and Novel, in

Epic, Lyric and Drama, so as to constitute a valid part of Literature itself, both English and foreign, and make it necessary for the student of Letters to give it a place in his literary studies.

From the discussion thus conducted, certain important inferences and suggestions emerge—

(*a*) That, notwithstanding all relationship as thus described, there is an important sense in which each of these great departments of activity has its own specific Domain, a definite border-line of distinction lying between them, beyond which it is not desirable that either should pass. There is an intense personal life in literature which makes it essentially what it is, and with which no other mental form or product can be on intimate terms. It is the inner sanctum of letters and of authorship, where the esthetic or artistic reigns; where literary culture, so-called, has its home, and is far removed, as such, from the open and unrestrained methods that belong to political thought and life.

Naturally, we find this unique literary province and spirit more pronounced in verse than prose; and, in poetry itself, more pronounced in the subjective conditions of the lyric than in the epic and drama. Such a poem as Milton's "Il Penseroso," Cowper's "Lines To His Mother," Keats' "Eve of Saint Agnes," Burns' "Cotter's Saturday Night," Mrs. Browning's "Vision of Poets," and Lowell's "Cathedral," are examples in point, as are the great Elegies of English and American Verse, wherein the soul of the poet is intensely and devoutly moved, and what is written is written in the minor key, in the subdued spirit of sympathy and love and sacred meditation. In a word, whatever the relation of the literary and the civic, the literary should always be seen to control the civic and should never be in subjection to it. It is of literature primarily and not of politics that we are speaking, and literature, as such, in its specific type and function, should strike its own dominant note in every sphere that it enters.

(*b*) We note, further, as an historical principle, and as confirmed by our reflections hitherto, that Literature and Politics are best allied within the domain of Free Governments—where the great cardinal principles of individual and social and civic liberty prevail.

We speak, in these days, of Democratic Art. There is a vital sense in which the best literature is democratic, begotten of wholesome national conditions and demanding free scope for personal inquiry and personal expression. It is, thus, that English Letters give us the most fitting examples of the relation we have been studying, the limited monarchy of Great Britain, as historically developed and applied, furnishing practically all the free conditions of an out-and-out democracy. So, in Monarchical Europe, to the extent that Absolutism prevails, as in Russia and Spain, are the most wholesome political literary conditions repressed, and the utterances of the writer made to pass the censorship of the state, so that the rapid spread of republican principles in Monarchical Europe, in France and Switzerland, in Italy and Germany and the Netherlands, is full of promise as to the literary future of these respective countries in shaping political policy and in being shaped by it in turn.

In this connection, a question of interest arises—as to the Relation of a State to its Authors—its Literary Men, whether it is one of cooperative sympathy and practical aid, or one of reserve and neglect and repression.

The important subject of national and international copyright is here involved; the subject of the attitude of the state toward the establishment, maintenance and extension of Public Libraries, as, also, its attitude as expressed, practically and financially, in the tariff that is levied on Books and Literary Appliances. The attitude of the Court of Edward III. toward Chaucer, and of that of Elizabeth, toward Spenser, or that of the Stuarts and Queen Anne, toward the respective schools of letters, then flourishing, is an interesting study in this connection, as would be that of the Phillips in Spain, or of the Czar in Russia. The Commonwealth Reaction in England was as much a literary as a political revolution. In Monarchies and Republics alike, authors have a right to expect a generous consideration at the hands of the state, which they in turn amply repay in those various ways by which a sure and able literary development contributes to national honor, and well-being and national thought and taste.

(*c*) Hence, a final suggestion, as to the Mutual Influences of these two Departments on each other, for the more they are studied, the more it will be seen that, each, having, as we have seen, a sphere of its own, has something unique to contribute to the other. Tersely, it may be said that the office of Literature in Politics is to Elevate and Refine them, and that of Politics in Literature, to Invigorate and Inspire it. The presence, in the English Parliament of notable men of letters, and its organic relation to the University System of England is clearly in the line of such an ennobling and purifying influence, as the presence in English Letters of distinguished statesmen is in the line of strength and impulse. Hence, in this respect, The American Congress suffers sadly by comparison, in that our National and State Legislatures are so largely made up of politicians only, but few of whom deserve the name of statesmen, and still fewer, the name of authors or men of letters. The present composition of the American Senate is a sufficient commentary on the subject in hand.

Just here, the vital relation of Political and Literary Reform is evident, and the peril is seen in the open fact of the Decline of Modern Politics from a civic science to a civic craft; from a high vocation on behalf of the state to a personal profession on behalf of the incumbent. On literary grounds, if on no others, National Politics should be kept pure, as on patriotic grounds national literature should be kept pure.

We note, moreover, that the literature of the Future, as it is expressed in Free States, must of necessity become, more and more, a School of Life—a vital and practical expression of the best thought of the time. "The relation of an author to his age," says Whipple, "is the most important of his life." Even Emerson, transcendentalist as he was, insisted, as an author, on the discussion of Society and Social Aims. Whatever has been true of the past, the time has now come, when the author and the man must be expressed, as never before, in one and the same personality.

CHAPTER SEVEN

LITERATURE AND LANGUAGE

PROFESSOR EARLE, in his elaborate treatise on English Prose, devotes an entire chapter to what he calls, "The Bearings of Philology," its bearings as a science, a study and a practical art on the work of the English writer or on Literature, in general. Thus he writes, "Philology is one of those studies which must be taken into account in a treatise which has English Prose for its scope, because it is one of the instruments whereby a man's mind may be made better acquainted with the material out of which Prose is constructed," and he quotes no less an authority than Dr. Johnson, the great lexicographer and essayist, to confirm his opinion. He refers to the enthusiasm so often connected with philological study and its reflex influence for good upon literary work. He then goes on to speak of the dislike that has been shown to Philology by men of letters, and explains it by the fact that every new science has to pass through such destructive criticism before its claims are fully conceded. Even so technical a study as Etymology, he writes, is conducive to literary uses and culture, as begetting in the writer the faculty and facility of verbal discrimination.

It must be acknowledged, however, that the drift of opinion is adverse to Prof. Earle and inclines to the view taken by Dugald Stewart, that such a pursuit is "unfavorable to elegance of composition."

Thus an anonymous author writes,—"The Science of Philology has made itself less and less felt in literature. In the United States, there is not, I believe, a single philologian who is a powerful writer, and this is the case the world over," and yet, he adds,—"Modern Philology which now regards as unscientific anything savoring of the Belles-Lettres, owes its own original impulse to literature," as German philology is indebted to Goethe, and Diez, founder of Romance philology, to Byron and his School.

In England, the discussion has been agitated with special zeal, as seen particularly in Collins' volume on "English Literature at the Universities," wherein he protests against the prevailing usages as to English in Oxford and Cambridge. The language of the London *Times*, in commenting on the treatise, is directly in point, as it says of it, that "it succeeds in showing how the too exclusively philological study of modern literatures at present patronized by the universities tends to encourage a somewhat pedantic spirit and to divest literature, as such, of nearly all that gives it its abiding hold on the human mind."

Thus the controversy goes on, and a correct view of language and literature as related to each other is in reality essential to a clear understanding of either alone, as it, also, has an important bearing on the entire subject of literary art, as to its best methods, its intrinsic nature and its governing ends.

1. We notice, first of all, that there is a natural and normal relation between Language and Literature and, hence, that literary study, in some well understood sense, must be linguistic.

Literature is and must be expressed through language as a medium. It is the resulting product and visible form of such expression, careful distinction being made between the product, literature itself, and the agency by which it is produced, language; or to state it in the terms of logic, the first cause of literature is the author himself, and the second cause is the language in which he embodies his thought. Hence, language is a means to an end and a means only, and is never to be confounded with the end. It is the instrument or agent by which the author works, and, yet, being an agent of mind and not of inert matter, the connection between it and the literature which it expresses must be a vital one rather than mechanical.

If we inquire, more specifically, as to the ways in which language enters into literary study, we answer: in diction and structure, in idiom and grammar and vocabulary and synonym, in securing, according to Swift, "the right word in the right place."

Hence, an author should be thoroughly acquainted with the history of his vernacular, from first to last; with its grammatical and logical structure; with its constituent elements as native and foreign; with its capabilities as a written and spoken tongue; with what is called the genius or spirit of the language, lying below any verbal usage or external feature.

More than this, he should be a student of language as well as of a language or his own language; should be conversant with that which makes language what it is as a means of communication; should clearly understand linguistic methods and uses and be an adept in the knowledge and use of words.

What Gould calls, "Good English," expresses very

tersely this close relationship of language and literature. By such English is meant that which is good in the linguistic sense and the literary sense and in these two senses in combination. So Dean Alford, in his "Queen's English," as Mr. White of our own country, in his "Words and their Uses," has reference to this unity of the agent and the product, of language and literature in one expressed form. Archbishop Trench in his "Study of Words," writes as an author as well as a linguist, and has in mind the best literary results in the work of those who study him. To say—as he does—that language is "fossil poetry" and "fossil history" is but another way of saying that it is fossil literature and is not to be studied as a something altogether apart from such literature and for its own sake. Hence, the authors of any nation are accepted as the standard in the use of their vernacular. English authors are the accepted authority as to English Language usage, so that here, if nowhere else, the bond of connection is seen.

Mr. Whipple, in his volume on "Literature and Life," in a critique on Roget's "Thesaurus of English Words," takes occasion to discuss the subject of the "Use and Misuse of Words," and to insist that their right use is found in detecting and developing their literary character and their abuse in neglecting this. As he says, "Expression is thought in the words and through the words and not thought *and* the words"; in fine, language has a relation to letters and letters to language.

Authors may be classified as to the way in which they have observed or violated this principle. Archbishop Trench himself is a notable example of a literary linguist, of a man who has used language as a medium to literature and that only, so that his numerous publications in the sphere of English Literature are in reality literature expressed in good English.

George P. Marsh and F. A. March are, also, to be cited as prominent examples of the principle before us. Acknowledged by all authorities as scientific English Philologists, their English, apart from manuals designed to be technical, is literary English. The same is true of Whitney, of America; and Müller, of England; and of Jacob Grimm, of Germany, and of all those professional teachers of language who have written in a literary spirit. No better instances of this could be found than are found in that long list of college and university professors in England and America and on the continent, who, while devoted to the technical study and teaching of their respective vernaculars, have written as authors as well as linguists. So, Curtius and Jebb and Jowett and Blackie and Earle and Morley. Special emphasis has been laid upon the fact that the late Ernest Renan, of France, the great Orientalist and biblical critic, did an invaluable work on behalf of the French Language and Literature. A master of the Semitic tongues and a master of his vernacular, he spoke and wrote the choicest French, and as if he had never made language a study for any other than literary purposes. An acute and a profound philologist, the scholastic side of his language study was concealed in his popular writings and he penned his thoughts with the freedom and naturalness of a child.

Lowell and Longfellow, of our own country, are witnesses in point, especially, as for years they were professional teachers of language from the critical and exegetical side, and we might expect to find in their pages prosaic evidence of such a vocation. There is nothing, however, of this. Wealth and accuracy of linguistic knowledge are displayed, but always presented in any but philological form, so that the author as an author is ever kept prominent above the etymologist.

There is then a true nexus, a priori and historical, between Language and Literature. Whatever their differences may be, there is a common middle ground where they meet and interact, and he is the true author and the wise linguist who recognizes it.

2. It is now in place to note the dangerous extreme to which the linguistic study of literature may be and has been carried.

The definite form which the discussion assumes at this point is, shall Literature be studied mainly on literary methods, as a literary product, or mainly or equally on linguistic methods, as a linguistic product, our present object being to insist upon the former as the preferable and only legitimate method and, conversely, to condemn the latter.

(*a*) If we seek the evidence of this extreme philological tendency, we find it, first of all, in Literary Criticism, fast assuming the form of linguistic criticism. An author's language is examined with painstaking minuteness. Each word of his vocabulary is taken by itself and made the subject of miscroscopic inspection and dissection, as if any author, writing from the purely literary side, could be expected to abide such a test. The literary critic, so called, is thus seen to narrow his area of investigation until he becomes nothing more or less than a professional verbalist; a mere analyzer of words and phrases; working in his verbal laboratory as the botanist and chemist work in their scientific laboratories. As he opens a volume of prose or poetry, the questions that are uppermost are not the old questions of style and taste, sentiment and spirit and esthetic law, but the newer questions of roots, derivations, prefixes and suffixes, text and context, past meanings and possible meanings, the balancing of conflicting opinions as to the use of terms and the force of particles, and a score of other related questions as to the purely verbal art which the author displays or fails to display. Precisely that is done which the French Academy of the time of Richelieu at length succeeded in doing, and which the unworthy imitators of Goethe and Schiller succeeded in doing, in Germany, in the eighteenth century. Literary criticism is made so linguistic that a Moliere must protest against the formalism of a Boileau and insist that the examination of authorship is more than a mere study of words.

(*b*) This tendency is, also, especially visible in our literary manuals. Text-books in literature are now prepared for schools and colleges, more and more, from the linguistic side. The criticism of text, the notes, explanations, definitions and critical data are prepared and presented mainly with the idea of philological precision and of cultivating in the student verbal aptitude. The attention of the student is held so intently to the line and the letter, to nice discriminations, to the history of critical opinion and disputed points of text, that but little time is left to take a comprehensive view of the author's work as a specifically literary product. One of the best features of Mr. Rolfe's editions of the Shakesperian Plays is seen in the fact, that he has thus far resisted, to a good degree, this technical process, so that, while securing the results of accurate scholarship along the lines of philology, he has also been mindful of the higher interests of dramatic literature. No careful student of English literary manuals can fail to note the growing influence of this philological passion, until it has become in certain quarters a cult or craze, if not an editorial hobby. Undoubtedly, the increasing attention to Old and Middle English is in part accountable for this, it being forgotten that while the study of Old English must be mainly philological, that of the New English, as Oliphant calls it, need not be. Because we must study "Beowulf" and the "Ormulum" as language-texts, this is not to say that Ben Jonson and Milton must be so studied, living, as they did, in specifically literary eras. Even so early an author as Chaucer, standing at the opening of national English, should be studied, chiefly, from the side of literature. Surely the "Canterbury Tales" were not written for a textbook in English Etymology, and only to afford a basis for the comparison of fourteenth-century English with that of to-day. No English author has been so misused as Chaucer at this point, for his verse is as fresh and as free as the air we breathe, full of the very juice and marrow of literature. Technical criticism has its place. Editors must see that we have a correct text and an intelligent interpretation. This secured, however, the author should be allowed to talk to us in his own way and not always through the mouth of the scribe. If literary students are accused of becoming fastidious, never so happy as when they find a colon where there should be a comma, and quite silent as to the genius of the author behind the text, we must lay the blame largely at the door of this etymological method, by which authors are examined as those who have left so many volumes of verse and prose for the study of the linguist, and who deserve, at their death, what Browning calls—"The Grammarian's Funeral."

In a word, these "anatomists of literature," as Mr. White styles them, have reduced literature to the plane of a commentary, and Addison and Milton and Macaulay and Tennyson must be so overburdened with Notes and Foot-Notes, Addenda and Emendations, that one is at a loss to know, meanwhile, just what he is studying—literature, grammar, a lexicon or a syllabus.

It is to this that Prof. Moulton refers in his volume on "Shakespeare as a Dramatic Artist," as he says—"The idea, I believe, prevails that anything like the discussion of literary characters or dramatic effect is out of place in an educational work, is indeed, too indefinite to be examined on," and he adds, by way of refutation, that he has had "ten years' experience in teaching literature apart from philology."

The influence of Germany, as a philosophical and literary center, has undoubtedly been powerful in this direction. The German mind, naturally philosophic, has easily passed over from a safe and moderate philosophic method to that of a hypertechnical and abstruse one. Philosophy itself is presented more in the form of a logical technique than in a readable and attractive method. Theology is studied and presented from the side of dogma and the speculative reason rather than in practical forms for practical ends.

Language is pursued from the scientific side as an end in itself and one of the many topics for analysis and erudite study, so that, when literature is made the subject of investigation, the method of the schools is easily transferred. Style, taste, sentiment and final objective effect are ignored or underrated and the text of the author is the subject-matter, and this, despite the fact, that the common folk of Germany are of simple tastes and are quick to discern and enjoy the strictly literary quality of authors. There is no nation in Europe where the commonalty so appreciate the simple folk-lore, the national ballads and tales, where such a poet as Schiller is more enjoyed. If Goethe is the author of German scholars, and "Faust," especially in its second and more abstruse part, captivates them, Schiller and Herder and Heine and Richter and Hans Sachs are the authors of the people. It is a singular and somewhat inexplicable fact that, when the influence of Germany in the eighteenth century came in upon England, it came in the twofold form of impulse and criticism, producing, on the one hand, a genuine literary awakening and, on the other, an undue emphasis of the abstract and technical in literary art.

It was a romantic and a classical revival in one. The influence of the French critical school was somewhat similar, as seen in Pope and the correct authors in the Augustan Age, while, as the science of Modern Philology has advanced with unwonted rapidity from its crude beginnings to its perfected form, literature has for the time been somewhat in abeyance, and reduced, at the best, to a science of expression.

One of the strongest proofs of the essential unsoundness of this textual method in literature is seen in the fact, that it prevails in eras of literary decline, partly, as the cause and, partly, as the consequence of such a decline.

This is seen very clearly in the literary decadence between Milton and Addison, when the artificial canons of the time restricted, in large measure, the open progress of literary thought and taste by substituting verbal niceties for poetic inspiration. No amount of high eulogy by such a critic as Mr. Gosse can suffice to redeem such a literature in the eyes of discerning students. True, indeed, Modern Philology had not taken on, at this time, its present expansive forms, but the critical and exegetical method had already appeared in extreme form, even in so representative an author as Dryden, and the encroachments of the linguistic on the literary had already begun. Dryden's fame as a prose writer rests mainly on what are known as his "Critical Prefaces," in which criticism often became too textual and technical and served as such to modify and lessen literary effects. With the second and third rate authors of the day, this error was, of course, pushed to even more dangerous extremes. Injurious wherever found, it is especially so in the sphere of verse, as seen in the couplets and epistles of Pope. What De Quincey has called "Mechanology" took the place of "Organology"—the letter ruled the spirit, and correctness of diction, structure and versification was the final aim. By this process, literature is reduced to a something that is neither strictly philological nor literary, but is an arbitrary compromise between them, and fails, thereby, of producing the best effects of either.

What we have called the differentia of literature, its ideal or idealistic element, is hereby eliminated, and hence it is, that poetry is most of all the sufferer, as representing the imaginative side of literature, the tendency being to reduce all its forms to the didactic, the least poetic of all, or to make the dividing line between verse and prose almost a vanishing factor.

The "Faerie Queene," "Othello" and "Comus"

must thus yield to Pope's "Essay on Criticism" or "Essay on Man," while, even in the province of prose expression, the lighter and more flexible forms of narration and description and miscellany are made subservient to what may be termed the educational and disciplinary, the least literary forms.

If these things are so, then it follows as a safe and practical instruction that Language should be taught, in the main, on the side and in the light of its literature, and not as an end in itself.

There are exceptional instances, indeed, where the aim is purely technical and scholastic, and where the method of study as minute and detailed may be justified as such, but for the purposes of the student of literature, the literature should always take the precedence.

We are living in the day of excited discussion as to the exact influence of classical teaching and study, in their relation to the Modern Languages of Continental Europe and the vernacular English. Must the classics go, or, more specifically, must the Greek go, are the questions mooted. It is not in place here to enter upon this discussion, but it is in place to say, that much of this agitation has been occasioned by the fact that, in the majority of instances, these older languages have been taught purely or mainly from the linguistic side, with little or no reference to their literary nature and qualities. Hence, the teaching has been prosaic, hypertechnical and tedious, instead of being instinct with personality and life. In this respect, these languages have justified their name, The Dead Languages, and have thus occasioned a reaction that has as yet by no means spent its force. Even Modern Tongues may be presented and pursued on this soulless method, as made up merely of grammar and lexicon; of roots and stems; of particles and vocables, and not as the embodiment of modern thought and taste. It is precisely this to which Whipple refers in his invective against words for words' sake, and on which Emerson lays such emphasis as he contends for naturalness and strength in literary art.

An able paper on "Philology and Literature in American Colleges and Universities" goes so far as to say, by way of challenge, that there are not a half dozen institutions in America, where it can be said that Literature is taught as literature, the implication being, that it is taught as Philology, as a body of words and sentences adjusted on correct linguistic principles and nothing more. The writer pleads for the diffusion of a better method, the subordination of language to literature, if so be American students are to perpetuate the literary work and spirit of the earlier school of authors.

No better example of this higher method can be found in American Letters than that furnished us in the old Knickerbocker School of Bryant and his friends, in the writings of Cooper and Dana and Drake and Halleck and Morris and Paulding and Washington Irving. Of these writings, as a class, that can be said that Wilson says of the "Salmagundi" Essays, that they are "sunny and good natured." Irving himself is a brilliant example of this school of life, where literature was studied and published as literature and for literary ends with no thought of any specifically critical purpose. Irving's "Sketch Book" and Bryant's "Thanatopsis" would have long since passed into oblivion, had such a method characterized them.

Such a method is especially needful in the present

age, not only because the science of Philology is making such advances and is encroaching more and more on literary domain, but because other influences as well are working in the direction of the unliterary. A bold and gross industrialism is militating, as far as it goes, against a high type of literary taste and all literary forces are to be mustered to resist it.

There seems, moreover, to be even among authors a satisfaction of scholarly ambition when letters are approached from the scholarly side, and the critical method in prose and verse is emphasized. They thus seem to separate themselves, as they suppose, from the vast horde of scribblers who write superficially because uncritically, and have not the learning or insight to show in their writings that they understand the scientific meaning of the words they use.

This is a plausible error in that it is forgotten that literature may be philosophic without being technical; learned without being pedantic, and scholarly without being scholastic.

Language, then, is one thing and literature another. Whatever their relation, their methods and aims are diverse, and can not be safely made to coalesce. Literature is a verbal art, but it is a something more. It is the language of the author's vernacular, but a something more. It must be grammatically and linguistically correct, but far more than this. It is an assemblage of terms and phrases and constructions, but far more. Literature can not be reduced to a verbal exposition, and when Dowden and Mabie and other critics speak of the interpretation of literature, or of literature as an interpretation, infinitely more is meant than that literature is merely a verbal exegesis.

"Thoughts that breathe and words that burn" can not always satisfy the severe demands of the philologian, but they are none the less the content and soul of the best literature. There is nothing better in literature than the spirit of life, so that it becomes to all who read it a mental and an emotional stimulus. Much discussion is being given at present to the question whether or not literature is a truly disciplinary study and pursuit. If by this is meant that it is to be disciplinary as the study of science or mathematics or metaphysics is such, then, we submit, that to make it such would be to modify it from its original status and purpose. Literature is not a branch of pedagogics, nor was it ever designed to be a discipline in the sense in which what are called the disciplinary or educational branches are such, and here we meet one of the main differences between language and literature.

Language, as such, is a disciplinary study—so understood and so pursued, its object being, to cultivate what may be called, the language nature or faculty. It has to do therefore with the discrimination of words, with their analysis and exposition, with structure and lexicography, and it is only when studied and used by the author that they subordinate their educational element to that which has to do with art and taste and final effect; with imagination and feeling and beauty. Literature is thus a science and a philosophy, but is also an inspiration. It must be developed through language as a medium, but has, also, to do with impassioned thought, with imaginative outlook, with sublimity of word and phrase. It is a recorded text for comment, but, also, an embodied soul for appreciative study and enjoyment. It is a creative as well as a constructive art, a sphere in which "the vision and the faculty divine" may have fitting scope and reach their most pronounced results.

One of the somewhat puzzling spectacles of modern times is brought to view in the apparent decrease of literary insight and spirit as linguistic insight and spirit increase, forcing the question upon us whether, after all, there are elements existing that make them mutually exclusive.

The cases in which there goes on a corresponding development are historically rare. If the authors quoted —such as Marsh and Renan, are examples of the union and interaction of the two, they are but notable exceptions to the general principle, so that it is now scarcely expected that they shall coexist. Such a divorce is unscientific and unnatural and is begotten of that tendency to extremes so potent in human history, and, hence, the difficulty of men of letters as of linguists in minimizing differences and magnifying common elements, if so be that the highest influence both of language and literature may be felt. The few representative men who have effected such a combination are sufficient to prove its possibility and open the way for a more general illustration of it.

Be this as it may, however, literature can not safely become philological in any professional and pedagogic sense, while, at the same time, able and ready to use in its own way all the latest and best results of philological criticism.

The author has to do with words only as they are the common carrier of thought and life, of faith and truth, of insight and outlook, of the spiritual and eternal in human character. When Carlyle tells us that "Literature is the thought of thinking souls," it is but another way of saying that literature is the expression of the mind, mediated through the entire nature of the man—his imagination, feelings, and taste. Literature is the expression of human personality, the written embodiment, in artistic form, of the intellect and life of the race.

CHAPTER EIGHT

LITERATURE AND LITERARY CRITICISM

WE are living in a critical age, an age of criticism, induced, partly, by the fact of the rapid multiplication of books which are supposed to form the occasion and basis for the critical art and, partly, by certain manifest literary tendencies in the direction of technique and the study of literary theory, the increasing interest in what may be called the speculative side of literature. Hence, the growth of critical bibliography, sufficient in itself to constitute a library; books about books; authors about authors. We have, thus, the Principia of Literature, as Newton prepared a "Principia" of Science. Such a treatise as Saintsbury's "History of Literary Criticism" or Gailey and Scott's "Methods and Materials of Literary Criticism" is sufficient to reveal the wide province now covered by critical science as applied to letters, the large number of students engaged in its study, and the increasing demand, on the part of the reading public, for fuller instruction along this specific line of intellectual effort. In so far as English Literature is concerned, this revived activity dates back to the days of Matthew Arnold, while a corresponding general movement in European Letters may be noted. Nor is it meant by this that Literary Criticism is now pursued abstractly as a science and for its own ends, quite irrespective of the authorship that lies behind it and which has, indeed, induced it; that a school of criticism has arisen for speculative purposes only, and as a kind of diversion from the more serious and original work of literary production. On the contrary, the renewed interest is a thoroughly normal one, the necessary expression of authorship itself, and for a better understanding of its merits and defects. It is to the special praise of Arnold, and of the living critic Brunetiere, that, in their view, criticism is but a means to an end, and can never be safely allowed to stand upon its own merits.

CRITICISM

We are dealing, first of all, with Criticism, as distinct from any other form or branch of literary study with which it might be confounded, such as, narrative, descriptive and forensic discourse, or miscellany, in its most general sense. We speak, and speak correctly, of critical miscellany, as distinct from that which is uncritical or non-critical. Hence, what are known as sketches, history, travels, written forensic addresses, and the various types of prose fiction are examples of non-critical literature. Thus, Masson classifies the writings of De Quincey into three generic divisions, the second of which is called, "The Speculative, Didactic and Critical," in which division these three terms are used synonymously. Dryden's "Critical Prefaces" are thus distinctly marked from other British Miscellany, as Addison's review, in the "Spectator," of Milton's "Paradise Lost" is distinguished from the more general papers of the series. In this sense, American authors, such as Lowell, and British authors, such as Coleridge, have written criticism.

LITERARY CRITICISM

Still further, the subject before us is, Literary Criticism, as distinct from that which is philosophic, scientific, theological, or political. Such critiques as Addison's, on, "Tragedy and Comedy," or Johnson's, on, "The Lives of The English Poets," or Lamb's, on, "The Artificial Comedy of The Last Century," are thus literary as contrasted with such dissertations as De Quincey's, "Political Parties of Modern England," or Matthew Arnold's "God and The Bible," or Lowell's "Democracy," or with any discussions in which the taste and artistic quality are not prominent. Linguistic criticism is one thing; Literary criticism is another. While, here and there, an author such as, George P. Marsh, or Francis A. March, or the late scholarly Whitney, or Earle, or Arnold, has written on philology in a literary way, the instances are so rare as not to invalidate the principle stated. So, forensic criticism is not, as a rule, literary, tho Burke has written on British Politics, and Bryce, on American Politics, in a literary manner. Even "speculative" authorship, as De Quincey uses the term to indicate the metaphysical and technical in the sphere of mental science, is not, generally, literary, even tho Berkeley and Cousin and Descartes have written philosophy on literary methods. When De Quincey writes on The Human Brain, and on Plato's "Republic," and on Kant's theories, as a metaphysician, he is not writing distinctive literary criticism, as when he writes on Carlyle and Goldsmith and Goethe.

Jonathan Swift, in his "Tale of a Tub," writes of three different kinds of critics—those who collect and systematize the principles of esthetic art for the guidance of others; those who devote themselves to the restoration of learning from the "graves and dust of manuscripts"; and those whom he calls "the third and noblest sort, the true critics" whose mission is "to travel through the vast world of writings" and discuss the qualities of books and authors. However these orders of critics may differ, as to emphasizing merits or defects or investigating ancient or modern authorship, they are alike in being literary in the sense that we are pressing.

As to the different species of literary criticism itself, there need be no prolonged discussion, even tho some variety of opinion exists regarding them. Masson, in his classification of De Quincey's works, already cited, separates his critical writings from those that he calls—descriptive, biographical, historical and imaginative, and, yet, each of these divisions of authorship offers, in a true sense, some sphere for literary judgment, inasmuch as in type and spirit such forms of authorship are literary. Hence, we have what may justly be called, descriptive criticism, as in De Quincey's Sketches of Coleridge, Wordsworth and other authors, and in such modern American writers as Holmes, Warner and Curtis. While in these examples criticism is presented in its most general and popular form, quite divested of anything like the didactic, analytic and logical, such literature has still enough of the judicial in it to give it the character of a running comment on books and authors. Hence, also, we speak, and correctly so, of historical criticism, not meaning thereby a criticism of history but a literary criticism historical in its form and spirit. Writers in the special sphere of the history of literature, such as Hallam and Craik, Morley and Tyler, have illustrated this type, or De Quincey, in such papers as "The Cæsars," "Charlemagne," "The Essenes" and "The Pagan Oracles." Even within the sphere of the imaginative, a kind of criticism enters, as is plainly evinced in the accepted phrase, poetic criticism, as distinct from that which is philosophic, historical and didactic. The phrase, esthetic critisism, at present so current, is so far widened as often to include every form and application of the examination of literature, tho specifically used to apply to that order of examination which views the subject in hand as a work of art in its relation to the faculty of taste.

At times, we hear of logical criticism, which seems to refer to a study of the validity or falsity of argument. So, verbal criticism emphasizes the language of authorship. It is textual or exegetical, rather than subjective and mental.

In these and kindred terms, of whatever diversity, literature is the fundamental conception, and the order of judgment is essentially literary. The phrase, Literary Criticism, may thus be defined to be, that science and art which has to do with the examination of the quality and form of literary authorship. As a science, it gathers and formulates critical principles, and as an art, it seeks to apply those principles to concrete examples of authorship in prose and verse. Criticism as a literary form has thus its own place and function, and as, in the nature of the human mind, it will express itself after one method or another, it is highly important that its method be the best. When Carlyle, in referring to Criticism in Germany, writes, "that it stands like an interpreter between the inspired and the uninspired to clear our sense that it may discern beauty" he at once lifts the art of literary judgment above the plane of the commonplace to a level of mental and moral outlook and power.

When it is remembered that its radical elements are literary and intellectual insight, a profound and delicate affinity of spirit with all that is best in authorship, and a conscientions fidelity to truth and justice in the examination of literary product, it will be evident that its requisitions are of the highest order, and that the charlatan, novice and morally indifferent are out of place in the execution of its trusts. "The critical function" writes Professor Richardson "is as legitimate as the creative, and, in a true sense, it is as high. Some criticism is creative literature in the best sense." To the same effect, Matthew Arnold contends, as, does Mr. Stedman, of our own country. The fact that criticism is found, at times, in verse, as in Pope's "Essay on Criticism" and Lowell's "Fable For Critics," and that many of the ablest critics of England and America, as Arnold and Poe, have been poets as well, detracts in no whit, as some allege, from the mental quality of criticism as an art, but rather shows its wide-reaching function in the sphere of literature and its happy combination of genius and artistic taste. He should be the best critic of prose or verse who has written acceptably in each province, while not a few of our representative English authors have done their best work and won their highest place and repute along the line of criticism, rather than on that of any other form of prose expression.

There is criticism, as we know, and there is criticism. There is an ignorant, an unsympathetic, a superficial and partial censorship of books and men of letters, but there is, also, a science and an art of literary inlook and outlook; a sane and sober method of interpretation as well as of observation; a study of mind and art as related; a study of mind in art and of art in mind; of esthetic genius as revealed in the province of imagination, sentiment and taste; an investigation of causal agencies working behind and below what is called literature on the printed page. This is the criticism of which we speak and brings into play every finest faculty of the complex nature of man.

Of this high order of personal judgment more is urgently needed among us, partly, to minimize the distance between the production and the examinatien of literature and, partly, for its own sake, to make sure those high results within the realm of letters which the judicial faculty and habit are supposed to guarantee.

More than this, of all men, the critic should be the humblest, and the readiest to sit in judgment and with fullest severity upon his own creative work or his work as a critic, as it is not until he has developed this generous and lowly temper that his conclusions are valid for himself or others.

It is in this spirit that Lessing and Saint Beuve, Coleridge and De Quincey, Lowell and Whipple wrote and judged and, for this reason, if for no other, their decisions have commended themselves to the literary world.

Lord Kames, in his "Elements of Criticism," calls special attention to the object and varied advantages of the critical art, the prime purpose being, in his view, the expression and development of taste, and its benefits, lying in the line of esthetic pleasure, the formation of the habit of literary discrimination, and its effect on character and conduct in elevating and purifying the entire nature of man.

All true literary criticism, as to its object, it may be said, is constructive and positive rather than destructive and negative; synthetic more than analytic; and, thus, serves to stimulate and encourage authors rather than to rebuke and repress them. Swift's satire, in his "Tale of a Tub," on those critics whose chief delight is in the detection and exposition of errors is well deserved, and points to the better method by which what is meritorious is magnified and all demerit reduced to a minimum. Hence, what are known as, the Canons of Criticism, should be determined from this point of view, such as that of Matthew Arnold's, that criticism has to do "with the best that is known and thought in the world"; or that of Stedman's "that a critic must accept what is best in a poet and thus become his best encourager." "The thing to know of a writer," says Arnold, "is, where he is all himself and his best self," if so be, we may thus do him no wrong in the way of a captious fault-finding. In a word, what has been termed, the function of criticism, is thus seen to be positive, incitive and catholic, free from negations, discouragements and .mental narrowness. Criticism, as such, should thus take its place in literature as a commanding art for the worthiest ends; should invite to its service the best minds of the time, and be an important factor in general intellectual life.

This, indeed, it is now doing. Better work has never been done in this direction than that which is now in process. Literary critics are asking somewhat as the old masters, Longinus, Cousin and Lessing asked—What are the conditions of all successful criticism? What are its possibilities as an adjutant to literary study, and what its limitations? What are its best methods, and how can the manifest errors that have obtained hitherto be nullified or lessened?

In fine, how can the science be delivered out of the hands of its enemies and be kept under the control of competent guides? It is gratifying to note, that, in the solution of these problems, literary criticism is receiving valuable aid from all other related provinces of criticism, philosophic and linguistic, scientific and sociological, so that the unity of truth shall be preserved, and the examination of literature be conducted on principles and by methods common to all other leading departments of study.

I. We are now prepared to enter, somewhat more specifically, into the discussion before us, and inquire, first of all, as to The Primary Purpose of Literary Criticism. According to Arnold, its purpose is "to see the object as in itself it really is," or, as he elsewhere states it, "to learn and propagate the best that is known and thought in the world." Brunetiere, of France, insists, more definitely, that the purpose of criticism is threefold, to explain, to classify and to judge. This explanation involves what we mean by the exposition or elucidation of an author, a book, a literary movement. The classification involves the assignment of the author or book to its legitimate place as related to other books and authors. The judging involves a final and an abiding determination, an estimate of quality and spirit and purpose, this last object, that of judging, being the one to which the others are preparative and subordinate. Criticism, as the word implies, is a Judgment.

Thus Dryden, in one of his "Critical Prefaces," says of Criticism—"that it is a standard of judgment, whose purpose is to enable us to observe those excellencies which shall delight a reasonable reader." Its purpose says Hennequin, "is to show the relations of any work to the author of it." Lowell tersely expresses it, "The object of criticism is not to criticize but to understand," or as Maurice states it—"to discover what is true and permanent." Thus the varied views might be cited at length, while, in the last analysis, they can all be safely reduced to a few cardinal propositions. As far as our present purpose is concerned, and in the light of literary history, the Final Purpose of Literary Criticism may be best expressed by the words—Interpretation and Decision. The critic is the Interpreter and the Judge, his office being to examine and disclose the quality of the literary product before him and, in the light of it, to give his decision.

As Lowell intimates, it is the critic's object to understand the subject himself and to make others understand it, and so to widen the bounds of human knowledge. It is evident, therefore, that if this is the aim of criticism, the special qualities that the critic must possess are clearness of conception and the ability to embody his conceptions in definite and conclusive form. What Arnold has called "straight thinking" is needed, absence of mental crookedness, bias and narrowness, the skill to see and study and state the thing as it really is. At no point are the intellectual demands of criticism more clearly seen.

II. As to the Methods of Criticism, also, there may be and has been a valid difference of opinion, the point of importance in such diversity being as to which of these methods should at the time prevail. The German author, Urlichs, and others speak of all methods as reducible to the Higher and Lower, it being left to the judgment of the critic as to just how this classification shall be made. We shall mention four distinct methods:

1. The Historical. Any literary history, so called, as Hallam's or Sismondi's is clearly of this order, wherein

the history being literary is as such critical, the historian as he passes on from point to point, pausing, as he deems best, to comment on what is under review, precisely as the civil historian fulfills the function of a political critic. Such a book as Masson's "Life and Times of Milton" or Tyler's "Literary History of The American Revolution" is of this type. There is a sense in which it may be said that Historical Criticism lies on the border-line between the higher and the lower orders, it being somewhat easy for the critic to pass from the work of criticism proper to that of ordinary historical narrative.

2. A further method is the Textual, confining itself to the letter of the book in hand. It is the grammatical, verbal or exegetical method, dealing with authorship only and not with authors.

By this method, the literature examined must be made to stand the test of correct verbal usage, of correct structure. It must conform to the statutes laid down. Words, sentences and figures must be appropriate. Textual Criticism is, in a sense, syntactical, having, as might be expected, a much wider scope in linguistic subjects than in those purely literary, where the commentator must deal with texts and manuscripts and insist upon absolute fidelity to the accepted canons of the schools.

3. Esthetic Criticism magnifies the sentiment and spirit above the letter, detects and appreciates the beautiful wherever found, and insists that literature is, first and last, artistic, involving grace and finish and all that is expressed in the word—Form. Especially in poetry as a Fine Art is this order of criticism applicable, wherein, on the principle of poetic license, the poet must have scope

and privilege, and not be held, as in the textual method, to the most minute conditions and restrictions. One of the most natural applications of this method is seen in the spacious province of Style. As an English critic expresses it—"Criticism is a search into the primary laws of good writing." This is the dominant feature in Arnold's work as a critic, apart from which he can not be understood. In his treatise—"The Study of Celtic Literature" he discusses Style; insists that the absence of it in German Literature is conspicuous; shows how it appears in Dante, Virgil and Milton, and remarks—"that the turn for style is perceptible all through English poetry" noting, as its essential elements—Simplicity and Dignity. What he calls, "the grand style," is notable for its serious decorum, for what Longinus calls "elevation of spirit."

Hence, the copious literature on this subject from Plato and Aristotle down to Ruskin and Pater—what it is, what its relation to literature is, what its relation is to the thought behind it and to the author, and how it may best be cultivated. The esthetic method with all its merits has not always escaped the special peril that besets it, an undue emphasis of the merely formal in literary art and style.

4. Hence, the need of the Philosophic Method. It is the application of thought to criticism—the Intellectual Method proper and especially adapted to the best forms of Prose. Here the critic inquires—What does the author say and mean? What is the value of his message? Is it original and does it add to the content of existing truth? So, in the study of an epoch, he inquires—What is its literary meaning? What principles are at stake at

the time and how does it affect other epochs? In short, the critic is now dealing with the foundations of literature and with all those basal problems that emerge as the foundations are examined. The method is retrospective and profound, as seen in Spencer's "Philosophy of Style" and Courthope's "Life in Poetry and Law in Taste." It is this method that brings criticism into vital relation to all the highest forms of mental action and coordinates it with literature itself as but one of its manifold phases.

We speak of Literature and Literary Criticism, and, yet, we are to remember that properly interpreted, the product and the study of the product are alike literature, the critic and the author, the one personality. If, as we are told, literary criticism has not yet reached the "scientific stage" of its development, it may be safely asserted that through the application of this Philosophic Method this "scientific stage" is practically reached.

III. An additional inquiry awaits us as we note—The Results or Benefits that accrue to Literary Criticism when properly understood and applied.

1. The first of these is a fuller Appreciation of Literature, with all which that involves, such as a keen and an unerring sense of the artistic; a close discrimination between the true and the false in authorship; the possession of what Hazlitt calls "a refined understanding"; in a word, literary taste and tone and spirit, a sense of companionship with the best literature so that as soon as seen it is known to be the best. Without this result both to the critic and the reader, criticism is a failure, thwarting us just where we look for success and need it the most. It is this appreciativeness which will guide

the mind in that Choice of Books of which Mr. Harrison speaks, so that by a kind of cultivated instinct or affinity what Maurice calls, The Friendship of Books, will be enjoyed.

2. A further Result is seen in the Enlargement and Enriching of Literature itself as its historical development goes on in any age or nation. This, indeed, is the ultimate aim of all literary comment, to lessen and, if possible, eliminate all existing defects and make an open way for the realization of the best ideals. No just and catholic application of critical canons should be long continued in any nation's literary history without its being soon followed by the unerring signs of literary improvement both in scope and quality. The critic, at this point, is the accepted guardian of the nation's literary interests; draws from the past both encouragement and warning; indicates the ways in which the good may be conserved and the objectionable avoided, and by holding up an ever higher literary standard serves to give steadiness and consistency to literary progress. This is something more than literary appreciation. It is literary effort and expression on the part of those to whom, for the present, a people's literary reputation is entrusted and whose duty it is to leave the literature better than they found it.

3. Another natural Result of all true criticism is seen in its relation to the General Reading Public, in the line of the Education of the Public Taste. This is something different from the subjective Appreciation of the critic or the objective Enlargement of Literature. It is the application of critical canons to the outside world of

every-day life ; to the street and counting-room ; and shop and farm ; to the body politic proper, so as to make it, in so far as possible, a literary constituency, exerting, as such, a wholesome reactionary influence on the critic and the author. We speak of the literary world. This should mean more by far than the limited circle of authors and critics by profession and the comparatively limited circle that frequents the library. It should include the intelligent public at large, the middle classes proper, indirectly and, yet, potently affected by the mere prevalence of sound principles of criticism and the diffusion of good taste. Literary Criticism, thus interpreted, should go far to make good literature a general commodity, attractive to the people in the mass. It should secure General Culture. From the discussion thus presented, various problems of interest emerge. As old as the Art of Criticism is, dating back to Aristotle, it is, also, as new as the latest literary deliverance in the pages of a contemporary magazine. Literary Criticism is said to be, at present, "dynamic." This means that it is more conscious than ever of its inherent power and feels more fully than ever the consciousness of its growing strength. "An appreciative curiosity," it is added, characterizes it. This is but another way of saying that the whole history and character of literary criticism is now recasting, that it must be reopened and studied from new points of view, that much that was true in Aristotle's time may not hold good in the present century of European Letters. Old questions long ago considered settled are demanding readjustment and new problems are emerging under new conditions, so that in criticism, as in literature itself, the impartial student is kept busy in noting and interpreting the signs of the times. As to what these Problems specifically are, a wide difference of opinion may prevail. Some of them, by way of example, may be stated. Precisely what is the Province of Criticism—its scope and its limitations? What is the exact relation of Criticism to Creative literary Production, and how and why do eras of Criticism and Production appear and disappear as they do? What is the relation of Literary Criticism to other critical types—Scientific, Philosophic and to what extent is it justly linguistic? What are the necessary Conditions of Criticism and the necessary Qualifications of the critic?

Is a School of Criticism such as the French Academy under Richelieu desirable in its literary effects? What is the Comparative Merit of the great critics of literature? What is the legitimate relation of Criticism to Journalism, and what are the most apparent needs at present in the line of advancing the interests of the Art? Such questions as these indicate the scope of the subject in hand and the interest that attends any proper discussion of it.

A suggestion or two must suffice.

(*a*) That Literary Criticism must ever be kept in vital contact with Literature, and never be made an end in itself. It must have the pulse of life in it; must be an organic process and not the official method of an expert.

(*b*) Further, Literary Criticism must be kept in the hands of Literary Masters and never delegated to Novices. No great author is too great to assume the critic's function, and no work that he may do is more important than his critical work. There are great critics and great critical masterpieces as there are great poems and great plays. Critical Genius is a distinct order of genius in the realm of letters.

CHAPTER NINE

LITERATURE AND LIFE

THAT might be said of Literature in general which Courthope says of Poetry, "that it is as much the reflection of the growth of the national mind and circumstance as history is the record of the national life. We ought to be acquainted historically with the general laws that seem to determine the progress of popular imagination." To this, Vinet, the French critic, responds, as he says—"Literature has man for its subject and end. The aim of the poet is to see life steadily and to see it whole. . . . The author is to be impregnated with the social movement." As a matter of fact, we might say, that Literature has hitherto been regarded by many critics and by the popular judgment as a something separated widely from the common life of the respective eras in which it has flourished,—the peculiar province of scholars or men of letters, the study of the school, the cloister and the select circle, the exclusive pursuit of the cultured and the higher classes. In earlier European history and, especially, in that of the Middle Ages, not a little sanction was given to this view by the necessities of civilization. Learning itself was not diffused. Manuscripts, before the invention of printing, were rare. There was a clannish tendency among authors as among tribes and peoples, and it was not until the Revival of Learning, in the sixteenth century, when the classics were diffused, and the modern nations took on a new life, that literature itself became less exclusive and sought to identify itself with all the external activities of men. Then sprang up what Possnett has called, a World-Literature. The "Voices of the People," as Herder states it, were now heard. Literature became what Mr. Arnold has called it,—a "criticism of life," including, in its progress, an ethnological element, a catholicity of type and function altogether alien to it in the former time. So pronounced is this new departure that literature and civilization must now be studied in the light of each other, as they are so studied by such comprehensive authors as Guizot and Draper and Buckle and Scherer and Hallam and Sismondi. The student of national progress is struck at the outset by the vital manner in which literary events and civic events mutually affect each other. This is especially illustrated by noting the way in which Literature has been affected by Revolutions, inasmuch as national life in such crises is expressed in its most intense form. Prof. Dowden, in his able volume on "The French Revolution and English Literature," applies this principle to one European Nation, when the Reign of Terror was occasioned by and also occasioned a type of literature as extreme and impassioned as was the civil struggle itself. The same could be shown in Germany, in the Thirty Years' War, and in the later struggles of the Empire to secure its confederation. In English Letters, from Chaucer down, this influence is notable—in the French and English Wars; in the Wars of the Roses; in the Reformation of the sixteenth century; in the Revolutions of 1640 and 1688, and in the influence of the American Revolution of 1776, and the French Revolution of 1789, on England and English authors. Such authors as Coleridge and Wordsworth and Shelley and Blake and Byron evinced this effect of

French life on English in so marked a manner as to color the entire literature of the opening of the nineteenth century.

What Mr. Whipple has called, Literature and Life, are here so related that the study of the one not only involves that of the other, but the study of the one is the study of the other, and they are to be viewed as two volumes of one and the same book, giving an account of the sayings and doings of man. There is what Triggs has called, The Social Imagination. Hence, we notice, at the outset, the relation of History to Literature, history itself, in reality, being one of the forms of literature. By the term, history, however, we mean now civic life, as revealing itself through the successive centuries or as recorded on the page for the study of the scholar.

In the Preface to Courthope's "Liberal Movement in English Letters," we read, "My intention has been to trace historically the manner in which the movement in behalf of liberty during the present century has affected the order established in the sphere of Imagination." Here the author applies national life in one of its phases, the movement toward civil liberty, to literature in one of its phases, Poetry. The application, however, is as broad as national life and literature in their widest reach, and can be tested satisfactorily at any point along the line of what we call, the historical development of a people. There is an Historical Method in Literature, an examination of literary data, of facts and opinions and incidents and events with reference to reaching intelligent and safe conclusions. There is a survey of literary progress as there is a survey of historical progress, conducted after the same manner and affecting each other at points innumerable.

This is true, whatever the process may be, chronological or logical, the latter being in literature as in history the higher process, and the two processes fusing into one in all the best forms either of history or literature. There is then a History of Literature,—a record of literary life as it has been lived, as there is a History of Philosophy and of Science and of the Arts and of Language.

There is, moreover, what we may term, The Historical Spirit in Literature,—the spirit of research, inquiry, and an impartial purpose to reach and diffuse the truth. Hallam, in his "European Literature in the Fifteenth and Sixteenth Centuries," has so written, as Schlegel has in his "Philosophy of History," as Henry Morley has done in his "History of English Writers," and as all historians have done who have aimed to exhibit authorship in vital contact with the life of the time in which it was developing.

Not that the study of Literature should be confined to a study of its History. There is a manifest danger here to which too many students of literature have already yielded, of subordinating the spirit and purpose of literature to its facts and dates, of studying the life and times of an author more than the author himself; of being thoroughly acquainted with the record of opinion as to English Prose and Verse, and being essentially ignorant of the prose and verse itself.

There is too much of this recitative, annalistic process by which the heart and soul of the literature are missed. All this is necessary, but with it and as germane to it, there is to be that wider process by which Literature as a life as well as a statement is to be examined and the inner impulses of literary movement to be seen and felt. The very phrase,—historical progress—indicates life and change, and change ever for the better. Literary History is in the making even as we study it, and, tho there is a sense in which the historical record of the old literatures is a finished record, this is in no sense true in the great historic literatures of the spoken tongues and of modern times, instinct, as they are, with life, and requiring on the part of him who examines them a keen discrimination to detect every element and form of progress and to separate the living from the dead. English Literature has its permanent and its variable phases, and it is in the region of this latter series of movements that the eye must be ever open to note the order and quality of the change. A brief reference, at this point, to the celebrated threefold theory of Taine will be of interest as setting forth still more clearly this sociological element in literature, in the relation of Letters to Life.

1. There is, first, the relation of Literature to Race—the racial element in literature, as Mr. Freeman applies it to Language. Hence, if we contrast two such peoples as the Shemitic and the Aryan, such a relation is at once apparent, the difference between Asiatic literature or Hebraic literature and that of Germany and the Goths being as marked as the racial difference. The literature of the Shemitic races is the embodiment of Oriental life, as that of the Indo-European races is of Hellenic and Teutonic life, while within the separate province of either of these great families, the same influence is noticeable, the Latins as a race expressing one form of literary life and the North Europeans as a race, quite another, tho each is alike Indo-Germanic.

In Great Britain itself, Scotch and Irish and English Literature are quite distinguishable as types, expressing, as they do, distinctive, tribal, and racial differences, while American Literature, whatever its features of similarity, has a type and mission of its own, as the exponent of the American branch of the English-speaking peoples.

2. So as to Literature and Environment. There is such a thing in literature as the local factor—the *genius loci*, begetting a certain kind of literary life. The mere position of the English Channel is enough to account for some of the phases that mark English Literature, as contrasted with that of the continent, where peoples live closely together and infringe upon each other. What is called, the Scotch Literature of Northern England could not well have flourished in Kent or even in the central shires, as that of Wessex and the Thames could not have done on the upper side of the Humber. The bold Sagas of Scandinavia are differentiated in space as well as in quality from the soft and tender virelays of Brittany and the Loire. We look for "Beowulf" and the "Cid" just where they are actually found. There is such a thing as literary and non-literary localities. We speak of the Lake School of English Poets, in which usage the literary and the topographical are intimately connected. The poems of these authors, of Wordsworth and Southey, were Poems of Places, as Longfellow has used the term. Dr. Holmes, in his Life of Emerson, speaks of "the academic races of New England." These races were favorably situated for the development of literary life. Dickens' novels of London life owe much to London surroundings, while the realistic school of modern literature is largely local in its type. All writers whose works deal with natural scenery—such as Chaucer and Burns and Thoreau and Whittier—are, of course, notable examples

of this salient principle, while outside of merely descriptive literature, locality has often much to do with developing literary type. Iceland is too cold for the presence of lyric verse, as South Europe is too tropical for such an epical drama as Faust. Climate, as a local element, has an important part to play in literature as in language, and often determines whether we are to have verse or prose; epic or lyric; the bolder or the more subdued side of authorship.

3. So, as to Literature and Epoch, as conditioning Literature and Life. This is the time factor—the Zeitgeist of the German school, the spirit of the age, of which we so often hear.

"Literature depends," writes Possnett, "on contemporary life and thought." In fact, we speak of contemporary philosophy and contemporary literature, philosophy and literature developing contemporary with the age and revealing its spirit. So, Shairp, "It is one of the most characteristic things about our literature that the spirit of each time has passed into our poetry," to which we may add, into our prose, also.

"Had Shakespeare lived in the fourteenth century, his powers would have been to a great extent stunted in their growth," says Devey, and, we may add, had Chaucer lived in the sixteenth, tho civilization was two centuries in advance of Chaucer, we should not have had and could not have had, The Canterbury Tales. "There must be a resemblance," says Shelley, "between all the writers of any particular age and an influence from which the meanest scribbler nor the sublimest genius of any era can escape."

Golden Ages in Literature are thus rational cause and

effect, as are barren periods. The dearth of good English literature in the fifteenth century is just as explainable as the wealth of it in the sixteenth and nineteenth, and explainable on the same principle, as the times were unpropitious or propitious. The Sturm and Drang period in Germany gave rise to a certain form of literary life, as the more settled eras that followed produced a corresponding type. In the Reformation epoch, we have Reformation literature and vital literature; in the early part of the eighteenth century, it is more formal and, later on, again, more impassioned.

4. To these three relations, one might add a fourth and the most important—that of Personality,—the author and the man. Altho, as Schlegel states it, "Man can give nothing to his fellow-men but himself," that, if properly developed, is quite enough to give, and will invest with permanent vitality all he says and does. Possnett calls this Personality "the principle of literary growth." It is this principle, which, according to Lanier, makes the English Novel, especially in George Eliot, what it is as a vital factor in English Letters and history; national and individual personality, manifesting itself, in one form or another, in every page and line. Such are the great conditions of literary life and change —race and place and time and individuality, each acting separately and, when conjointly working, well-nigh irresistible.

Not that these are as wide-reaching as Mr. Taine insists and are to be viewed as causes rather than conditions, nor that, at times, literature may not thrive apart from such conditions and in the face of adverse elements, but that these are laws generally operative and especially noticeable whenever literature takes on varied and cogent forms.

In the light of these laws, it is clear that literature and life are related, and that the student of the one must make himself familiar with the other. If thought, as expressed in books, is so dependent for the type and effect of its expression on nationality and personality, on time and place, then is the man of letters driven out, perforce, from his retreat into the broader area of men and things, where history is forming and the world is working. Certain phases of this development he may examine within closed doors, but certain other phases demand individual inspection where they are, and must be sought out in order to be understood.

If what Mr. Symonds has called, "Democratic Art," as applied to literature, be a correct appellation, then must the world be allowed to enter the author's study or the author leave his desk and learn of the world the teaching that it has for him.

Such authors as Thiers and Grote and Spencer and Clarendon and Mill and Temple and Wayland and Walker have so written, on the side of Sociology, while, more specifically, such writers as Burke and Disraeli and McCarthy and Gladstone have written English literature as vitally connected with English life—civil, social and individual. Such a treatise as Bryce's "American Commonwealth" is a significant example of civil and political truth presented on its literary side—of the true relation of literature and life.

Such a man as John Morley, opening a discussion in Parliament on Home Rule, on one day, and, on the next, superintending the "English Men of Letters Series" or writing his "Life of Voltaire," is an equally notable instance of the normal relation of the author and the man; of literature and life.

To the degree in which such authors as Bancroft and Motley and Hawthorne and Lowell have acted, also, as civil representatives in foreign countries, is there evident this close connection of the esthetic and the political.

As to the importance of such a combination, no serious question can be entertained. One invaluable result is that it makes literature timely—gives it an interest that renders it attractive and readable. In proportion as literature and life are related, prose and verse are vital and, therefore, popular and pleasing.

Far back in the fourteenth century, "Piers the Plowman," as written by Langlande, was a poem hailed with delight by the people because it was a true transcript of the religious and political life of the time. It was read and relished, not merely because it was a satire, but because it was suffused with energy and life. The same principle explains the wide currency of the "Canterbury Tales" of Chaucer, in that the description of the pilgrims on the way to Kent is as real as if one could see them, to-day, starting out from the Tarbard to visit the tomb of Becket. So Shakespeare and Milton, while writing for all time and all peoples, were true exponents of the life of their respective eras. So Addison and Steele wrote the "Spectator," and Burke, his fiery prose for the political exigencies of the hour. The great British and American Essayists are notable examples of this vital and vitalizing style which made the pages they penned palatable and instructive.

So, on the other hand, the literature of the fifteenth century was inane and inert and, therefore, unreal and useless, while, in all the periods of English Literature where authors wrote merely for the sake of writing, or with reference to finish and adornment rather than practical effect, their writings are deservedly long since obsolete to make place for those that deal with living issues.

"The greatness of a poet lies," says Arnold, "in his powerful and beautiful application of ideas to life," and he rates Wordsworth among the supreme poets of the century because he so succeeded in doing this.

Hence, the permanence of literature as well as its pleasure depends on this energizing principle. There are dead literatures as well as dead languages. There are obsolete and obsolescent poems and prose works as there are such words, and the explanation in each case is the same, viz., that they are no longer needed, and not needed, simply because thought is active and authors are demanded who write under the stimulus of intellectual life and with reference to the mental needs of men.

If we inquire as to the special Forms of Literature that illustrate this presence of vitality, we shall find them to be clearly distinguishable.

1. One of these, strange to say, is Fiction, the precise purpose of which is the exhibition of human life and thought from various points of view.

We speak of certain divisions of Fiction, as the Historical, Descriptive and Sentimental Novel, but they all agree in this—that they are designed to set forth life. A certain type of fiction is said to be realistic. All fiction is, at bottom, realistic, in that it purposes, in terms of imagination, to treat of the life of man. The mere fact that these truths are set forth in symbolic form does not prevent them from being vital and dealing with vital topics.

Hawthorne wrote a type of fiction especially figurative and imaginative, and, yet, the "Scarlet Letter" is so full of reality and lifelikeness that its pages fairly palpitate with life, and we seem to see the characters it portrays moving in person before us.

Even that form of fiction known as philosophic or ethical is thus real and vital, as in George Eliot's "Daniel Deronda," in that the weightiest moral problems are stated and discussed therein. It were desirable that some other name than Fiction might be given to this species of literature, which is and ever will be a popular form of literature because of its representation of life. Philosophically speaking, it might be called presentative or representative literature—its object being to set forth fact and truth and incident and life in symbolism, and, yet, as really as if embodied in history and didactic prose.

2. So, in the sphere of verse, if one form is selected, it must be the dramatic, as that in which Literature and Life are most closely joined. The very name, drama, implies action. All dramatic authors and critics have proceeded on this idea as fundamental. As Schlegel expresses it, its central principle or quality is, earnestness, which, as he uses it, is but another name for vitality. Its object is, to "hold the mirror up to nature"; "to body forth the forms of things unknown"; by way of impersonation and characterization, to reveal man to himself and the age to itself. It would be difficult to say whether this is done most effectually in comedy or tragedy or in some of the great historical plays of literature. In each and all, it is life that is depicted, whether in the passionate language of Macbeth,

in the sparkling pleasantry of Falstaff, or in the highly wrought utterances of "Julius Cæsar" and "Richard III." No better test of dramatic literature is found than is found here—in the presence or absence of life—its absence obliging the critic to assign it to some other sphere of literary art.

Hence it is, that a national drama, from its earliest to its latest forms, is a reliable picture of the progressive history of a nation, and, most especially, at its critical epochs. The Elizabethan Drama is a representation of English life in the time of Elizabeth, whatever may be its general characteristics and teachings. So, as to the French drama of the classical period.

3. In Lyric verse, also, we have life at the center of literature, dealing, as it does, with the innermost joys and sorrows of the soul. More subjective and personal than the drama, it seeks to embody human experience in song. Nothing in literature is more lifelike than the best examples of its Odes and Sonnets, such as we have in the heroic stanzas of Milton and Wordsworth; in the pastorals of Spenser and Thomson; in the stirring lines of Burns, and the Elegies of Gray and Tennyson.

Genuine sentiment is always vital—from the soul to the soul, and critics are fast inclining to the belief that lyric verse as the conspicuous exponent of human life is second to no other in its range and richness.

In noting the relation of Literature to Life and the desirability of such relation, there is one danger to which literature is liable and against which authors are to be guarded, the unduly practical or mercantile theory of letters. If, as is held, literature should represent life, why not make it, after all, one of the useful arts—simply one of the human industries, to be classed among the bread and butter sciences. Hence, we read of Socialistic Literature—where the extremest good of the body politic is the main end. Hence, the discussion by Dowden, of what he terms, in almost contradictory phrase, "Democratic Art," a literature for the masses rather than the classes, of which Thoreau, at his Brook Farm, or Whitman, among the American Soldiery, would be the best exponents.

The leading expounders of this theory scarcely know what they mean by it, but this much they mean, that literature, as hitherto interpreted, as a fine art, in the hands of the cultivated for purposes of taste and esthetic ends, must give way for an out-of-door authorship, where men stand face to face with the world, and acquainting themselves with the needs of the race know how best to meet them. All this is in place within due limitations, but, when pushed to extreme, deprives literature of its central quality and reduces it to the plane of a handicraft. There is in all literature what Cardinal Newman calls, "a note of dignity," what Mr. Arnold styles, the "sense of beauty," and especially visible in the sphere of verse.

There is a meditative cast about it that unfits it for the wranglings of the market-place and hustings, and bids it seek a quieter sphere and contemplate different ends. Socrates, out in the streets asking and answering the pressing questions of common life, was a philosopher and man of affairs more than an author. Emerson, in the undisturbed contemplation of his Concord life, penning his suggestive essays, or Tennyson, in his retiracy at the Isle of Wight, penning his equally suggestive poems, are better representatives of that literary spirit which, while vital and vitalizing, instinctively shuns the "madding crowd."

The application of this subject and this caution to the young but rapidly developing literature of America is a matter of serious interest. Have we a literature at all, is the question that was started at the opening of the century by Sidney Smith and the *Edinburgh Review*, and a question strangely still under discussion by not a few English and Continental critics who are supposed to know what is and what is not literature. The Americans, we are told, are too matter-of-fact, too practical, to have either the time or taste for the elegant arts. Literature and Life must be united, 'tis true, but, here, we have a surplus of life and a corresponding decrease of the true spirit of letters. Commercialism is the word, they say. Men must pass by the Exchange to reach the library, and authors and publishers must be viewed as men of trade and business as much as if they were handling pig iron or cotton goods. Hence, the old sarcastic query—Who reads an American book—that is, who reads it for purposes of literary taste and training?

Moreover, it is urged, that as this American tendency in civilization is increasing rather than diminishing, the outlook, as Mr. Stedman terms it, is all the more foreboding, and we must look, then, as now, to the Mother Country for men of letters and literary books. There is some point in this and, yet, more British prejudice than point, while England herself is in danger of the same onrushing tide of commercialism which threatens to drown out the inner spirit of letters, and must with equal vigor resist it.

To all such superficial questions and objections, whether relating to British or American Letters, there is one sufficient answer: that, rightly viewed, there is and can be no valid conflict between literature and life, between literature as a mental and an artistic product, and literature as a vital product for practical ends. It is only among inferior authors, working on erroneous principles and methods, that any such conflict is visible. Herein lies, indeed, one of the essential tests of genius in authorship, of literary sanity and symmetry, to strike the "note of dignity" as a writer, and, yet, to make it so natural and sensible a note that the open ear of the intelligent public will quickly hear it and quickly respond thereto. Genuine literature, dealing in a real way with real things, will always be in good form, and commend itself at the same time to sensible men. With all the masters in prose and verse, literature is, first and last, a reality, and because a reality, admits of no disparity between things that should not differ. Readers of *The Atlantic Monthly* have been refreshed by some pertinent suggestions, under the caption, "On Being Human." Authors, above all men, should be intensely human; men first, and then authors; natural, if naught else; speaking out, in frankest manner, the thought that is in them. If we have reality in literature, we shall have as a result the "note of dignity" becoming the author in "the quiet and still air of delightful studies" and, also, the note of practical purpose becoming the author as a man of the world.

Thus it is that Macaulay and De Quincey, Matthew Arnold and Walter Pater, Bryant and Hawthorne, Emerson and Irving, wrote on the most practical topics in a literary way and on the most literary topics in a practical way, and so wrote, we may add, mainly because they wrote normally and naturally and with vital aims in view.

The first question with regard to an author's style, says Mr. Whipple, is, "Is it vital? Has it life?" This is the first question we submit with regard to literature itself. Is it vital? Has it life? Is it real? Has it reality?

This is the Realism in Letters for which the modern reading world is waiting, and herein our authors will be seen to keep in closest touch with the life that is about them and, also, in closest touch with the highest requirements of literary art.

CHAPTER TEN

LITERATURE AND ETHICS

In this caption the word "ethics" is not used in any technical sense, referring to what is known or studied as the formal subject of moral philosophy, but rather in the more current and the wider sense of morality, as designating that which is true and pure and in accordance with the established principles of right and goodness. Perhaps the adjectives, the literary and the ethical, would more nearly convey our meaning. Judging from the attention which this topic has received from the very beginnings of modern literature, and the increasing attention given it in the last two decades of European and English history, it is well worth the while of every student of letters and of morals to acquaint himself with the history of opinion thereupon, and to examine for himself the grounds of such opinion so as to be able to give a good reason for his personal views respecting it. So extreme are the positions taken by different critics that it would seem well-nigh impossible to secure any common ground on which conflicting interests might meet.

Such an author as Selkirk, in his admirable discussion of, The Ethics and Esthetics of Modern Poetry, speaks of the "correlation of the religious and the poetical instincts"; as if, indeed, the one were the necessary complement of the other. "I only demand of the poet," writes Vinet, "that he be true and do not interest himself in vice," the supposition being that it would require an actual effort of the will for an author to be other than moral in his writings, and he adds, "When thought is nothing more than the slave of matter there is nothing literary." So that concise statement of Bacon's, that "poetry has a participation of divineness," brings into exercise what Wordsworth, with the same idea in view, has called "the vision and the faculty divine." Nor is such opinion confined to the sphere of poetry; it finds its expression applicable as well to prose, where the author, according to Mr. Arnold, must deal with "the best that is known and thought," and must be possessed of that "sense of conduct" which, in its place, is fully as important in letters as the "sense of beauty." Even so free an author as Chateaubriand asserts that "unbelief is the chief cause of the decline of taste and genius," arguing, *per contra*, that in an age of positive and sound convictions literature might be expected to flourish. It needs but a casual glance at the pages of literary history in Europe to find the confirmation of this statement. It was so especially in Roman letters when the empire was socially and civilly corrupt; so in Arabia and the East under the blighting influence of Mohammedanism; so in France in the days of the Encyclopedists and freethinkers; and so in England in the middle of the seventeenth century under the degrading influence of the second Charles. When the church has been untrue to her trusts, and a false theology has begotten a false theory of life and conduct, contemporary and subsequent literature has always revealed the presence of the decline. So has a false philosophy begotten a correspondent type of authorship, while in its morality and immorality the history of European art can be said to mark the history of

European letters. Archbishop Trench raises at this point the practical question whether what is known as, The Renaissance, referring to the revival of art at the time of Francis the First, can in justice be called a renaissance, or new life, in that the art which was revived was pagan, and not Christian, and thus calculated to lower rather than elevate the tone of life and letters. If it be asked, What is meant precisely by the ethical in literature as a principle or method? it may be answered, The indissoluble union of literature with truth and faith, with the highest and best interests and instincts of man, correlating it with all those departments of thought and forms of personal human activity which have to do with the raising of men to a higher level of life and outlook. It is a study in literature, and by it, of character and motive; of those great influences, individual and general, which tend to regenerate and uplift. When Possnett speaks of literature as "a spiritual reality" he states this truth in most emphatic form. A phrase used by some critics of prose fiction, "the novel of purpose," has special reference to the same generic idea. Most of the references in literary criticism to the inner spirit of literature and to its controlling tone and tendencies magnify this principle. When a modern writer in referring to Arthur Hugh Clough speaks of his "conscientious skepticism" he is discovering the ethical side of his verse, as he must do who speaks of that "honest doubt" to which the late English laureate refers in the pages of his "Elegy." When we are told that authors as a class "aim at a purely artistic effect" the lesson to be learned is that this is not enough to constitute true authorship, an essential element—the ethical—being omitted.

One of the best evidences of the normal relationship of

the literary and the ethical is found in the fact that literature has always given it a commanding place despite all desire that might have existed to evade it. In the department of history, such authors as Clarendon and Hallam, Mahon and Lingard, Palgrave, Knight, Stanley and Turner have recognized it, while even on the side of skeptical authorship the ethical has played a most important part in the pages of Hume and Gibbon, Buckle and Taine, John Morley and John Stuart Mill. Biography, as the history of personal character and action, must, in the nature of the case, be of this cast. The large circle of philosophic or didactic authors have necessarily dealt with this element, as Paley and Bentley and Boyle and Warburton and Locke and Cudworth, Hobbes and Butler, Maurice, Coleridge and Emerson, while most of the miscellaneous prose of England has evinced it, as in the pages of the great British and American essayists—Landor, Forster, Arnold, Newman, Addison and Burke and Lowell. In poetry, as the expression of human life and feeling, we naturally seek it, whether in the profound study of character, as in the Shakespearean drama; in the stately and serious course of the Miltonic epics; in the reflective verse of Wordsworth; or in such a philosophic elegy as "In Memoriam." When Milton speaks of poetry as "passionate" it is but saying that it treats of human character. It is certainly a striking fact that in the development of modern prose fiction, where we would, perhaps, least expect to find the province of moral teaching, this tendency is more and more conspicuous.

If, as Lanier insists, the prime object of the English novel is to detect and reveal human personality, what is this but saying that the prime object is a moral one?

Hence it is that such a novelist as George Eliot, whom he selects as the representative of this theory, is scarcely more or less than a moralist in fiction. Such examples as "Daniel Deronda," "Adam Bede," "Middlemarch," and "Romola" we call philosophical; and so they are, but especially on the side of conduct and character. The very word "characterization," applied either to the drama or the novel, is significant, as expressive of the dominance of character in these types of literature, the dominance of soul and purpose and motive. A great play, such as "Othello," or a great novel, such as "The Scarlet Letter," might fittingly be called a study of conscience, a study in ethical philosophy, only that the imagination is more distinctly prominent than in other forms of literature. Russian fiction in the person of Tolstoi represents the same tendency. So pronounced is this drift that much abstruse theological discussion is now contained in the pages of what is called fiction, as in Mrs. Ward's "Robert Elsmere" and her later works, "David Grieve" and "Helbeck of Bannisdale"; in Mrs. Deland's "John Ward, Preacher," and in Celia Parker Wooley's "Rachel Armstrong" (Love and Theology). Charles Reade, in his "Never Too Late to Mend," is a moral teacher, as is Charles Kingsley in all his attempts to lead the way in social reform.

In Mr. Stedman's latest discussion of poetry, under the title "The Nature and Elements of Poetry," four out of the eight chapters are on the distinctly ethical side of verse, namely, "Poetry and Truth," "Poetry and Faith," "Melancholia," and "The Faculty Divine," while even in the other four it enters as an important factor. An explanation of this is not far to find, since the ultimate object of the author is the ultimate object of the philosopher and moralist—the obtaining of the truth, the realization of ideals and, more profoundly still, the solution of the great problems of human character and destiny. Nowhere else as at this point do the highest literature and the highest ethics meet, so that when the author sits down to pen a poem or an essay, he has in hand—only by another method—the purpose of the moral scientist in studying the fundamental truths of God and man and the visible world. One of the most characteristic expressions of this common purpose is seen in the attraction that literary work has always possessed for the clergy, in the union of the Divinities and the Humanities; the seeking and finding and teaching of truth being prominent in each, the sacred and the secular. Stopford Brooke has called the attention of scholars to "The Theology of the English Poets" as it is seen in Pope, Cowper, Burns, and Wordsworth. Such a theological tendency on the part of authors has been fully reciprocated in the literary tendency on the part of the clergy and theologians. Meeting one another in the spirit of brotherhood, theology and literature have alike been the gainers and done a more beneficent work.

In treating of this relation of literature to ethics a caution is in place, lest at any time the literary become too subordinate and the author take the place of the mere moralist. "A certain kind of preachment," writes Stedman, "antipathetic to the spirit of poesy has received the name of didacticism. Instinct tells us that it is a heresy in any form of art. An obtrusive moral in poetic form is a fraud on its face and outlawed of art. Pedagogic formulæ of truth do not convey its essence." What the American critic here applies to poetry is applicable to literature in general, and it is safe to say that just as all art is to be concealed art, so as to have the freshness and force of nature, so all didacticism or ethical teaching in literature is to be so concealed as to have the reader feel that the author is not so intent upon pointing a moral as upon expressing his thought and feeling and taste. Often the best way of doing good is by seeming not to be too intent upon doing it, and more is accomplished by indirectness than by directness. The history of literature affords suggestive examples of this undue consciousness of the ethical intent on the part of authors. In southern Europe, and in France more particularly, it took the form of Pietism, or Mysticism, carried to such an extreme as to repel those minds honestly intent upon seeking the truth, and to offend the taste of those who, when they came to literature for literary purposes, were more than displeased to find themselves inside a conventicle where they were obliged to sit in silence and listen to the homily. In the British Isles, especially at the middle of the seventeenth century, it expressed itself at times extremely in the form of Puritanism, when Baxter and Bunyan and George Herbert and Jeremy Taylor and Fuller and Sir Thomas Browne set the form of authorship in the line of the homiletic and didactic. Even John Milton wrote his prose pamphlets mainly in this ultra ethical spirit. One of the special reasons why Izaak Walton's "Complete Angler" holds such a high place in literary miscellany is that it was absolutely free from professional ethics, expressing in a genial, natural and readable manner what he had to say on the art of angling. The correct and over-careful school of the time of Queen Anne has not escaped censure in this particular, as carrying poetry to the extreme of professionalism and making prose too prosaic and proper. Students of English criticism are familiar with the stinging comments made by Taine upon the moralizing in which Addison indulges in the pages of *The Spectator*. It is clear that the English essayist lost his influence with his French critic by trying too laboriously to reach his conscience and correct his morals. Here, again, Daniel Defoe, in his "Robinson Crusoe," relieved this moralistic monotony very much as Izaac Walton relieved it in the days of the Commonwealth. Later on, in the Georgian era, we have what has been called the prolonged and pious descriptions of Thomson's "Seasons," the somewhat forced and overdrawn teachings of Richardson's "Pamela" and "Clarissa Harlowe," Thomson's "Castle of Indolence," Johnson's "Vanity of Human Wishes," and the prosaic morality of Edward Young's "Night Thoughts." When Voltaire was asked what estimate he placed upon these he sharply answered, in the line of what we are emphasizing, "Very good for night thoughts." The extreme literary libertinism of such authors as Savage and Smollett and Sterne and Bolingbroke is partially a reaction from the stilted and conventional ethics of the time, and readers preferred, if they must choose, "Roderick Random" and "Tristram Shandy" to Shenstone's "Schoolmistress" or Akenside's prosaic poem on the Imagination. Equally severe have been the strictures at this point upon the poetry of Wordsworth, who is represented by his critics as literary for a purpose—to reform the English morals of his day. Hannah More may have been an able and estimable woman and authoress, but the average Englishman and the average man is too worldly, it is urged, to enjoy his literature prepared and dispensed just as she insisted on giving it. Cowper and Blair, Campbell and Maria

Edgeworth and Jane Austen and Martin Tupper came, to an extent, under the same condemnation, while, by way of literary and mental relief, the Englishmen of that day betook themselves to the natural and sprightly pages of Goldsmith and Sidney Smith; of Sheridan and Burns and Lamb and Scott, even at the risk of passing to the other extreme. The immense influence of Lord Byron in his day and later is partly attributable to this same opposition to the professionally ethical. Recent critics have not hesitated to question the method of so pronounced an educator and author as Dr. Thomas Arnold, of Rugby, in keeping his ethical intent so prominently before his pupils and readers as at length to reduce it to what Taine calls, the commonplace, and awaken thereby a feeling of aversion. It is not altogether aside from truth to suggest that the opposite course assumed by his gifted son, Matthew Arnold, may have been in part occasioned by this indiscreet procedure. All this is necessary by way of caution, and in no sense militates against the theory that literature in its essential nature and purpose should conserve and express truth and purity, should be ethical in spirit and final result, it being the part of its best exponents to keep this side the line of the professional moralist and not to make a show of goodness in their character as authors.

A brief examination of literature as related to doubt and unbelief is in place. The reference here is to literature as denying that there is any essential or even formal connection between letters and morality. Any such element is ignored; with the inevitable result that such a type of literature is found at length to be an outspoken exponent of infidelity and skepticism. The denial of the ethical leads to the assertion of the unethical. Not that there is an inevitable tendency in the highest literary art to take on such form, which has sometimes been asserted both as to philosophy and letters, nor that the skeptical element or tendency is at all the dominant one in the ablest literature, but that in Continental and English literature there is enough of this to demand the careful examination of the student into its causes, the varied forms and periods of its manifestation, the results of it in literature itself and kindred spheres, and the best means by which it may be minimized or eliminated. As to its causes, apart from the inherent human tendency to misinterpret or evade the truth, an unethical literature is generally the fruit of a skeptical philosophy or science, or due at times to those exceptional crises in national life and history when the very foundations of morality are shaken and all the worst elements of society come into prominence. Hume in philosophy, and Priestley in science, and Voltaire in French national life are sufficient proofs of this connection. As to forms and periods, they may be said to be as diversified as the forms of thought and the different eras of historical life. Literary skepticism has thus been expressed in the forms of stoicism, or gross materialism, or in sensualism, or in pantheism, while it often takes the type of negation and indifference. The results are evil, and only evil; not only within the province of literature itself, in the lowering of its tone and the impairing of its rightful influence, but in all related departments and spheres of thought, so that an unbelieving literature is at once the effect of antecedent conditions and the gauge and test of general national life. The remedy must needs be found in a new order of philosophy and science and in purified public opinion; in the prevalence of Christian as distinct from pagan or antichristian principles. The original and historical trend of English literature has been a sound and wholesome one, as initiated by Cædmon and Bede and Alfred and Wiclif, and any existing tendency in a counter direction is in despite of precedent and the best interests of the English race. Such gifted poets as Tennyson and Whittier evince the presence of this historical tendency, as Swinburne and Whitman belie it. One of the most decided and one of the saddest forms of literary doubt is found in the line of literary despondency, where faith has given way to unbelief and hope has given place to moroseness, or where, apart from any preexistent belief, the mind has been, from the first, under the control of error. The most significant recent example of this declension on the side of melancholia is found in the person and work of Arthur Hugh Clough. Such of his poems as "Qua Cursum Ventus," "Qui Laborat Orat," "The Shadow," "In Venice," "The Stream of Life," "Where Lies the Land," and, "Say Not the Struggle Naught Availeth," clearly evince the truth of this statement. As he says in his "Perchè Pensa":

> "To spend uncounted years of pain,
> Again, again, and yet again,
> In working out in heart and brain
> The problem of our being here;
> To gather facts from far and near,
> Upon the mind to hold them clear,
> And, knowing more may yet appear,
> Unto one's latest breath to fear
> The premature result to draw—
> Is this the object, end and law,
> And purpose of our being here?"

Tho Clough's skepticism was sincere, and partly constitutional, it was none the less harassing. It almost shipwrecked his sensitive soul. Out on a wide waste of waters, and anxious to make the right port, he tossed about aimlessly and verily died at sea. Goethe, in the pages of "Wilhelm Meister," and "Faust," and especially in "The Sorrows of Werther," was the victim of the same mental and moral unrest, and never found that "More light" for which it is said that at the time of his death he longingly asked. So Byron, in his disappointment as to all things human and his desire "to quit the scene," as affording him no peace of spirit or satisfied ambition.

There is, then, a valid connection between literature and ethics and Christian faith. He who ignores it is unwise. Truth has its claims on every man, and insists upon asserting them and demands their acknowledgment and satisfaction. The natural and the supernatural are so involved in each other in the present order of things that he essays no easy task who attempts to disjoin them and write and speak on the level of a purely worldly philosophy. The "mundane" school of literature and art has had its day and place and is still in being, but always under the protest of the deepest instincts and interests of men. The best literature must rest after all on what we now term "the primary human convictions," and must find its fullest and most natural expression in what the British poet Watson has called "the things that are more excellent."

CHAPTER ELEVEN

LITERATURE AND THE ARTS

A. THE LIBERAL ARTS

THE use of the word, liberal, as applied to the Arts, necessitates, at this point, a clear distinction as to the classification of the Arts. One of these, and a valid one, is that of the Arts as Liberal, and Practical or Applied. By the latter of these, the Practical, sometimes called The Mechanical or Industrial Arts, special reference is had to the fact that the amount of knowledge needed for their successful application is that which pertains only to the particular Art in question, as the art of building or ship-making or weaving or carving. Each of these, as to knowledge needed, stands alone, and may be skilfully prosecuted on the basis of the particular training incident to the Art. One may thus be an expert builder and know little or nothing outside the sphere of his special work as a builder.

It will thus be seen that the scope or sphere of the Applied Arts is a comparatively narrow one and contemplates specific and practical ends. What are called, the Trades, illustrate them.

The Liberal Arts, on the other hand, are so called because they take for granted, on the part of him who prosecutes them, an antecedent general preparation, a comprehensive survey of the spacious area of truth, as it contains the varied departments of human knowledge. Hence, we speak of a liberal training, in this sense, as being that quality and scope of study included in the curricula of so-called liberal institutions—the collegiate training as given in our American colleges.

The Liberal Professions are proof in point, meaning those pursuits or callings based on something more than the mere knowledge of the calling itself, that something more being a general discipline and a general scope. Not that, as a matter of fact and possibility, a good degree of excellence in professional work may not be found apart from such preceding preparation, but that, as a theory, it is not so and, as a fact, found to be so but exceptionally. As a rule, the best jurists and physicians and teachers of the truth are those who have been wise enough to base their respective vocations on the broad foundation of liberal study.

Here we see the place of literature as an art, that in its correct interpretation it is a liberal art rather than an applied or a mechanical art; that the author in theory and right reason, at least, should be the well-informed, the broadly trained, the fully educated man, knowing far more than literature itself, and working within the literary sphere with his eye widely open to all related spheres and teachings.

With this classification in mind, it is interesting to study the history of literature as to its possible confirmation, the literature of England being prominently in view.

If we run over the roll of the great Prose Writers of England and America from Bacon to Carlyle, we note that the large majority of them were university men, such as Bacon himself, Hooker, Milton, Dryden, Swift and Addison, Samuel Johnson, Coleridge, Burke, De Quincey, Macaulay, Matthew Arnold, Carlyle and Sir

Walter Scott, Thackeray, Lowell and Emerson; while, in the sphere of verse, in addition to many of the names already mentioned, who wrote in verse as well as in prose, we find such names as Chaucer and Spenser, Byron, Wordsworth, Browning, Tennyson, Holmes and Longfellow, bringing to literature, as they did, all their gifts and acquirements, and, thereby, enriching, all the more, the minds of their readers.

If it be asked, what the special advantages are which come to the literature from the liberal arts and by which literature itself is of right termed a liberal art, the answer is plain and manifold.

(*a*) There is, first of all, the Knowledge which is thereby acquired, the actual contribution of material, which tho other than literary, whatever it may be, may have literary elements and possibilities in it for the use of the author as an author. The relations of Literature to Philosophy and Science and Ethics and History and Sociology are evident, and it is as the liberal student furnishes himself with stores of knowledge from these and kindred realms of investigation, that he becomes richer for any work to which as a student of truth he may be called.

When we think, for a moment, of the vastness of this field of truth, it will appear what a privilege is opened up to the inquiring mind and how such truth may be utilized.

(*b*) But, further, there is secured by this process a Comprehensiveness of mind more valuable by far than any special branch or department to which the student of letters may give his attention—that mental scope and breadth and freedom of view which, next to the truth itself, is important.

Liberal study, as liberal, opens and elevates the mind; sets the faculties free to range at will and to do their best work; stimulates, thereby, all the dormant energies of the soul; vitalizes, so to speak, all the mind-space at the student's command, and enlarges that space and makes it possible for him ever to do better things than he has, as yet, done.

Liberal culture is essentially liberative, and is thus the best preventive of mental bigotry and narrowness. To the author this is invaluable, as it ennobles him, and obliges him to study letters as but one expression of the human mind, and but one method of realizing ideals.

(*c*) It may, further, be noted, in the line of benefit, that scholarship and authorship are thus connected, and sympathy awakened between them.

Instead of being, in any sense, antagonistic, as, at times, they have been, they find themselves able to stand on common ground, with many interests in common, and feel, at least, that the highest ends of each will be best secured by a deferent regard for each other.

Nothing will more surely or rapidly correct the prevalent tendency to superficial authorship than this insistence upon the status of literature as a liberal art, in poetry as well as in prose; in the lighter as well as in the weightier forms of literary product,—so that the pen shall ever be viewed as the exponent of intelligence and reason and logical process and permanent good. As the scholar should borrow fluency and grace from the author, so should he, in turn, secure that breadth and depth which comes from patient study and research.

By way of possible objection at this point, it is argued, that many authors of eminence have been devoid of such training, to which it may be answered, that such cases, as seen in Pope and Burns and Bunyan and De Foe and Dickens and Whittier, constitute the exceptions to the principle, and, further, that we are, beyond question, proving more than we wish to prove when illiteracy itself, as in the case of Bunyan, is accepted as a warrantable ground of excellence in letters. Shakespeare, as the incomparable genius of English dramatic verse, may be said to be a law unto himself, and who knows but that, in the case of most of these uneducated authors, literature would have gained in the end, had they entered upon their work by the way of the university. Literature, certainly, upon the lowest interpretation of it, is no exception to the principle that general culture is a most desirable possession for any one who pretends to be an expounder of truth.

A further objection is sometimes urged, that the natural expression of thought is impeded by these educational processes that belong to liberal training. This is but one form of that objection made to all discipline on the ground that nature must have its own way, despite all precedent and direction. This will answer as a theory, not as a fact, nor is it practically applied in any other art. Master musicians, painters and sculptors reach their best results through the slow and patient processes of personal discipline, and so must he do who is to wield his pen with skill and make literature what it ought to be, a power and an impulse. It is, in fact, only a false training that begets a restricted and stilted authorship. If such training is broad and thorough, it enters as a vital factor into the entire mental life of the student and, when it expresses itself in literature, does so in freest and most natural manner.

It is here, as elsewhere, that the "little learning is the

dangerous thing," not the comprehensive learning, so that as Bacon expresses it, the author, to be a true author, "must go abroad into universality."

That is an utterly erroneous view of literary culture and of any culture which puts a premium upon limitation of knowledge by the theory, that, the more we know, the less capable we are to vitalize and utilize our knowledge.

The error is not in the knowing, but in the method of the knowing, so that the student of literature as a student of the liberal arts must emphasize the fact that they are liberal and not restricting, and acquire them as vital elements in the prosecution of his work as an author.

The more knowledge the better, only that it be assimilated and adjusted and rightly applied, not in the mechanical manner of an artisan, but in the natural manner of an artist.

A word is here in place as to Literature and The Liberal Professions. Literature itself is often spoken of as a Profession, tho Frederick Harrison stoutly objects to that term as unsuited to a calling such as Literature. It may be an art, a vocation, a pursuit, but not a profession, as that term is currently used. If, indeed, it is such, such an author as Shepard in his "Authors and Authorship," has shown from numerous facts that it can not be called lucrative.

Attention might be called to the relation of the Divinities to Literature, as seen especially in those who have combined the two pursuits of Letters and the Ministry.

As to Literature and Law, the closest point of contact is in the sphere of judicial and forensic prose, while, even here, the emphasis is to be laid upon the oral rather than upon the written form of the thought.

Many of the great parliamentary and congressional orators of England and America have written but little. Such authors as Kent and Story and Blackstone and Marshall and Hamilton and the leading constitutional and civic jurists have generally confined themselves to the didactic exposition of the law rather than to its literary interpretation.

Literature and Medicine, explain it as we may, seem to represent a more intimate union. It would be an interesting study to run through the records of English Literature and select the names of those practitioners who either in connection with their medical work or after it have engaged in authorship; such as John Brown, and Sir Thomas Browne, author of "Religio Medici," Hopkins and Arbuthnot and Cowley, while American Medicine is illustriously represented in the poems of Abraham Coles, author of "Man a Microcosm" and of a version of "Dies Iræ," and in Oliver Wendell Holmes, successful alike as an anatomist and a writer.

Erasmus Darwin, author of "The Botanic Garden," was a physician by profession, and the poet Keats left Medicine for Literature, the leisure often found in the pleasant paths of a rural practise being congenial to literary meditation and production.

In each case, however, that of law and medicine, the central principle is that of professionalism on the side of the formal and technical, and this is distinctively opposed to the spirit of authorship.

The question is at present under sharp discussion as to whether or not Journalism is entitled to the name and rank of a Profession. If affirmatively decided, then we find, at this point, the nearest relationship between the literary and the professional. Journalism, with all its imperfections, has, in theory, at least, a literary side. There is such a thing as journalistic literature, coming to prominence in the editorial columns, and to special prominence of late in the matter of literary criticism. Full and often accurate reviews of current and even scholarly authorship are now found in English and American Journals, by which the tone of such journals is greatly elevated.

The long connection of William Cullen Bryant with the *Evening Post* gave it a literary cast. Journalism has certain unliterary or anti-literary elements and tendencies by reason of the mercantile spirit that pervades it, on account of which the popular taste, whether high or low, must be satisfied. This apart, however, there are elements of decided literary merit, while, if in Journalism we include the large province of the Magazine issues of the time, its character as literary is greatly increased, it being the rule rather than the exception that the contents of these periodicals take the later form of books and treatises. The weekly papers of the time of Addison constituted the best literature of the time.

The question of the relation of Literature and Education also arises here, on the ground that teaching is now taking rank as a profession.

There are here two distinct views that may be taken. On the technical side of teaching as an art, there is no vital connection between it and literature, but rather exclusive elements exist. Teaching is necessarily didactic, and the form that authorship would naturally take and does take, on the part of educators, is that of the manual or text-book, purposely devoid, as it is, of any pronounced literary feature.

On the other hand, there is an untechnical side to education, which may be designated by the term, culture, and here we touch literary ground. It is, thus, that there is at Oxford and Berlin and Cambridge a high degree of literary influence, a literary tone and habit permanently expressive and making itself felt over wide areas. Thus Thomas Arnold and Timothy Dwight, Mark Hopkins and Francis Wayland, were educators and, also, literary in their work and influence, while it is not to be forgotten that many of our most distinguished authors have been connected with collegiate duty, such as Longfellow and Lowell and Holmes, of our own country, and Dowden and Masson and Morley, of England. Not a few of those names adduced to represent the connection of the editorial and the literary, may, also, represent the connection of the educational and the literary, in that they combined in one personality the three related functions. All true literature, while it need not be didactic, should be, in the best sense, educating.

B. FINE ARTS—ESTHETICS

Here we meet another and an equally valid classification of the arts, into the Fine and the Useful, the basis of the classification being that of the ultimate purpose in view, in the one case, artistic effect; in the other, immediate and practical use. Literature, we have seen, if correctly interpreted, is a Liberal art, based on general training, and is saved, thereby, from becoming superficial, while here we note that it is, also, a Fine Art, and saved, thereby, from becoming unduly prosaic and uniform.

According to Mr. Symonds, Every art-type has a certain history. First, the idea is prominent; then, the form; then, the latter supersedes the earlier, and the type disappears. This, we may say, is true in part and to this extent, that in Literature there are both the idea and the form, neither of which ever disappears, the one securing vitality and permanence; the other, flexibility, interest and popular effect.

Literature is thus an esthetic art, having to do with what is called the Study of Authors, with culture, in the literary sense of that term. It is thus that Vinet writes—"It is only Literature that cultivates." A modern American critic speaks of "Poetry as a Representative Art." So is Prose and all Literature an art, having to do with the faculties and forms of expression. "Culture and Anarchy," as Matthew Arnold uses the phrase, would seem to be a virtual contradiction.

There is then an artistic principle or method in Literature as an art, and may be best expressed in the word—form. "Form-giving," as has been said, is the essence of art.

Literature has a specifically structual or architectural side, as much so as architecture itself. There is such a thing as building a poem or prose work. Authorship is not only a production, it is a construction, and involves the element of technique. Style is architecture.

Tho not as important in itself as the strictly intellectual side of literature, it fills a place that nothing else can fill, and is of such value that no degree of purely mental excellence can atone for its absence.

More than this, there is in literature, as a fine art, an artistic spirit or purpose, a something less mechanical than method, and relating literature to the highest and best uses. This is what Arnold means by the, "sense of beauty" or the "instinct for style."

This is that, which, to use a word coined by Bagehot,

makes any production, "litaresque," or available for literary purposes. It is something which can not be borrowed or counterfeited or secured by study and labor and cost of any kind, that inherent art-life which marks a poem or essay or novel as beautiful, in good form, answering every demand of the most scrupulous taste.

What is meant by this and by the lack or the inferior expression of it may be clearly seen by comparing two such authors as Ruskin and Dr. Johnson, or Sir Joshua Reynolds and Edmund Burke. In each of these authors alike, all the intellectual qualities of high authorship are found. Each of them pursued literature as a liberal art, but it was reserved for Ruskin and Reynolds to express in their works the artistic side of letters, of which the burly Johnson and the parliamentarian Burke knew but little.

Longinus and St. Beuve, Keats and Cousin instinctively illustrated it, so that, as Johnson said of Addison, they wrote "in elegant but not ostentatious" English. Elegance, in the best use of that word, is a proper function of literature, one of its essential elements, and can not be ignored with safety by any writer, be his endowments and attainments what they may.

In discussing Literature as a Fine Art, there are two dangerous extremes at present noticeable. The one is best represented in what Mr. Allen calls, "Physiological Æsthetics," the material side of art, the "fleshly school" of modern times, as represented more particularly in the department of Southern Continental fiction and in the verse of Whitman.

Contradictory as such a type and tendency may seem to be to the inner meaning and purpose of the ornamental arts, every age of letters has inclined more or less to its expression, while it has been reserved for nineteenth century literature to give it special prominence.

Just as psychology is becoming largely a physiological study, and the laboratory is made the center of mental experiment, so literature as an art and, thus, presumably supersensual, is taking on these material and realistic forms.

The other and more manifest tendency is in the direction of undue formalism or technique, the dominance of the form over the subject-matter, "art for art's sake," making an end of verbal finish, and reducing all the intellectual faculties to that of taste.

In the light of this theory, beauty of presentation becomes a prime essential on the part of the writer, and decoration takes precedence of meditation. What is known, in the history of literary art, as Polite Literature or Belles-Letters, is in the line of this extreme, borrowed, in part, from the lighter forms of French and Italian Letters, and, yet, finding a congenial soil in Great Britain.

Based on the false assumption that the only end of literature is to please, or that, if there are others, this is the chief, it insists upon giving to mere adornment the main attention.

Hence, the beneficent work that has been done in all literatures and, especially in English, by those solid writers who tho possessing the instinct of the beautiful have expressed their thoughts as they lay before them with the primary aim of enlightening and impressing the minds of their readers. It thus becomes a question of interest, whether Thomas Arnold is not a much more valuable personality in English than his gifted and cultured son; whether such authors as Bacon and Dr.

Johnson, are not more indispensable than the correct and classical Macaulay; whether, in the region of verse, Pope and Keats and Grey must not yield to Burns; and whether, after all, the Poet Laureate himself would not have done a more masterly work, had the hand of the technical workman been oftener concealed.

Emerson is far less of a literary artist than Poe, but a far greater potentiality in American Letters, while Thomas Carlyle has conferred a lasting blessing on the England of his day in expressing the thought that was in him in his own way, tho not always in obedience to the formulated canons of the schools.

This is not to place a premium on literary carelessness, or to say that the artistic has no place in the personality of the author, but it is an earnest protest against the abuse of terms and the reversal of things primary and secondary, and means to say, that literature, while both a liberal and a fine art, is more of a liberal art than a fine art; more of a principle than a method; more of a creation than a construction, and is a fine art only to that extent to which its subject-matter shall be in harmony with the requirements of good taste, so that, indeed, it shall not be unartistic.

It may be said, moreover, that the expression of Literature as a Fine Art is different in different literary spheres: more pronounced, and rightly so, in poetry than in prose; more pronounced in poetical prose than in forensic; more so in narrative and incident than in critical and philosophic miscellany; more so in description than in discussion. Hence, in those authors, such as Lowell and Emerson, Scott and Milton, who have written both in prose and verse, we expect to find the artistic element more apparent in the verse than in the prose;

while, still again, in the sphere of prose, art is more conspicuous in Lamb's "Essays of Elia" and in his study of the "English Dramatic Poets" than in Locke's "Essay on The Human Understanding" or Burke's "Orations." There is a fitness of things here as elsewhere, and art as art is subject to conditions and environment.

If we inquire as to the grounds or causes of such an extreme in the direction of the ornate, we find a partial explanation in the erroneous view that is taken of literature in general or of the vocation of the author; not among the illiterate classes only, but far too much so among the enlightened is this found to be true. Literature in their esteem is reduced to Culture, and Culture is the possession and prerogative of the few.

The Humanities, despite their name, are said to be for the study and the cloister and the library and not for the people or for those with whom life is a serious reality, if not indeed a struggle and a sorrow.

Hence, the identification of Literature with the accomplishments, with the enjoyments of the favored and privileged classes; suited indeed for men of elegant leisure, and finding its place in the mental market of the world only under the head of luxuries.

This is that drawing-room theory of literature that has wrought untold harm in every age, and which unfortunately receives a personal endorsement on the part of those authors who have no due conception of their work, and pen what they pen for personal pastime or the pleasure of the cultivated only.

We find the other explanation of this error in the equally erroneous view that is taken of all the fine arts of which literature is but one; of art as art, sharply differentiated from science or from any one of the utilities.

Here it is said that all art is merely cultivating and refining and has no relation, the most remote, to any practical and definite end. Hence, Painting and Sculpture and Architecture are commendable as arts only in so far as they are ornamental, while Music and Poetry and all literature are of the purely esthetic order only, having no element of utility.

Wrong views of truth are best refuted and displaced by the infusion of correct views, and it is the duty of students of letters, first of all, to show the essential unity of the arts,—their common purposes and ends, and then to show the unity of literature as a liberal and an ornamental art, and its intimate relation to the highest progress of the race. As the great dramatist tells us:

> "There is an art that doth mend nature,
> Change it rather.
> But the art itself is nature."

Right conceptions of nature and art; of the natural and the artistic; of the creative and the constructive, are needed in order to view either aright and see the truth in its oneness.

Shelley's "Hymn to Intellectual Beauty,"—expresses the right relation of the intellectual to the esthetic, while Mr. Dowden, in his "Mind and Art" of Shakespeare, succeeds in showing their logical unity.

Literature, then, is an art, in the widest sense of that term and in the highest sense, bringing into play all the faculties of man's total personality—will, conscience, affection, reason and taste, and contemplating as its object the development of those powers with reference to their noblest uses.

Edwin P. Whipple, the American critic, said of

Agassiz, the great student of nature, that he was not only "a scientific man but a scientific force." So it may be said, that Men of Letters, who are worthy of their name and place, are not only literary men, but literary forces—potential and active factors in the world's progress, and taking their place as such among those agencies to which humanity is most indebted for what it is and what it has.

Shakespeare and Milton and De Quincey and Tennyson and Lowell and Emerson were such literary forces, and, when we speak of literature as an art, no interpretation must be given it out of keeping with this high conception. That conception of the author which makes him nothing but an artist in the superficial sense of the word —a verbal decorator and designer—must give place to that more comprehensive interpretation by which as an artist he represents all liberal as well as ornate learning, and unifies the scholarly and the popular, the useful and the esthetic, in such wise that every high faculty of his nature is brought into play and every worthy end contemplated in his work. It is in no wise contradictory to say that Literature is an intellectual art

CHAPTER TWELVE

THE MISSION OF LITERATURE

ONE of Emerson's most characteristic essays he entitles "The Uses of Great Men"; and he goes on, in his inimitable way, to state and discuss those high offices to which great men, because they are great, are called, and to show under what odium they should come who are either ignorant of the character of their calling or untrue to what they know to be its exalted demands. Among the great men whom he eulogizes are Shakespeare, the Poet, and Goethe, the Writer; whereby he specifically asserts the greatness of literary men, and the nobility of the mission to which they are called. It is in such connection that he says "that men are born to rule." "Society has no greater interest than the well-being of the literary class." "Talent alone can not make a writer. There must be a man behind the book," and so on. We find him devoting separate essays to distinctly literary topics, such as, "The Man of Letters," "The Progress of Culture," "The Poet," "Literary Ethics," and "Literature" itself, as if he would feign express his high appreciation of all such work and of those committed to it. He speaks of "the power and the joy that belong to it and its high office in evil times."

It is a matter of sincere regret, as well as surprise, that many of the views of the purpose and mission of literature now prevailing are either base and belittling or, if legitimate, far below the standard of correct literary judgment.

With some, the necessities of life are such that they are led to reduce literary work to the level of the industries, and to wield the pen as they would ply a trade or perform the drudgery of professional and perfunctory service. Not a few English writers, Spenser, Dryden, and Dr. Johnson, for instance,—not to speak of such an author as Savage, who died a pauper with pen in hand, —have been thus obliged to write for bread and to reduce the theory of literature to a purely practical and economic art.

With others, desire for fame is the only end of letters; and prose and verse are but media through which they come to the realization of their worldly ambition. Hence, when they write, immediate or ultimate success, in the sense of personal popularity, is the governing motive; and they are the veriest slaves of what Milton calls, "that last infirmity of noble minds." Here, the man of letters is on a level with any other aspirant for distinction, and has no higher claim to the respect and gratitude of men.

Still others accept the common opinion—in itself legitimate—that the end of authorship is the pleasure of the reader, the gratification of taste or one's sense of beauty. This is the esthetic or cultured side of literature,—good as far as it goes, but far below the most desirable standard of authorship. Even in poetry this is a subordinate motive; and more especially is it so in the great department of prose.

Again, it is said, with conscious pride, that self-expression is the end of literature—the unveiling of the author's innermost self and thought simply for the sake of the self-revelation. As Schleiermacher, the great German theologian, said that he would be satisfied and ready to die, could he but give utterance to himself, so here, the author is an exponent of his own personality, and literature is, in the best sense, an autobiography. Of all the possible purposes of literature thus far stated, this is, beyond question, the worthiest, in that it has a mental and a spiritual side, and exalts literature above the plane of the mercantile and artistic. Still, it is in its essence a selfish end, and has this element in common with all the others. It is, as stated, the autobiographical or egotistic side of literature, and, in an extreme and exclusive way, would examine literature only in the light of the personal equation and as a record of personal experience.

All these ends—economic benefit, fame and gratification, taste and individual utterance—literature, when properly viewed, may and does have; but, if it have nothing more than these, it can scarcely be said to take its place among the great activities of the world, nor to enter as a factor into the world's best civilization.

The interesting question, then, that here arises is: What constitutes the real mission of literature,—what makes the man of letters and his work potential for good? We answer: (1) The conception, embodiment, and interpretation of some great idea or principle. (2) The correct interpretation of the spirit of the age. (3) The interpretation of human nature to itself and to the world. (4) The presentation and enforcement of high ideals.

1. *The conception, embodiment, and interpretation of some great idea or principle.*

We are here in the sphere of the intellectual in literature, and of genius, also,—of original and independent thinking on the part of the author. There is nothing here that savors in the least of the commonplace, or of servile imitation of the reflections and opinions of others. The author, in this view of his work, feels that he stands alone, and is responsible for his own thinking; that he must have a special message to his fellow men as constituting a reason for his utterance; and that, in the true Baconian sense, he is to add to the sum of human truth. He must be, as Emerson states it, "a man capable of ideas,"—capable, we may add, of so embodying them as to meet the demands of educated taste.

It is by this standard that all literatures may be tested as superior or inferior; and to this court of final appeal must all books and authors be summoned. Have they or have they not some intense, germinal, comprehensive idea that gives them vitality and character, and insures their perpetuity? Are they so instinct with thought or personality as to throb and pulsate with it, and to seek to deliver themselves of it to those who are waiting for and needing it. Of such qualities are: Dante's "Divine Comedy," the "Iliad" and "Odyssey," "Paradise Lost," "Beowulf," "Evangeline," and the "Idylls of the King." Such are the great tragedies of Æschylus and Racine and Lessing and Shakespeare, the "Comus" of Milton, and the "Cathedral" of Lowell. In prose, Bacon's "Advancement of Learning," and the great essays of De Quincey, of Burke, and of Thomas Carlyle are such. The essays of Emerson, with scarcely an exception, are of this high character,—proofs in point of his conscientious desire to realize his literary ideals.

Tennyson's "In Memoriam" is as notable an example as modern literature affords of this first and noblest mission of letters. Tho entitled an "Elegy," and written to commemorate the virtues of the poet's personal friend,

—and, in this sense, appropriately restricted in its range, —it takes up and develops the great ideas of God and the universe; of man and the soul and duty and destiny; of life and death and immortality; of good and evil, right and wrong; of science, philosophy, ethics, and religion; so as, in a word, virtually to cover the spacious area of truth, and to make the reader feel that he is dealing with the profoundest problems of earth and heaven. Hence, "In Memoriam" is something more and greater than a mere poem. It is a kind of compendium of theology and philosophy, of the Divinities and Humanities in new and striking form; furnishing food for thought to every thinking man who reads it.

Hence, to our mind, the fame of Tennyson and its permanence rest more upon such a product as this than upon any other of his works. "Maud," "The Princess," "Lady Godiva," "Enoch Arden," are choice and attractive poems, but scarcely to be cited in the same connection with this poetic masterpiece.

Similarly rich in these qualities is the marvelous genius of the Shakespearian drama; making that classification just which insists upon placing Shakespeare by himself, as having no legitimate rival in the province of English literature. Most of the Shakespearian plays evince this first condition of literary greatness, in their respective embodiment of some great thought.

Milton's "Paradise Regained" and "Samson" are unworthy of the author of "Paradise Lost" and "Comus"; and the illustrious Puritan poet often descends to a still lower level of poetic art. So with Browning and Tennyson and Longfellow and Lowell. But Shakespeare is uniformly great; and the question with the critic is, which, among an extended list of notable poems, is the most conspicuously so. Such is the first purpose of literature,—to propagate great ideas; the only condition being that they shall be presented in literary rather than in technical or educational form.

The difference between Bacon in his "Essays" and in his "Novum Organum" lies not in the presence or absence of ideas, but in the literary presentation of such ideas in the one, and their philosophical presentation in the other. There is the same difference between Mill's "Autobiography" and his "Treatise on Logic," or, in general, between any work that is textual and didactic and one that is offered in the accepted forms of prose and verse. Literature is thus the embodiment of ideas. As such, it is suggestive, stimulating, and inspiring, and commends itself to all who aim at mental discipline and the study of truth.

2. *The correct interpretation of the spirit of the age.*

It is here important to note that literature embraces two purposes—in a sense, separate, and yet, in the last analysis, united. The one contemplates general and remote effects; the other, those that are more specific, local, and immediate. The one has reference to the literature of a nation in its sum total, and in its historical influence from first to last; the other views it as operative in any particular age, and notes the manner in which it affects the thought and feeling and activities of that age. The mission of English literature may thus be examined as a consecutive and permanent influence from the beginning,—from Chaucer to Tennyson and Lowell, —or it may be studied in its successive and separate stages—Elizabethan, Augustan, and Victorian—as representative epochs of national and literary life.

In the discussion before us, it is not important sharply to distinguish these two types of influence, seeing that they are virtually one. Literature is to interpret the spirit of the age, either at any one period of its national development or all along the line of that development; and the more fully that a literature does this continuously, without serious and abrupt cessation or decline, the more fully does it subserve its purpose and hold its claim to eminence. What are called "golden ages" in letters are so partly because of the fact that, at such eras, authors have the most fully succeeded in catching and embodying the spirit of the time; interpreting correctly its great historic and social features, and thus making their work at the same time a cause and an effect of such special development. Such was the Augustan age in Rome and the Periclean in Greece.

Nor is it only in eras of special excellence that such a principle is seen. The fifteenth century in England may be said to have failed signally in producing any high type of literature; and yet it would be untrue to hold that its literature failed to reflect at all the temper of the time. The literature was inferior because the age was such. A high order of prose and verse at such an era would have been as much out of place as mediocrity in the days of Elizabeth or Anne.

What is demanded of authors, however, in periods of depression and decline, is to rebuke and reform the age at the very time of revealing its type and spirit, instead of assuming an attitude of indifference toward it, or resting content in simply being its representatives and exponents. It is thus that in every such decline there have been always a few choice spirits who succeeded in pointing out to their generation a higher way; insisting that they should enter and follow it. Such men were Lydgate and Malory and Skelton and Caxton, between the death of Chaucer and the coronation of Henry VIII.

Critics speak of literature as a social and civic force. This is but another way of stating the point in question. It was so in Greece, as the government was democratic or despotic; in Rome, before and after the fall of the Empire; in Arabia and Spain, under the influence of the Caliphs; in Northern Europe, especially in England. English prose miscellany, as Drake has traced its history, clearly reveals this side of the mission of literature; so that Addison and Steele, in the *Spectator*, the *Tatler*, the *Freeholder*, and the *Guardian*, may be said to have photographed the manners and politics of the day. So did Swift, in his "Gulliver's Travels" and "Drapier's Letters." So has Lowell done, in the "Biglow Papers," and Curtis, in his "Potiphar Papers."

3. Closely connected with the last-mentioned mission of literature is another—*the interpretation of human nature to itself and to the world.*

This is the subjective office of literature as a revealer of interior and personal life. In this sense, literature is a psychology; a manifestation of mind and will and conscience and character; a study of man and men; a full-sized portrait of the joys and sorrows, the faults and follies, the strength and weakness, the whims and fancies, the struggles and achievements, the glory and the shame of man; a disclosure of him at his best and his worst. Hence it is that literature demands, at this point, a master-hand to delineate humanity correctly. A development of mere esthetic taste will not do; a superficial acquaintance with men and books will not do; nor will anything do, in the line of necessary equipment, save a catholic and comprehensive mind, a keen and sympathetic insight into men and things, and an unswerving purpose to be true to facts.

There are two or three departments of literary work in which this particular function of literature may be and has been best expressed—viz., the drama, fiction, satire, and humor. In each of these forms of verse and prose, the interpretation of human nature to itself and to the world is the primary motive. So far as the drama is concerned, it is best evinced on the side of comedy,—what is called specifically the "comedy of manners," wherein, according to Shakespeare, the mirror is held up to nature, and "all the world 's a stage and all the men and women merely players." In this sense, the dramatist is simply a delineator or portrait-painter, and seeks to do with his pen what the artist does with brush and pencil and chisel.

So in fiction, on its realistic side, whether we speak of the novels of fact, of feeling, of manners, or of purpose,—of Scott, of Charlotte Brontë, of Dickens, or of George Eliot. Revelation of the inner man to his fellow men and to himself, by an impartial observer, is the object. In fiction, as in the drama, impersonation and characterization are the end, which very terms indicate the point in question.

In the spacious field of satire and humor also, and in the manifold forms that they assume—the serio-comic or mock-heroic, sarcasm and innuendo, repartee and invective,—representation of what is beneath the surface is the end. Thus it is that "Hudibras," the "Dunciad," "The Battle of the Books," and "The Rape of the Lock" set forth the cardinal characteristics of human nature in those days in such striking form that men were obliged to rebuke and ridicule themselves.

The permanence and the popularity of these special forms of literature are assured, in that their object is to portray human nature, which from age to age offers an increasingly inviting field.

4. *The presentation and enforcement of high ideals.*

Courthope, in speaking of the literary outlook, says:

> "What is wanting is the genius to conceive and construct some ideal. The bias of Englishmen to practical skill has reacted on the national mind. They respect the fine mechanical forms even in their song. The tone of colleges, scholars, and literary society has this mortal air. Even so-called philosophy and letters are mechanical in structure, as if inspiration had ceased. The English have lost sight of the fact that poetry exists to speak the spiritual law."

What the English critic here applies to verse would apply to all literature; and he emphasizes the fact that what is wanting in these commercial and practical days is the spiritual and unmortal view of letters,—the exaltation and realization of the ideal in literature as distinct from the visible, tangible, and merely mercenary. Not only, as stated at the outset, must literature involve in its mission some great idea or ideas, but great ideals as well. It may be said, indeed, that the two should be found together; great ideas begetting or springing from correspondingly high conceptions.

In reply to the inquiry what is meant by this particular requisition of literature, it may be stated, that it includes the imagination in its supremest function; a conscientious sense of the dignity and responsibility of literature, and a serious purpose to execute it.

Here, again, is one of the tests of literature; and on this basis, as much as upon any other, are the masterpieces classified as such. The Dantean, Homeric, Shakespearian, and Miltonic conceptions of literature are of this extra-mundane order, having "no mortal air" about them. This it is, more than all else, that gives to such an author as Emerson his potency, and goes far to nullify any errors of method and detail that may exist in his writings. Matthew Arnold—all his faults conceded—possessed and illustrated this conception of literature; always penning what he penned under the influence of the ideal.

It is this which gives to the poetry of Tennyson its supremest quality, as it comes to its best expression in the "In Memoriam."

The literature of the Restoration was what it was because, save in Milton's work, it had no such inspiration and aspiration; and, in the realistic tendencies of the day, the danger is that sentiment may be displaced by facts and figures, the imaginative by the realistic, and that authorship may be reduced to the level of the trades.

Literature can not live by bread alone, but must find its main sources of strength in thought and feeling, in motive and aspiration, in converse with the unseen and infinite.

Whether Literature, Continental or English, is realizing these conditions of literary success, is a question of pressing interest. Is literature fulfilling its mission? While such a critic as Morris—himself a poet—speaks of the present epoch in letters as an "empty day," and not a few others despair of reaching the scope and dignity of what they call "the epic age," there are still some who take a more hopeful view and anticipate the dawn, at no distant date, of a broader and better economy. Thus Stedman, in discussing the latter-day singers,—Swinburne and his school,—discovers a serious and recently renewed effort to sustain and perpetuate the glories of English verse, and thus to make the close of the nineteenth century worthy of its opening and middle years. Reviewing the American side of English letters, he writes of the dawn which may soon break upon us unawares, "even tho as yet the older school of Longfellow and Lowell and Poe and Whittier is not even approximately reproduced."

Similar views are expressed by Richardson, in his "Perspective of American Literature."

"The future of poetry," says Matthew Arnold, "is immense, because in poetry our race will find an ever surer stay"; while Emerson is more than pained as he beholds what he conceives to be the lowering tendencies of the time. The truth may be found to lie midway between these extremes; and, while all the features constituting the highest mission of letters may not be found, enough may be found to give it place and worth.

If it is not the era of great ideals in literature, in the spiritual sense of that term, it is contended that great ideas are still seen to be present, and, above all, that literature is, as never before, an interpretation of contemporary life and of human nature. Our conception of literature and its mission, it is urged, must be modified somewhat, as times and conditions change; so that the great ideas as incorporated in Dante and Goethe and Milton may be no greater than those which find expression in the representative prose and verse of the nineteenth century, even tho these latter are expressed in more practical and objective form. The poetry of Robert

Browning may be as full of great ideas as is that of Homer, and the prose of George Eliot as much so as is that of Cicero and Bacon; while what is called the practical literature of the century may be as thoughtful as that preceding it, only embodied in more vital and pungent form.

To our mind, the main difference lies, as suggested, in the less conspicuous presence and power in modern letters of ideals rather than of ideas, by which the province of literature may be widened, but not heightened; by which quality and tone may be sacrificed to mere amount and result; and what is called the inner spirit of literature be somewhat in abeyance to the external and sensible.

If the poetry of the future is to be the poetry of Whitman, as some suggest, then it is clear that the idealistic will give way to the materialistic; culture and refinement, to the grosser expressions of verse; and literature become simply a medium for the semi-enlightened views of the lower orders of society. If, on the other hand, the Tennysonian conception of literature is to prevail, then it is equally clear that the ideal will have full scope, and literature be kept upon its higher levels.

Whatever the tendency, however, the mission of literature is a distinct one; and the mission of the man of letters is correspondingly clear: To hold literature to its original purpose as one of the liberal arts, expressed in the form of a fine art, so as to secure, at the same time, what is most needed,—the union of strength and beauty.

If the facts be fairly stated, it must be conceded, that modern tendencies are in the main unliterary, tho, perhaps, not in any hostile sense anti-literary. The attitude of the modern mind toward letters may be expressed as one of unconcern,—the absence of any keen and inquisitive interest in the development of national taste in letters. The great majority of writers themselves, whatever their preferences may be, are, of necessity, working on the lower planes of literature rather than the higher. Instead of an epic or a philosophic age, the age is one of lighter miscellany, produced in forms the most manageable and marketable. This has its place and purpose; but it is not the ideal type as embodied in the great productions of the older peoples, pagan and Christian.

One of the deteriorating influences of modern times flows from the fact that quantity, rather than quality, is so often accepted as a measure of merit. The voluminousness of modern authorship is one of its greatest dangers; and we are living, more than ever, in the age of books. Publishers are besieged by authors; and their shelves are burdened with the rapidly increasing issues of the press. Libraries are multiplying and enlarging; and bibliography—the mere collection of volumes—has become a science, a separate department of study and investigation. All this tends somewhat to modify and lower the original standard of letters, and makes it appear a comparatively easy matter for one to pen his thoughts and secure for them a general reading. It is only the emphasis of the qualitative in literature that will save it, at this point, from rapid and permanent degeneracy.

Possnett, in his "Comparative Literature," draws an interesting picture of what he calls "The World Literature," as distinct from that of any separate class or nation; embracing the best efforts of all civilized peoples as well as the fundamental principles of Christian doctrine and faith. Just as church historians speak of the possible unity and federation of all religions on some broad basis of common agreement, and as Max Müller writes of the possible reduction of all languages to a few of the great historic languages of the world, so it is contended by some that the mission of literature will not be and can not be fulfilled till this principle of federation or confederation is to some extent realized. Goethe, in some of his works, seems to be looking forward to it, as does Herder also. "Let us conceive," says Matthew Arnold, "the whole group of civilized nations as being, for intellectual and spiritual purposes, one great confederation, bound to a joint action and working toward a common result,"—"an ideal," he adds, "which will impose itself more and more upon the thoughts of our modern writers." In a word, what is here meant is the spirit of fraternity in letters,—the recognition, on the part of authors as a class, of common relationships, common interests and aims, whereby literature, as a great world-force and civilizer, might more effectually do its beneficent work. We speak of the brotherhood of letters. This is not confined to one people, but may have a range as wide as the brotherhood of men.

Of the four great offices of literature mentioned, all but one are, in fact, of this cosmopolitan character. Great ideas, human nature, and great ideals are universal in application, and serve, at once, to show that, in these respects at least, all literatures deal with common principles and have common purposes, as true in Homer as in Milton, and in Emerson as in Lucretius and Pascal.

It was thus that Shakespeare wrote his dramas, not simply as an exponent of the Elizabethan age or even of the English people, but as an author—within the province of general literature and the specific province of the drama—depicting character in "Macbeth" and "Lear" and "Othello" and "Imogen" as character for all peoples and all time, so that when translated from English into the language of any other people, they seem to that people to be the masterpieces of one of their own authors. There is in these works that "one touch of nature" that "makes the whole world kin," and the presence of which in any work marks it as the work of genius.

No master-spirit in any literature has ever written prose or verse purely from the local or national point of view; and herein lies the difference between genius and talent or mediocrity in letters. Chaucer wrote for all men and for all time. His contemporaries, such as John Gower, wrote for the England of their day. Shakespeare, Milton, Burns, and Tennyson wrote for all men and for all time. Prior and Thomson and Campbell and Crabbe wrote for the England of their own generation. There is a contemporaneous literature, the product of literary talent, and one that is permanent and intellectual, the product of genius; and it is he only who produces the latter who has a due conception of the mission of letters, and is gifted of God for its realization.

Hence, literature has, as its highest mission, in common with every noble science and art, the conception and expression of the truth for the truth's sake, if so be the thought and life of man may be perfected and enlarged. Herein lies the unity of all truth; and herein is literature, in its final purpose, the artistic embodiment of the "best that is known and thought in the world."

PART SECOND

CHAPTER ONE

THE AIMS OF LITERARY READING AND STUDY

WE are using the term, literary, in this connection, in its specific sense, as distinct from such terms as scientific, philosophic and linguistic; as distinct, indeed, from any order of reading that is technical or professional. In any true definition of literature, it is emphasized that it must be presented in untechnical form, and, as such, be fairly intelligible and interesting to the general mind. Hence, those books which are justly entitled to the appellation, literary, must be thus unprofessional in content, method and purpose, the free expression, in written form, of the author's thinking, such thinking being always mediated to the reader in apprehensible and comprehensible forms, the imagination, feelings and taste being especially prominent. The term, literary, being thus defined and applied, it is in place to state, that at no period in the history of our American Institutions of learning has this particular subject now in review been more prominent in the eye of the educated public—what the objects, direct and indirect, of our reading are; what its best methods are as gathered from the wisest counsel and experience; what, above all, should be the subject-matter of our reading; what authors in the almost limitless variety should be emphasized as essential and what avoided; and what relation such an order of reading is supposed to sustain to our general intellectual life and work. Naturally, these topics are now at the front; partly, as the result of that general mental awakening or revival of learning which marks the beginning of the present century; partly, the result as well as the occasion of that decided increase of interest in American Libraries that now obtains; and, also, because an extensive and an intimate acquaintance with literature has come to be, as never before, the essential mark of an educated man. To be well read is as important as to be well bred and well trained; the liberally educated man, above all, being quite inexcusable for any neglect in this direction. When Thomas Hobbes, the great English philosopher, remarked—"If I had read as many books as other men, I should be as ignorant as they are," he was by no means condemning extensive acquaintance with books, but only that far too frequent order of reading which surrenders all independent judgment as soon as it consults an author, and misses the very end in view by a servile imitation of the opinion of others. Bacon's Essay, "On Studies," which is really an Essay on Reading, strikes the true note on this subject, at the very opening of Modern English Letters, by insisting that every intelligent man shall, as such, be conversant with standard authorship and, most especially, with that of his vernacular.

Coming now to the special discussion in hand, we may inquire, at the outset, as to

WHAT THE PRIMARY AIMS OF LITERARY READING ARE

First of all, is Information or Enlightenment. We are to seek facts and truths for practical use. As Bacon states it—"Reading maketh a full man, so that if a man read little, he had need to have much cunning to seem to know that he doth not." Literary Equipment is the first need of the student of letters, and this determines the first purpose of his work. What are the most available and important literary data is the question at issue, so that the student of books shall have at his command the knowledge he needs. It is just here that one of the most important functions of a Library as an educational agency is seen, in that it is, in Old English phrase, the storehouse of books, the treasury of information for the inquiring mind, the base of supplies, always accessible, and ever inviting the seeker to new discovery of fact and truth. All that is meant by a Library as a place of research or investigation, either for the novice or the mature inquirer, is here involved, and the fuller its facilities are in this direction, the richer will the results be to those who frequent it. We speak, by way of special usage, of a Library of Reference, a place for consultation on the part of scholars. Every Library is, in the best sense, a Reference Library, a place of resort for the literary investigator. It is in this spirit that Lowell wrote his suggestive paper on "Books and Libraries," as he said—"After all, the better part of every man's education is that which he gives himself, and it is for this that a good Library should furnish the opportunity." It is the home of a student's mental and general educational life to which all his acquisitions converge and from which he is constantly taking his bearings. If it be asked, what specific order of reading is here the most pertinent, it is manifest that Prose is far more essential than Verse, and that, among the different forms of prose, the Historical is fundamental, a province of reading open to the student which it is not optional with him to neglect. Facts must be sought where facts are to be found, and it can not be emphasized too strongly that historical reading, as it demands the student's earliest attention, also demands his later and continuous attention. To the English student, English and American History should be an open book in itself and its manifold relationship to Continental History. He should be acquainted with its facts and incidents; its beginnings and unfoldings, and, to some degree, at least, conversant with those great historic principles that underlie and determine it. Nor are we speaking of Annals and Chronicles, Outlines and Compends, which may be said to contain the material of history without being History Proper; nor of History in its wider meaning as applied to any department of knowledge embodied in narrative, as Leckey's "History of European Morals." We speak of Civil History as a form of literature, conceived and presented with primary reference to literary ends, as Macaulay's "History of England," or as Tyler's "Literary History of The American Revolution." Freeman's "Outlines of European History" is not strictly literary, as his "Norman Conquest" is, the point of view materially differing in the respective volumes.

A second aim is Culture, a word that is sometimes used in the wide sense of general mental training, but which we are now using in the narrower and well-understood sense of specifically esthetic training. It refers to the education of the taste, in its distinctive nature and function as a faculty of the soul. Arnold calls it, "the sense of beauty" or, as applied to authorship and criticism, "an instinct for style." It is a faculty, discerning what is beautiful, and a sensibility enjoying it. As it has a nature and an area of its own, so it has its own laws and processes, its own forms of expression and methods of cultivation, its own ideals and purposes, and must thus be regarded by those who seek to realize its ends. Here, there is no contrast, as in History, between the literary and the non-literary. Culture is, first and last, a literary term, and from the earliest days of Greek and Roman Letters has been so conceived and applied. The cultured man or people is, as such, conversant with books and authors, with literature as a subject. Here, the student is introduced into the province of the Fine Arts, as contrasted with the Mechanical or Useful Arts. Here, Literature itself is reduced to a Fine Art, whatever its more practical aims may be. Here, the beautiful is studied and exalted for its own sake, as well as for the beneficent ministries which it serves in an age and nation so devoted as ours to material interests, and insists that education fails of its primal purpose to the degree in which it underrates the artistic side of authorship and life. It is thus that Bacon, philosopher that he was, tells us, that "Studies serve for Ornament" as well as for "Ability," and that the symmetrically developed man can not afford to neglect this phase of human training. Hence it is, that Literature itself has, at times, been interpreted, by way of extreme, in the light of Culture only, as Belles-Lettres or Polite Literature; while the Germans have been inclined to pass to the other extreme of the didactic and speculative, the plane of rational opinion lying midway between these two positions.

If it be asked what order of literature is here in place for perusal, we enter at once the province of Poetry, this fact revealing the scope of the area which Culture covers. It is an essential factor in Poetry as distinct from Prose, that it mediates the thought of the author not only in metrical form, but through the channel of the imagination, feelings and taste. Poetry is, first and last, artistic, a product in which form assumes an importance of its own, in which the expression of the author's taste and the qualification of the reader's taste is a vital factor. In this respect, it has no peer or formidable rival, the only kind of prose that at all approaches it being the romantic, as seen in fiction, and the descriptive, as seen in the lighter miscellany. "Poetry as a Fine Art," writes a modern critic, "is possessed of qualities that make it a means of culture far beyond the utmost possibilities of prose." Observing students of modern educational tendencies must have clearly noticed the growing purpose to elevate Poetry to its proper level as related to Prose. It is urged that neither shall be sharply contrasted with the other, but that they shall be allowed conjointly to effect their beneficent ends. Far back in Elizabethan days, Sidney opened the argument for the Defense of Verse, which Dryden and Shelley continued. To no one author more than to Matthew Arnold is the English world indebted for an insistence upon its charms. With this branch of literature, therefore, the student of literature must be conversant. He must know its content and spirit; its laws and structure; its masterpieces and masters, and how it enters more and more fully into the thought and life of the age. No one can familiarize himself with the Literature of Verse and not be a cultured man. By the very force of daily conference and contact, the reader will take on the esthetic type and habit of mind, become imperceptibly the man of taste and of the finer forms of feeling. His poetic imagination will be quickened and refined; his literary outlook, enlarged; and the whole man be gradually brought into a fuller intimacy and sympathy with the beautiful.

An additional aim of Literary Reading is Discipline, in the fullest sense of that term. It is all the more important to press this principle in that the drift of current criticism runs in the opposite direction. Close and unwarranted distinctions are made between literary reading and literary study; the one being, it is said, informal, recreative and discursive, often having no other end than personal entertainment or diversion from more serious pursuits, while the other is a substantive intellectual process and, as such, quite aside from the primary purposes and ideals of literature. Such a theory, it will at once be seen, is narrow and superficial and inconsistent with facts, covering but a part of the area properly compassed by the word, literature, and failing to coordinate it as a department with all other related intellectual pursuits. It is not aside from truth to say that most of the errors of popular opinion as to the scope, nature, the underlying principles and purpose of literature are due to this initial, radical error, whereby, as we conceive it, the very heart of literature is emasculated, and nothing is left but its lifeless and useless encasement. Literature, indeed, contemplates personal pleasure as one of its ends, and, in not a few of its forms, as in fiction, the lighter miscellany, lyric and descriptive verse, emphasizes the entertaining, recreative side of authorship. This, however, is but one of its aims, its least distinctive and controlling purpose. We are now using the term Literary Reading, as Bacon used it, in the sense of Literary Study. As he says "Studies serve for ability" or in more specific phrase, "Read in order to weigh and consider." Hence, he insists that while some books are to be "tasted" only, that is, rapidly and informally read, others are to be "chewed and digested." In a word, reading is to be studious. It is to be made a business or vocation to the exercise of which a man may bring his best abilities, and through the medium of which he may expect to make such abilities even more pronounced and effective. Literature is the expression of thought. Hence, if it be asked —what order of literature is now to be consulted and made a part of the reader's daily work, we answer, Disciplinary Books, books which make us "weigh and consider," the thought-containing and thought-producing books, by contact with which, all the faculties of the mind are awakened and the entire mental being quickened and enlarged. Prose on its philosophic side is here in place, and the department of Critical as distinct from Descriptive Miscellany. Even Fiction, in its philosophic forms; Epic and Tragic Verse, as distinct from lyric and descriptive, belong here. The higher classes of Historical Prose are in place here, where great generic principles are discussed as applied to states and empires. In fine, the strictly intellectual expressions of prose and verse are now the ones sought, where the matter dominates the form, and mental impression is the final purpose of the writer.

The final and crowning Aim of all Literary Reading is Incentive, Impulse, Mental and Literary Inspiration,— the deep and pervasive moving of the soul of the reader in such wise that his emotive and intellectual self is electrified and impelled to quicker function. What we have in mind, just here, is best indicated by the term— Stimulating Literature, a literature that stirs and fires the entire personality of the reader and awakens all his dormant energies. The reading of the great Biographies of literature, such as that of Milton, Burke or Cromwell.

will accomplish this result. The careful study of a great Historical Event, such as The French Revolution, or a great Historical Scene, such as The Battle of Waterloo, will affect it. The absorption of the soul in the gradual unfolding of a great Tragedy, as Hamlet, or King Lear, will do it. The study of the great Orations of literature, as those of Cicero or Webster, will do it. In fine, the study of that species of literature which beats and throbs with the principle of life will do it.

These, as we conceive them, are the Primary Purposes which the right-minded student of letters has in view as he sits down to examine its content. Information, Culture, Discipline and Incentive; the gathering of Knowledge to furnish the mind for its work; the refining of the taste whereby what is best may be seen to be the best; the positive strengthening of mental power, and the infusion of a new spirit into every faculty and function. If, therefore, the question be asked, more comprehensively, what books and authors are to be consulted, we answer, The Great Books of Literature; the Masterpieces of every age and nation; with special reference to those of one's own nation, those authors whom Robertson has edited under the caption—Great Writers; great in thought and language and general style; great in the truths they convey and the manner in which they convey them; disciplinary to taste and intellect, imagination and will. It is thus that Lowell insists on the choice and mastery of such books as these, as he states it—"communing with the choice thoughts of choice spirits and unconsciously acquiring the good manners of that supreme society." When asked to recommend a course of reading, Mr. Lowell answered—"Confine yourself to the supreme books in whatever literature." To the same effect, Emerson pleads with us to lay aside the local, "municipal" literature of the day, and to acquaint ourselves with that which is sublime and catholic and expanding—with Plato and Plutarch and Pascal and Goethe and Shakespeare and Milton; with books, as he says, in his inimitable way, "that work redemption in us"; "that take rank in our lives with parents and lovers, and passionate experiences; medicinal, stringent and authoritative books"; with books that give us "the perception of immortality"; books of "believing men that had atmosphere and amplitude about them," by which a man is lifted to higher levels and set in harmony with all that is good.

In fine, read Helpful and Wholesome Books, books that are sane and sound throughout, free from unhealthful influence, full of guiding and safe suggestion, full of beneficent purpose, written by authors in sympathy with their fellows and wholly intent on the bettering of human conditions; written less for gain than for good, less for the author than for the reader. Such books address themselves with serious purpose to the solution of the pressing problems of life, deal with fundamental questions in a fundamental manner, and do much in their way to clear the atmosphere and make it easier to live aright.

CHAPTER TWO

THE GENESIS AND GROWTH OF LITERARY FORMS

ONE of the most interesting studies in the sphere of literature is from the point of view of its expression as permanent and variable,—the elements and phases of literature. There is such a thing in literature as a settled condition and manifestation of literary life,—what the student of events would call an historical continuity from age to age, so invariable as to be assumed as always existing, and to be anticipated and utilized as such. Every great nation has, thus, its characteristic literary history, life and personality which marks it from all other nations. Thus, Germany or France or Spain. When we speak of the Teutonic Literature of Europe as a comprehensive type, we know precisely what we mean, while such a type preserves its identity from age to age as clearly as the Teutonic physiognomy preserves its type of form and feature, as distinct from the Latin or Asiatic.

The law of literature at this point is just what it is in nature and in the various fields of intellectual activity. There is and must be an invariability on the basis of which facts and truths are examined and a status or condition from which all observations are made. This is not necessarily uniformity in the mechanical sense, nor a blank and lifeless monotony. It is rather the principle of unity, stability and self-consistency, by which primary types are preserved and certain radical and cardinal principles hold their place amid all disturbing influences.

Mr. Courthope, in speaking of the "conservatism of the eighteenth century," must have this in mind. He means by conservatism, the retention of the historical and literary traditions, so that the connection between any two periods is sustained, and the one line of development preserved from the earliest era to the latest.

Old English thus passes naturally into Modern English, and Elizabethan, into Augustan and Georgian English, not merely because one follows the other in the order of time, as one century follows, necessarily, the preceding, but because there is a closer and a higher nexus, a philosophical and a literary as well as an historic sequence, that continues the succession and gives it common type and function.

All this is true, but it is, also, true and equally true, that Literature has a variable type and life. This is best seen perhaps in what are known as Literary Transitions, illustrating, in part, what Hunter has called "arrested progress" in the life of letters.

The transition in German Literature which took place when Luther completed his version of the Scriptures, or in the literature of Greece, after the downfall of the Republic, or in that of France, at the time of the great Revolution of 1789, or in the sixteenth and eighteenth centuries in England—all are instances in point of this principle of variation or development in literature.

Apparently abrupt and unnatural as we first examine them, these variations come at length to assume historic prominence, and seem to obey a law of regularity, as to time and place and character. "Movements in Literature," says Courthope, "are as distinct and definite as what are known in religion as the Methodist and Tractarian movements and, in politics, as the liberal and radical," and, we may add, in science and philosophy, as developments induced by evolution.

This is a strong way, and, perhaps, an extreme way, of stating it. Movements, however, there are, more or less radical and far-reaching, and the student of letters intent upon the examination of what he calls a settled product or body of authorship, must be alive to these great and often rapid changes which form a part of the literary history of every advanced people, alive to the evolution of literature.

The general and special types of such changes, to which we wish, in the present discussion, to call attention, are those included under The Rise and Growth of Literary Forms—the different ways in which literature may and does evolve and express itself in order to reach its legitimate ends.

Thus, first of all, as to Prose and Verse. Of these two great divisions of literary art, we speak, naturally, as if they occurred at the same time, developed after the same methods, and in equal degree. When we examine more minutely, we note that in every historic literature, verse precedes prose, expressing itself, as it does, at the very dawn of national and even tribal life. The songs and odes of the bard and the strolling minstrel are the first forms that are manifest, and these in connection with music itself as a necessary adjunct or medium. Thus it was in Southern Europe, in the Chansons and songs of Trouveres and Troubadours; in ancient Greece, in the life of the Rhapsodists; in old Celtic and Saxon Britain, when the gleemen with harp in hand went about from door to door and court to court for their own livelihood and the pleasure of those for whom they composed and sang and played. So marked is this priority of poetry that, in English letters, nearly two centuries intervene between our national verse and national prose,—between the Canterbury Tales of Chaucer and the Essays of Bacon.

There is reason for all this in the very constitution of the human mind, as well as in the history of language; in the effect of environment and in what is called the progress of civilization. Without endorsing Macaulay's extreme position that as civilization advances poetry declines, and that a certain crudeness of mind is necessary to the production of the highest verse, this much may be said,—that the natural and undeveloped mind, in its earlier life, chooses verse rather than prose as an outlet; that language, as an instrument of literature, first assumes this unstudied form; that the natural world of earth and air and sky and sea directly inspires it, and that civilization in its less elaborate and primitive types offers fewer barriers to its natural expression.

Prose is a more studied, deliberate and developed form, and is evolved under later and more complex conditions. It expresses, more fully, the strictly intellectual side of literature; is embodied in language when language has assumed its more stable character; is less affected by physical environment and is more in sympathy with an advanced and involved civilization. As to the development of prose literature, as well as to its genesis, the inquiry is interesting, taking a decidedly subordinate place in the Elizabethan period, while, in that of Queen Anne and the first Georges, it comes into special prominence, the present tendency being in the same direction.

So as to the different forms that prose and verse may assume. Let us examine this diversity and, if possible, arrive at some rational explanation of it.

1. If we divide the generic forms of Prose expression into Narrative, Descriptive, Forensic, Critical and Philosophic Prose, it is found, as a matter of fact, that the Narrative and Descriptive forms are the first in order of time, if not, indeed, of importance, and this is natural and philosophically reasonable. The first thing with which the human mind has to do is facts or events and objects or scenes. These it at once attempts to embody, in so far as prose is concerned, in story and portraiture. The events are narrated and the scenes are depicted just as they strike the mind and eye. Here we have the origin of historical and descriptive writing, and the explanation of it. Hence, in England, as far back as the days of King Alfred, in the ninth century, we have the compilation of the Old English Chronicle, and those sketches of persons and places that we find in Orosius and Mandeville, the chroniclers and travelers of Early English days, represented in Modern English, in Raleigh's "History of the World" and Sidney's "Arcadia."

History and Descriptive Miscellany are thus expected just where we find them, their subsequent growth or decline, also, following the well-established law of natural life.

Hence, there is good reason why we should have a great historical school in the time of Hume and Gibbon, and a great periodical prose school, in that of Addison and Steele.

2. So, in order of time, forensic or parliamentary prose comes later, following the course of civic life and the growth of government. Edmund Burke, in his great oration against Hastings, would have been out of place

in the sixteenth century, as, also, the great British and American orators would have been. The illustrious forensic productions of Greece and Rome, in the persons of Æschines and Cicero, came to their place in ancient history in the fulness of time, and could not have justly come earlier.

3. What is called critical miscellany and philosophic prose naturally develops last of all. Modern British literary criticism does not take form till the very opening of the last century, in the establishment of the *Edinburgh Review*, while English prose, on the philosophic side, has been a comparatively recent growth.

When these various forms first emerge and how; the way in which they take on vigor and function and the influences at work to modify and, for a time, to annul them,—all this constitutes a most attractive portion of that work that lies before the student of letters, and wherein, once again, literature is seen in its relations to philosophy and history and human life, and is seen to bring into exercise the fullest mental activity of author and critic.

There are one or two features of this historic prose development in English that may be especially commended to the ambitious student. We refer to Satire and Prose Fiction.

A. Satire is a form of prose peculiar in its origin, nature, method and purpose. With the classification given in mind, it is not strictly narrative, or descriptive, or forensic, or critical, or philosophical, but these in one. It takes from each what will best suit its purpose; follows its own plan, if it has any plan, and works steadily toward its end. It is the most personal form of prose.

As it is based on facts, it is historical ; in so far as it involves caricature, it is descriptive ; as it employs and addresses feeling, it is forensic ; as it expresses faults and follies, it is critical ; and as it probes to the bottom and is without fear, it is philosophic.

The questions for the literary student are,—Where did it arise and why, and how has it developed and why. As far back, in English Letters, as the days of Alfred and Hendyng we find it and, here and there, in Hampole and Langland and Wiclif and Latimer and Wyatt and Gascoigne it appears, until we come to Butler and Dryden and Pope and Addison and the great school of modern satirists. Why should "Hudibras" have appeared when it did, and the "Battle of the Books" when it did, and why did not Thomas Carlyle appear as the great censor of men and morals a century earlier ; and why should satire so often leave the sphere of prose and embody itself, as in "Hudibras" and the "Biglow Papers," in verse, and what is the bond that holds it to the Humorous.

B. So as to Prose Fiction—a department of prose thoroughly unique, tho combining in one form the three great departments of narrative, descriptive and philosophic prose. When did it originate in English letters and why ; what have been the varied forms of its manifestation, as in Scott and Thackeray and George Eliot and Kipling, and why should it so decline in one age and so develop in another. Is Lanier's theory that its purpose is the representation of personality correct or not, and what is the explanation of its modern ethical and theological tendency.

As to origin, it is stoutly contended by some that it dates no further back than the days of Sidney, in the pages of his "Arcadia," while others trace its faint, yet historical, beginnings in the days of Chaucer and in the earliest folk-lore of the English people,—even back in the old British myths and legends and traditions, as they manifested themselves in Teutonic form. What is "Beowulf," we are told by some, but a great novel in verse, the portraiture in Beowulf and Grendel and the prominent characters, of what occurs in every life,—the conflict of good and evil, the fight of every man with the dragon that threatens his soul.

Fiction, tho it be fiction, is one of the great facts of literature, and worthy, as such, of patient and philosophic study.

When we come into the region of Verse-Forms, this study assumes increasing interest and complexity, as shown, especially, by the fact that, even yet, many of the questions started long since are unsettled. First of all, the true relation of verse to prose, and just where the line is to be drawn that separates them, and just what is meant by poetical prose, as seen in Hawthorne, or prose-poetry, as seen in Whitman and Tupper and Pollock and Young. Is it proper to call such poems as Pope's "Essay on Criticism" or "Essay on Man" poems at all and, if so, how are they differentiated from the great masterpieces of English Literature.

For the purposes before us, these great poetic forms may be said to be—The Epic and Dramatic and Lyric, and it is the object of the literary student to determine their respective origins; their respective historical development; their respective influence; elements in common and elements distinctive; and the respective purposes they are supposed to serve in literature.

1. The study of Epic Verse might in itself constitute a

separate department in literary study, as it practically does in those quarters where the Homeric Poems, or Milton, or The "Cid," or The "Divine Comedy" or "Beowulf" form distinctive courses. The field here is a vast one and touches, at divers points, the larger field of English Literature and Literature in general.

One of the primal questions here is—What constitutes a poem an epic, besides the mere fact of its having a hero, and why is not the "Faery Queene" or "Marmion" such a poem as fully as the "Iliad" or "Paradise Regained"?

As to its origin in England, how far back must we go, and is it true to say that it begins with Cædmon and Beowulf, and that Chaucer's "Romaunt of the Rose" and the old Romance of "Sir Havelock" and "Sir Tristram" mark its later history.

2. So as to Dramatic Verse, on its Tragic or Comic side, and here the controversy is prolonged and intense. The beginnings of the English Drama is a topic in itself, whether its genesis takes us back of the Elizabethan Age and, if so, to what extent the representatives of those earlier times prepared the way for the elaborate development of modern days.

The Historical Antecedents of the English Drama involves the study of the old Miracle Plays or Mysteries, the Morality Plays and Interludes of the middle period between the Saxon "Chronicle" and the revival of learning.

In one form or another, dramatic representation is as old as the race, and in nearly every nation, even among the Hebrews, has had some kind of expression in literature. Such a work as Schlegel's "History of Dramatic

Literature" is nearly as extensive in its range as the history of literature itself, or the history of civilization. More specifically, such a volume as Symond's "Predecessors of the English Drama," traces the English history of the drama as far back as the beginnings of English literature, and aims to show a continuous sequence on to the days of Elizabeth. Hase and Pollard, in their discussion of the old Miracle Plays, connect the rise and progress of the European drama with that of England, and thus preserve the unity of the history. To what extent the Elizabethan drama, in its incipient form, is due to Southern Europe, and to what extent it is original and English is a question of interest, while it is equally suggestive to trace the subsequent course of English dramatic verse on to the time of Tennyson.

Why there should have been so decided a development in the sixteenth century; why the drama of the seventeenth century should have been inferior in quantity and quality, and why no later school of poets has been able to equal or even approximate the excellence of the Shakespearian art, are questions fraught with historical and philosophical as well as literary value.

Dramatic verse on the American side of English Letters invites attention, while the various subdivisions of such verse, as seen in farce and pantomime and masque and melodrama, deserve a separate study.

3. Precisely so as to Lyric Verse—the other great department of poetry. Here we enter a field as comprehensive as it is attractive. The question as to its origin, in so far as time is concerned, can not remain in serious doubt, it being conceded by all historians of literature, that as poetry is older than prose, lyric verse

is older than any other form, taking its rise in the most primitive conditions of life, and having for its object the most original and natural instincts of the soul. If we emphasize the term lyric, as the poetry sung to the lyre, it points to those earliest eras, when the minstrel with the song of his own composing went about with lyre in hand to entertain his hearers, or, if we interpret this form of verse as especially emotional, we are here, also, taken back to the earliest states of society, and have to do with the most spontaneous utterances of the heart. Lyric verse is thus contemporaneous with the origin of language, and is simply the most natural way in which man can embody and express his deepest self.

Hence, the large variety of forms which it has historically assumed—in ode and sonnet, in pastoral and elegy. Vitally connected with the epic in what is called the heroic ode, it manifests its presence in sacred as well as secular verse; in humor and satire and in the passion of love. So numerous are these varieties that they constitute a class or section of verse, as embodied in ballad and roundel, in virelay and villanelle; in chant and triolet, representing, respectively, the ingenious ways which feeling takes to give itself a fitting expression.

The relation of the lyric to the dramatic is a study fraught with interest. If, as has been done by some English critics, special attention is given to the Elizabethan Lyrics, in so far as found in the Elizabethan drama, the student will be surprised to find how vast a field he has entered. So close, at times, is the connection that no dividing line can be seen or drawn. This is signally true of the Shakespearian drama, while of such a poem as Milton's "Comus" it is difficult to state whether the term lyric or dramatic is the more applicable, so thoroughly does the one element fuse itself into the other, and constitute a poetic unit which is neither lyric nor dramatic but a something combining both and better than either.

From this examination of the Development of Literary Forms, two or three inferences of practical value arise.

A. Herein is seen the Naturalness of Literature in its highest and best conditions. Literature is not a something external to the thought and life of a people, arising and manifesting itself in some arbitrary manner, obedient only to its own laws and intent only upon the furtherance of its own ends, but is what it is as determined by some higher principle and necessity, and that is the demands of the nation and age that it aims to represent. As has been seen, whatever the permanent elements may be in letters, they adjust themselves to the genius of the people and institutions to which they are related, and to the temper of the particular times or epochs that go to make up historic life.

Critics have spoken at length of the relations of Literature and Life. Nothing could better confirm such a teaching than the fact that, as that life changes, literature in its extreme type and aim changes. Chaucer produced in the "Canterbury Tales" just what the England of the fourteenth century needed, and the intervening centuries down to the days of Wyatt and Surrey were what they were, in the line of literary barrenness, because, in fact, there was no time or call for high literary product. The nation was in transition from the old to the new; moving, so to speak, into new quarters; feeling its way through storm and strife and the bitter feuds of the time to a better home and outlook, and authors were not in demand.

For a similar reason of fitness and fulness of time and naturalness, the Elizabethan Age was essentially literary, and nothing could have been more germane to the new order of things and the breaking away from the old than that Spenser should have written a poem so medieval and Old English that the force of the breaking with ancient things should be gradual and less painful, and yet so modern that Elizabeth herself may be said to be the heroine of the epic.

So, we have seen the drama arose because it was the era of action and life. So, the literature of the Restoration, in its secondary type, expressed the secondary character of the age, as Victorian Letters is a good index of Victorian thought and civilization.

It is well to emphasize this fact, that literature is a growth and not a mechanism; a native product and not an exotic; that, as such, it is obedient to all those laws that control growth, and is as essential an exponent of a nation's personality as is the growth of science or plastic art or commercial activity.

B. It is further to be noted from this discussion that there is a Law of Evolution in Literature as in all other departments. The Literary Development of Europe as well as its Intellectual could be written and has to a certain extent been written. The reference here is not to the mere history of literature, as Carlyle has given it in his posthumous lectures on "The Successive Periods of European Culture," or as literary historians generally treat it. It is something higher and deeper than history, embodying a principle or law of development—an explanation of the genesis of form, a reason for literature being what it is, as we inquire, on the physical side of this law, for the reason of the existence of this or that particular species in the vegetable or animal world.

Mr. Symonds, in his paper on "The Application of Evolutionary Principles to Art and Literature," has embodied this principle, as he says, "Evolution, in its largest sense, may be defined as the passage of all things from simplicity to complexity by the action of inevitable law," and he raises the question, whether such a principle can rationally be confined to the sphere of the material, to biology and geology, and not be extended to language, society, literature and even morals. It is not our purpose here to enter into the details of Mr. Symonds' definition and application of evolution, nor to state the dangerous extremes to which it might conduct us. This much, however, is true, that there is this generic and governing principle of development in literature, not proceeding "by an inevitable law," inasmuch as the element of human and national personality enters in literature, but still proceeding by a law and on a method of its own. It may not be known how this principle acts nor what the method is, inasmuch as it acts within the mental sphere where law operates in consonance with personal freedom of will and motive, but still we know that it acts continuously. Hence, we speak of the evolution of the Attic or English Drama from what we might call primordial dramatic germs; of the evolution of the epic and lyric and satirical. "I have little doubt," says the critic, "that the Novel could be analyzed on evolutionary principles," and he states the law in its most comprehensive form, as he adds, "The evolution of the spirit seems to resemble the evolution of nature." The truth of the matter lies just here. It is another illustration of Drummond's "Natural Law in the Spiritual (or Intellectual) World"—in the world of letters as one exponent, among others, of the spirit and mind of man. Here again, we see how Literature as evolutionary adjusts itself to all with which it has to do in that it so fully illustrates the very latest theories of Modern Science.

Such men as Darwin and his school have done an invaluable work outside of the special scientific sphere in which they have been interested, by revealing the presence and uniform application of this great natural or supernatural law, and have, thereby, wittingly or unwittingly, done the best that could be done to unify all truth and disclose a special divine design in all things. At this point, Science, Philosophy and Art, Language, Literature and Life meet and obey the same great law, while even the religious life itself, on its natural side, confirms the principle.

C. Hence, a further inference is in place,—that literature is no exception to the law of decadence and death. As Gibbon has written, "The Decline and Fall of the Roman Empire," so must there be a decline and fall of Literature, as one of the forms of mental life. Thus do the critics speak of the decline of taste, of the decay of literary sentiment; of the "dissolution of the Elizabethan Drama"; of the disappearance of preexisting literary types and forms. All this is natural and necessary. The Revival of Learning implies a previous condition of decrepitude. The Renaissance of Art and letters involves a similar fact. There is in literature, as in life, a struggle for existence and a consequent survival of the fittest, a law of natural selection working as it works elsewhere.

Hence, not only authors pass away, but entire schools decline and disappear. The literary mode or cult of one age is not that of another. There is an obsolete literature as well as an obsolete language, and this obsolescence is as much a sign and condition of life as is the surviving product for which it makes way.

In a word, the ultimate purpose in the genesis, growth and disappearance of forms is the establishment and continuance of what is best in literature. Here, as in nature and natural life, there is supposed to be from age to age a general progress, despite all temporary retarding of growth or loss of particular forms. The English Drama is far inferior, to-day, to what it was in the hands of Shakespeare, but English literature, as a whole, was never stronger and richer and more of a factor in the common good. The area of literature has immensely increased, so that old canons of criticism can not be applied to it, but of its general advance there can be no question.

Moreover, it is to be especially noted that that which is more valuable than all in a nation's literature lives and passes down from age to age and does not die, because it can not. We mean the spirit of literature—its inner soul and sense, that which vivifies and saves it and gives to any one of its external forms—prose or verse, epic or lyric, all that it has of value.

More than the drama of Shakespeare is the presence of Shakespeare in English Letters, and Milton's great and lofty spirit animates many a one who may long since have ceased to read his works.

Chaucer's personality in Modern English Letters is so integral and pervasive that whether we know it or not, can read the Canterbury Tales or not, we are under the charm and force of it. The forms of literature, be they what they may, are valuable only as instinct with that invisible spirit of life by which they move and mold us.

In literature, the art of letters, how little, after all, of permanence and power is there in the letter only! Here, as in character and conduct, it is the spirit that giveth liberty and life.

CHAPTER THREE

PRIMARY POETIC TYPES

As to the possible forms of poetic expression, they may be as diversified as the forms of literature in general, or of style, as a mode. We may speak of Poetry as ancient and modern; as Asiatic and European; as Germanic and Latinic; as Continental and English; as Pagan and Christian; as Homeric and Chaucerian and Miltonic, and so on.

There are few questions, indeed, within the province of literary history and criticism that have given rise to a wider range of discussion, while modern opinion is inclined to multiply rather than diminish these possible classifications.

Before mentioning the threefold classification on which we shall insist, there is an historical threefold division that has obtained sufficient endorsement by English critics to merit a brief examination.

It is that given by Devey, in his discussion of "Modern English Poets," and is as follows:

1. The Oriental or Scriptural Type.
2. The Greek or South European Type.
3. The Gothic or Northern Type.

The first is what Mr. Arnold would call, the Hebraic School; Christian against Pagan, in which the doctrine of Providence is central; in which ethical purpose is dominant; a spiritual type of verse against the sensuous, seen, in special form, in such an English Poet as Milton, or Wordsworth, as distinct from Byron or Swinburne.

The second is what Mr. Arnold would call, the Hellenic, as specially significant of artistic form and possessed of the sense and spirit of beauty. It is the poetry of Paganism against Christianity; of man and nature against Providence; of human passion and sentiment, as seen in Shakespeare and the old tragedians, in Shelley and Keats and Mrs. Browning.

The third school is what might be called, the Germanic type against the South European. The crude conceptions of the Teutonic mind take the place of the delicate ideals of the Greek, while strictly Hebraic sentiments give way to a more worldly and practical order of expression. It is the poetry of Medievalism, midway between the ancient and the modern, as seen in Spenser's "Faerie Queene" and Moore's "Lalla Rookh."

FURTHER EXPOSITION

Convertible Terms. If this classification, as thus outlined and explained, were differently stated, we would have the following schools or types:

1. The Ethical, or Subjective School.
2. The Classical, or Esthetic School.
3. The Romantic, or Objective School.

By the first of these, The Ethical, Poetry and Truth are combined as, also, Poetry and Faith, confirming the language of Emerson, that Poetry is "the Piety of the Intellect" and that of Courthope, "that belief is the parent of poetry, and that all history shows that Poetry springs out of religion." Even Goethe tells us, "that in Poetry only the great and pure advance us," a sentiment stoutly opposed by Poe, who insists, that with the conscience Poetry has only "collateral relations," and that it is "heresy" to hold "that the ultimate object of

Poetry is Truth." When Longinus tells us, that it is the office of the poet "to hold up high ideals," he is describing the legitimate purpose of this Ethical School.

As intimated, what is sometimes called, the Subjective or Psychological School, is of this ethical order, dealing with the inner self and soul rather than with art or man or nature. Such poets as Shelley and Emerson often carry this principle to the verge of the mystical and ethereal.

In the second, or Classical School, the technique is prominent, and correctness of taste must be secured, whatever else is sacrificed. What is called, at times, the Alexandrine School, is here included, as also, The Art School, in which, as has been said, "the principles of design predominate over nature." Hence, such poets as Pope and Keats and Gray and Matthew Arnold and Poe fairly illustrate this second type, which is the strictly Greek type.

In the third, or Romantic, we have a phase of the Gothic, representing, in modern verse, a revolt against the formal school of art, and finding its genuine expression in Burns and Scott and Byron and the Lake Poets. It is sometimes called, the School of Feeling, or the Natural School, and insists upon the superiority of sentiment over mere correctness, and of the imagination over the slower processes of the reason. It is the Popular or Life School of Modern Verse.

ACCEPTED CLASSIFICATION

With this explanatory reference to existing divisions, attention may now be called to the three fundamental types or schools of verse in which the poetic mind may be said fully to express itself, and which, even in the sphere of prose, may be said to be substantially valid and exclusive.

I. The Creative, or Intellectual.

II. The Impassioned, or Emotional.

III. The Critical, or Artistic.

A word as to each of these types is in place.

1. *The Creative, or Intellectual.* This is what Mr. Arnold would call, The Poetry of Ideas. The older metaphysicians would have termed it, the product of Original Suggestion. It is inventive rather than imitative, indicative rather than exhaustive. It evokes into action that special function of the poet by which he is known as the maker, or in First English phrase, the Scop, the shaper of chaotic material into order and beauty. It is here that poetic genius finds its occasion and fullest expression. All the deepest and strongest intuitions of the poet's nature come here to their most healthful exercise. It is needless to state that such an order of mind is rare, and that the strictly creative verse of the world's literature may be included in a few volumes. We find it in those few epics that have received the general endorsement of critics, in the somewhat more numerous dramatic masterpieces of ancient and modern times, while, here and there, within the broader area of lyric verse, occasional examples of its presence are seen. The vast majority of the poetic product of the world has no perceptible trace of this inventive element, and is to this extent undeserving of the name of poetry. Even within the domain of the epic and the dramatic, its presence is but partial. Sir Richard Blackmore has had far more followers in English epic than Milton has had, while Shadwell is not the only English Laureate who has written inferior dramas. There is poetry and there is

poetry, and, the more one reads of the multiplied effusions of modern versifiers, the more he is convinced of the fact that the writing of "nonsense-verses" is not confined to the classrooms of English schools. Poetry is one thing, Poesy is another.

The poet produces. The poetaster reproduces. In that long list of Victorian and American Poets to which Mr. Stedman calls our attention, how few are they to whom the "vision and faculty divine" have been really given! Mr. Arnold is right in asserting "that a free creative activity is the highest function of man." It is, also, the highest function of the author and the poet, and is as infrequent as it is exalted.

II. *The Impassioned, or Emotional.* If we carefully analyze the constituent elements of the poetic nature and function, we come, first of all, upon this emotive principle. It is here that we see poetry to be preeminently the language of feeling, the most direct interpreter of the soul of man—his hopes and fears, his loves and hates, his joys and sorrows. So characteristic is this feature that, in the domain of the creative as the specific intellectual form, sentiment and passion appear in pronounced degree, as in the tragic side of dramatic verse and in the most majestic reaches of the epic. It is noticeable, moreover, that that distinctively spiritual element which is germane to the very essence of poetry is of this impassioned character. It is simply the expression of the heart in its religious life, the outgoing of the finite toward the infinite in devout aspirations and affection. Hence, the excellence and influence of inspired and sacred song, on its purely literary side. As uttering in fervid strain the profoundest feelings of humanity, it finds a quick response in the moral sympathies of the race. The theory of the older peoples that all poetry was divine in origin and aim emphasized this emotive element above all others and allied the minstrel to the prophet and the priest.

It is in the light of such facts as these that lyric poetry has been assigned by many to the highest place among poetic forms. Historically viewed, there is some ground for this opinion. There is, probably, more Lyric Verse in its various forms of Odes, Elegies, Sonnets, and Pastorals, than there is of any other representative order. The shorter Lyrics of Milton are, in their place, fully as important as are his epics, in theirs, while it is still an open question whether such a standard Lyrist as Burns does not evince poetic genius as unmistakably as any historic English poet. This much, at least, is true, that the absence of genuine passion is fatal to the highest examples of poetic art, nor can such an element be too pronounced and pervasive so long as it is under the control of a well-disciplined mind and taste. The poetry of the Restoration was what it was because passion was freed from rational control. The poetry of Elizabethan and of later Georgian days was also what it was because poetic feeling was never stronger and purer and never more clearly allied to mental and ethical vigor.

III. *The Critical, or Artistic.* One of the more frequent terms by which this type of poetic expression is designated is, the didactic, referring to all that order of verse in which instruction rather than esthetic pleasure is the final end. The word, critical, however, is, at present, the prevailing one. It is this special type that Mr. Arnold has in mind when he asserts that the main business of the poet is "the criticism of life," and that Goethe ranks above Byron, not so much because of difference in productive power as in the power of the critical discrimination of men and things. As far as English Literature is concerned, the representative era of this school of poetry is the Augustan age of Queen Anne and George I., while, in the last two decades of the Victorian reign, those days of strictly conventional verse are more or less reproduced. In reference to this poetic form it may be stated, that it unquestionably has place among characteristic types. It is thus that Pope emphasized the external finish of verse. It is thus that Keats and Gray are quoted as classical poets rather than romantic or emotional. The poetic workmanship is made prominent. They are accepted exponents of literary art or technique, whereby the verbal execution of the poem takes precedence of creative genius and emotive energy. Poetry and Architecture as Fine Arts are nowhere so closely related as in the pages of these English verse-builders. This critical poetry, however, is the least important of the three great divisions mentioned. Mr. Gosse, in his discussion of our poetry from "Shakespeare to Pope," has called special attention to this classical school, and has attempted to exalt its principles and exponents to a position of undeserved respect. We are not yet quite prepared to bow the knee in such adulation before the school of Waller and Carew. "In Literature as in Architecture," says Mr. Stedman, "construction must be decorated, not decoration, constructed. Invention must precede them both—so that, if imagination be clouded and the glow of passion unfelt, it is worthless jugglery to compose at all. Poetry is a spirit taking form." Here we have the logical order,—the creative, the impassioned, the critical. First, the subject-matter; then, the Spirit; then, the Structure. Any radical reversal or modification of this literary sequence of poetic types always leads to poetic decline. No poetic production can be rightly called standard in which there is the noticeable absence of original ability, emotional fervor and structural symmetry, nor can any such production be regarded as a model in which the relative position of these separate types is out of the order specified. The first essential, even in poetry, is poetic genius or intellectuality, and the next is poetic stimulus, and, tho no poetry can exist apart from that external mechanism called versification, this formal arrangement must ever be held subordinate to sense and spirit. While the poetic drift in Modern England is clearly toward the structural and technical, and, thus, clearly on the decline, the most hopeful outlook in American verse is seen in the fact that our younger bards, in loyal deference to Bryant and Whittier and the older school, are seeking to produce an order of poetry marked, above all, for what may be called—its intellectual fervor. It is evidently under the inspiration of such an outlook as this that Mr. Stedman has written his "American Poets."

PLACE OF IMAGINATION IN EACH TYPE

The special relation of the Imagination to each of these cardinal divisions is clearly seen. In the first, the creative, the Imagination is of the Philosophic or Mental order. It is the poet's eye in its widest outlook and function, "The Vision and Faculty Divine," according to Emerson, "A second sight."

In the second, the Impassioned, the Imagination is of the Excitive order, stirring and firing the soul of the poet to its profoundest depths.

In the third, the Critical, the Imagination is of the

Poetic order, proper, evincing itself in its sense of form, in its shaping and constructive and plastic work.

Thus it appears, that, whatever the poetic type may be, the Imagination is present and active as an essential element, while as in the highest products of verse, all of the three great poetic types appear fused into one, so, by a similar process of fusion, all of the different functions of the Imagination appear as a unit and the result is correspondingly unique.

TESTS OF THE CORRECTNESS OF THIS CLASSIFICATION

Seen—

1. *In the accepted Definitions of Poetry.* Poetry is defined in terms of each of these types, while the complete definition involves the three. For example, The Creative type is emphasized by Arnold, as he says—"Poetry is at bottom the application of ideas to life," or, by Devey, as he says, "A great poet must be a philosopher." The Impassioned is equally emphasized by Poe, in the declaration,—"A poem deserves its title only as it excites by elevating the soul. A long poem is therefore a contradiction in terms."

The Artistic is equally emphasized by Swinburne, as he says—"The two primary qualities of Poetry are Imagination and Harmony" and by Poe, when he speaks of Poetry as "the rhythmical creation of Beauty."

So we find these three types beautifully combined in Courthope's comprehensive definition—"Poetry is the art of producing pleasure by the just expression of imaginative thought and feeling in metrical language."

2. *In the accepted Specific Kinds of Poetry, epic, etc.* In the Epic, the creative type is prominent; in the

Dramatic, the Creative, in conjunction with the Impassioned, especially visible in Tragedy; in the Lyric and Descriptive, the Impassioned is supreme, while the Didactic, involves the critical type as conspicuous. Poetry itself, in whatever form, is essentially esthetic.

In such poems as Tennyson's "Idylls of the King" and "In Memoriam," where each kind of verse is, to an extent, illustrated, all the varied poetic types—creative, etc.—appear in union.

3. *In the accepted Purposes of Poetry.* If the aim is to illuminate and enlarge the mental horizon, the creative type is in order.

If to stimulate and move, the impassioned is in order.

If to please and charm, the artistic is prominent.

Hence, when Mr. Arnold says, that "the grand power of Poetry is its interpretative power," he is referring to its creative function, and it is to this that Emerson refers, as he says—"Whatever is best in literature is the affirming, prophesying, spermatic words of men-making poets."

When, on the other hand, Mr. Dowden speaks to us of the "Mind and Art" of Shakespeare, he is insisting on the union, in the poet and the poetry, of the creative and the critical purpose, while the modern school of culture, so called, magnifies this artistic element above all else as the final purpose of verse. When, still again, we read, "that the test of poetry is the extent and quality of the pleasure it produces" we are in the sphere of the impassioned. Here, as before, however, all great poems may be said to involve, in one way or another, the essential unification of these three varied purposes—mental, emotional and artistic.

'Tis so in Homer and Vergil; Fenelon and Racine; in Goethe and Schiller; in Shakespeare and Chaucer. Such poems as "Telemachus," "L'Athalie," "Maria Stuart," and the "Canterbury Tales," express in concrete form such a fusion of varied purposes in one all-controlling, comprehensive purpose—viz., the expression of truth to secure the best results.

4. *In the Accepted Sources of Poetry.* These sources may be said to be two, the Internal and External. The first of these involves what is called, Genius, whether referring to that element which is distinctively supernatural, or that which is involved in the natural endowment or personality of the poet. It is that inbreathing which takes the form of inspiration in song. It is that poetic impulse, insight or instinct, whatever we may call it, without which no high result can be reached in poetic product. It is what Whipple calls, "a certain vital force, a spiritual power" and that to which Emerson refers when he tells us, that the poet must "learn in the secret augury; that the inexorable rule in the Muse's Court is either inspiration or silence."

Hence, it is clear that this entire province of Genius as a source of poetic power is covered by what we have called, The Creative and Impassioned Types. It involves what the metaphysician would term, "original suggestion," in the expression of poetic sentiment; the happy union of the natural and supernatural,—the actual and the probable and possible, so as to insure the most pronounced effect. Poetic Genius is essentially creative and emotional.

If, on the other hand, we note the External Sources of Poetry, we pass at once from the region of Genius or natural endowment to that of cultivated or induced poetic power,—to the science and the art of verse, to a sphere in which there are applied those principles of poetic production which were formally established by Horace and Pope and Dryden and Boileau, and which involve the idea that Poetry is, to some extent, at least, the proper subject of education, by which the absence or modified presence of genius may be partially compensated.

Here, therefore, we come into the region of the Critical or the Artistic Type of Verse, into the region of the correct and conventional rather than that of the natural, where the esthetic is prominent over the creative and impassioned, and culture and good taste must, at all hazards, be secured.

Here, again, however, as in all masterful verse, the three primary types are seen to combine in organic unity of effect, so, also, are these two sources of verse seen to combine their respective excellencies and we note the fusion, in the same poem, of Genius and Art; of Inspiration and Execution; of the Vision and the faculty of song.

In Milton's "Comus," or in Mrs. Browning's "Drama of Exile," or in Bryant's "Thanatopsis," or in Longfellow's "Evangeline," no line can be drawn between the internal and external, between poetic instinct and poetic expression.

5. *In the Accepted Affinities or Relations of Poetry.* If we speak of Poetry as related to Prose, we have to do, at once, with the Intellectual or Impassioned Types of Verse, dependent on the special form of the prose, as Historical, Philosophical, Forensic and Descriptive.

If Poetry is studied in its relation to the other Fine Arts—to Music and Painting and Architecture—we have, at once, to do with the Esthetic Type of Verse, while the highest type of what is known as Poetical Prose, as in Hawthorne, may evince the effective combination of the intellectual, impassioned and esthetic.

From these several tests, therefore, that have been applied it is evident that the philosophical and literary correctness of the three primary types as stated have been fully confirmed—their correctness as to number and as to order of statement and poetic value, The Creative, Impassioned and Artistic—Subject-Matter, Spirit and Structure; Genius, Impulse and Execution, each essential in its place and resulting, when combined, in the finest and fullest product of poetic power.

SUGGESTIONS

(*a*) Such a classification of Poetic Types is suggestively illustrated as an exhaustive one, if applied within the region of our Vernacular Verse. All English poets of national reputation may here be safely and scientifically placed, the precise place of poets of the lower orders being a matter of comparative indifference. We see, at a glance, that Chaucer and Spenser and Robert Browning illustrate the creative type, as Burns and Byron, the impassioned, and as Pope and Keats and Matthew Arnold illustrate the artistic, while such many-sided minds as Shakespeare and Milton and Tennyson express the union of all these types in their most effective forms. The same principle is signally exemplified in other literatures, as in Germany, in its three greatest names, Goethe, Schiller and Lessing, in whom the three primary types are respectively seen in masterful form; as in Italy, in the persons of Dante and Petrarch and Boccacio; in France, in the poetry of Racine, La Fontaine and Boileau, while, in our American branch of English Verse, the names of Emerson and Whittier and Longfellow embody, in turn, the same great poetic types, it being reserved for such a comprehensive mind as Lowell to express in fitting relation and association the substantial oneness of mind and soul and art in the open province of verse.

(*b*) Poetry, therefore. wherever we find it in its best expression, is a gift or a passion or an art, or it is these three in one,—the trinal unity of power.

Without some one of these types in pronounced expression the poet, so called, is but the merest versifier, while the most brilliant and lasting results in Poetry can never be obtained save by the manifest presence of the first of these types—the gift of song—a something not definable in terms and yet clearly discernible by the sensitive spirit; a something between the lines of a poet's pen more suggestive and inspiring than that which is visible and legible. It is this species of verse that is written by poets who have been born such; who have been so suffused with the very genius and instinct of song that they have never been able fully to pen their inspiration, and who, in the vain attempt to embody in verse the sum total of their innermost experience, have felt those "poetic pains which poets only know" and have given us in their best efforts but a part and a very small part of their full poetic life and thought. We sometimes speak of the masterpieces of verse—of the world's greatest epics and dramas and lyrics—of the Iliads and the Hamlets and In Memoriams, as if they expressed in reality the fullest mental and emotional range of their respective authors. If the facts were but known, however, it would be found that what we have in these so-called supreme efforts of the poets, is but the veriest fragment of that spacious and profound poetic life which surged in the souls of these sons of song. "Paradise Lost," as we have it, is but an outline sketch of what Milton must have really seen and felt when he was penning it, and what would not the world give to have something like an approximate disclosure of those poetic insights and outlooks which Shakespeare had in producing his dramas but which even he had no language or genius to express.

In a word, in all true Poetry, there is a something infinitely greater than the Poetry, and that is the poet himself behind and below it—the thinking, feeling and living personality, permeated with the spirit of song; seeing visions and hearing voices that he can not tell to others, and able only, here and there, in an interval of inspiration, to record, in part, the experience through which he is passing.

Hence, it is eminently natural, if in portions of such a poem as the "Divine Comedy," or "Faust," or the "Tragedy of Hamlet," or "The Ring and The Book," the reader is often at a loss to know the meaning of the message, and the critics are still at variance as to what is written, for these poems were produced in the white heat of poetic experience, in the stress and struggle of conflicting feelings, and their authors themselves wrote what they wrote when fairly overawed by what they felt and said.

Hence, there is in English Verse but one Chaucer and one Shakespeare and one Milton and one Tennyson—one Elizabethan and one Victorian Age; one "King Lear" and one "Idylls of the King," nor can these poets and poems be produced at call. One in a century is enough to make the century epochal; one in a nation is enough to make the nation historic. There is poetry and there is poetry. There are lines containing so many feet and the feet, so many syllables, short and long, and there are, also, lines so alive with the genius and the soul and the art of song that they carry within them their own credentials as of natural and supernatural origin and their own inherent right to live as long as thought and language live.

Of such Poetry, England has her rightful share, and it is with such poetry and such only that the aspiring student of English Letters has anything to do.

CHAPTER FOUR

PRIMARY PROSE TYPES

THE Primary Poetic Types of Literature have already been discussed, the Creative, Impassioned and Critical, illustrated in the more particular forms of the Epic, Dramatic, Lyric, Descriptive and Didactic. We are now dealing, and in natural, chronological order, with the corresponding Prose Types and with those that are accepted as Primary. We may call them Primary, both as to time and character, appearing in the developing history of literature after a somewhat established order of sequence, and appearing, also, as one or the other type when the literary demand for the respective type is the strongest. As Primary, they are thus both natural and historical types, strictly representative, and, as such, demanding the attention of the student of letters. Moreover, they are called Types in that they represent the form or mode in which Prose Literature most normally and fully discloses itself. They are the ways of Prose Expression, it being emphasized, that because they are the expression of the mind of the author, they are far more than mere modes, and take on, to some extent, the subjective quality of the thought behind them. Thus it is that in literature, as in physical nature, a type, tho mainly external and visible, a phenomenon, is, also, in part, a something internal, a quality and characteristic. As to the classification of these Types, various principles, more or less acceptable, might be adopted. We might view them as the Poetic Types were viewed. We might classify by Periods, and speak of Classical and Modern Prose, and of Elizabethan and Augustan Prose; by Races or Nations, and speak of Asiatic and European Prose; of English and Gothic Prose; by authors, and discuss, in turn, Goethean or Carlylean Prose; or from the standpoint of Style, and speak of Prose as Clear, Cogent and Artistic. The principle, however, that will most safely guide us in classification is—What is the Final Purpose of the prose author at the time in his literary work? On this basis, we note several distinct types—the Historical, Descriptive, Oratorical, Didactic and Periodical, each of them having its own distinctive purpose and province, and, yet, all of them so interacting as to reveal their common literary origin and the poetical unity of all diversities of form. We shall briefly discuss them in the order of their natural evolution.

1. *The Historical Type.* This is often and properly called, Narrative Prose, where the element of time, in which events are supposed necessarily to occur, is the prominent one. The object of the author is to present the subject to the attention of the reader just as it unfolds itself in the successive stages of its historic development. It is the simplest and earliest form of prose, as the song is that of poetry, and commends itself to all classes and conditions, to all ages and phases. In what is called, The Metrical Chronicle, as Layamon's "Brut," and Robert of Gloucester's "Chronicle," we have the narrative poet and prose-writer in one and the same literary personality.

Historical Methods may be reduced to two—the Chronological or strictly Narrative Method, and The Logical or Reflective. Of these, the first is the earlier and the simpler, the most natural way in which a story may be told or events made known. It is a citation or re-citation of facts as they stand, with just enough of enlargement to give them literary form and effect, and, yet, not enough to conceal the presence and importance of the facts as such. Such an historian escapes the error of the mere annalist or chronicler, who confines himself to outlines, while, yet, stopping this side the province of the reflective and logical. Historians, such as Hume aud Knight, who follow the course of the centuries from the opening of the Christian Era down, are examples in point of this earlier method. Descriptive History, so called, is of this simpler order. The Logical Method is later, more complex and difficult, purposely subordinating facts to principles; all details and mere data, to generalization. Tho the author here as an historian is a narrator, he is something more, as he is seen to magnify causes and effects, laws and principles. Not content with a mere record of facts, he reasons and reflects upon them, follows them out to their legitimate conclusions. It is here that Froude and Grote differ from Hume and Macaulay. Hence, we speak correctly of the philosophy of history and of philosophical histories. As to the Province of Historical Prose, there are two divisions which it includes—Biography, and History proper—Civil and Ecclesiastical. Biography is personal history, a record of individual life as it gradually unfolds from youth to age, finding its limit where the personal assumes national or social form. In Autobiography, this personal feature is even more pronounced, as the author becomes the subject of his own narrative. The rapid increase of biography is sufficient proof of the essential validity of this form, as seen in such strictly literary biography as Field's

"Yesterday with Authors"; in such a union of the civic and literary as Masson's "Life and Times of Milton"; in such strictly civic narratives as Strickland's "Queens of England," and in the "Lives of the Nations," as in The American Commonwealth Series. One of the dominant literary features of the time is the increasing production of these Biographical Serials. In History Proper, however, we have the most pronounced example of Narrative Prose, either on its civic or literary side. Indeed, the civic or political element is the characteristic one, as in Hallam and Green, Guizot and Buckle. As Webster gives it, History is "An account of facts, particularly of facts respecting nations and states. It is a record of the founding and growth of nations." This apart, however, its province is a comprehensive one, illustrated in every department open to the work of the student as an author. Thus we have Literary History, by Hallam and Warton; the History of Language, by Marsh and Whitney; of Philosophy, by Lewes and Ueberweg; of the Church, by Neander and Mosheim; of Politics, by Freeman and Von Holst. The field, indeed, is limited only by the accepted classification of the Human Sciences, Arts and Philosophies. The historian as a recorder and narrator has access to all collected data, and it is his duty and opportunity to present them in acceptable, readable form. As to the Literary Qualities especially exemplified and needed in historical authorship, it is evident that Unity, Sequence, Simplicity, Dignity, Delineative Skill, Clearness and Accuracy are essential. The central facts must be so apprehended that they must be presented in their temporal and logical order, in a style devoid of artifice, with a good degree of graphic boldness, with an intelligibility that can not be questioned, with a due regard to the serious issues involved, and with a devoted fidelity to the truth. Whatever else may or may not be present, these features must be, and to the degree in which they are present will the record fulfill all accepted conditions and commend itself both to critical and popular esteem. It is because of these cardinal characteristics that History has ever ranked among the most interesting and profitable forms of literature, and must ever find its justification among all ambitious students of English Style. Literary students have a right to expect at the hands of the historian not only a truthful record of facts and events, but a record so presented as to take its place as a specimen of standard prose authorship.

2. *Descriptive Prose.* This has to do primarily with space and locality rather than with time; with objects rather than events; with portraiture rather than with narrative, and fulfills its final purpose when it places the reader at the author's point of view, and reveals to him through the medium of language just what he sees and how he sees it. It is a kind of verbal photography in the sphere of letters, a real pictorial art in its processes, ideals and results. It is thus an imaginative order of prose, re-presentative as well as presentative, dealing with symbols more than with facts, if so be ideas and images may be as veritably present and vivid, as if they had substantial being and function. Hence, as in Narrative Prose, we find the simple and the abstract form, the description of a visible object or scene in nature, as Wallace's description of Vesuvius, and Victor Hugo's description of The Battle of Waterloo, or that of an invisible object or scene, as illustrated in Hawthorne,

Ruskin and Irving. Just to the degree in which the author rises from the plane of the sensible and tangible to that of the supersensible and symbolic, does description involve a definite intellectual function and entitle its successful exponents to the rank of masters. It is thus that the description of a battle in process before the eye of the observer is a less difficult literary effort than that of the courage of the soldiery or the magnitude of the issues involved in the struggle. Thus, the description of European Morals by Leckey or that of Divine Retribution by Edwards marks a far higher order of delineative power than the representation of The Plague at Athens by Thucydides or of the Ruins of Pompeii by Bulwer. It is mainly by reason of this distinctive imaginative element that Descriptive Prose finds so large a place in the province of Fiction—what is called, The Descriptive Novel, the Novel of Life and Manners, being its most pronounced embodiment, as in Dickens, Thackeray, Reade and Bulwer. The department of Poetic Prose evinces it, as does Poetry itself in lyric and drama and in such naturalistic verse as Thomson's "Seasons," and such indoor domestic verse as we find in Whittier. In such sketches of travel as those given us by Irving and Hawthorne and Bayard Taylor, this feature is conspicuous. If it be asked what the Essential Qualities of this order of prose are, there are two of prominence—Vividness and Vigor, a lifelike and forceful representation of the object or scene depicted. Descriptive Prose is nothing if not vivid and vital, and hence it is that when properly executed by a master hand there is no order of prose more deservedly current and none more promising as to literary value and permanence. When, moreover, Narrative and Descriptive Prose meet and fuse in one organic literary product, as in the choicest History and Fiction, the result is correspondingly satisfactory, while each is seen in its best expression.

3. *The Oratorical Type.* We are now dealing wholly with written prose and, hence, with the term, Oratorical, as distinct from Oral Prose; with the work of the author as such in his study and not with the orator on the platform in open assembly; with the oration as a written product for the examination of the critic or general reader. Thus understood, however, it is to be noted that the word, oratorical, has a force and meaning of its own by reason of its close connection with that which is oral. It is that type of prose which, because it is oratorical, is possessed of elements making it adapted to oral delivery, a kind of middle form between the oral and the written. It is sometimes called, Impassioned Prose, as distinct from the dispassionate type of the narrative and descriptive, its primary object being to awaken or allay feeling. It is the most incitive and excitive species of Prose, aiming at inspiration and impulse rather than instruction or pleasure. It is known, also, as Persuasive Prose, contemplating the influencing of the Will and the Motives and the Conscience toward some objective act or line of action, involving the personality alike of author and reader, as is true of no other form. As Bacon states it—"It is the application of the reason and imagination for the better moving of the will" coming to its highest exercise when the oratorical passes over into the oral and the author becomes the orator in living presence before the people on some vital issue. There are three Forms of such prose that are especially manifest. The Forensic, the Judicial and the Popular. By the first is

meant a written literary product that is parliamentary or congressional in character, prepared with the rostrum in full view, the civic or political prose of modern states and peoples. Hence, its themes are practical and pending, dealing with great national issues on which the destinies of nations may depend. It is a kind of legislative prose, expounding great constitutional principles or enforcing their acceptance and application. The written orations of Cicero, and Mirabeau, of Burke and Adams, before they were pronounced in open assembly, are of this specific order, and clearly have a place within the province of literary prose. Judicial or Argumentative Prose, tho in the line of logical exposition, lying outside the area of oratorical prose as impassioned, lies within that area in the line of persuasive cogency and appeal. The great written debates of European history afford the best examples of this juristic writing. By it, the author becomes the impassioned pleader for general justice and the rights of man, seeks to defend the injured and speed the cause of truth and law. There is, indeed, no form of prose where the personal factor may more vitally enter and genuine emotion rise to higher levels, for here the author becomes an unselfish advocate of the interests of others and the end that he seeks is the maintenance of law.

Popular Prose is a form in which the author is neither the statesman nor jurist, but rather a man among men, a representative of the public good. The Senate and the Bar are now less in view than the hustings from which the writer studies the needs and ambitions of the people at large. Public Opinion is now in process of formation and expression, and the oratorical author is seeking to shape and control it. This is the form most germane to Free Governments, the most liberal and democratic type. It is, thus, an eminently English and American form, signally illustrated, also, in the stirring days of the Greek Republic, as in all those crises of Continental Politics when the people protested against any invasion of their prerogatives and insisted on the claims of the masses against the classes. As to this kind of Prose, two suggestions may be noted.

(*a*) It is the least artistic of all the types, in that it borders so closely on the conditions of oratory itself, gaining, however, in power and pointedness where it loses in grace and esthetic finish, and starting a question ill to solve, whether it does not meet thereby fully as successfully as other forms the final purpose of the author.

(*b*) Hence, a second Inference, that Impressiveness is its dominant quality. At this point, it has no superior or approximate rival. It is alike affective and effective, primarily designed to meet an immediate issue and incite to immediate action. From first to last, it is impressive, so much so that as we read it and come under the power of it, we find ourselves, perforce, ardent advocates of the policy it proposes. Our understandings and our feelings are alike enlisted and we are ready at call to evince of sincerity by an actual committal of ourselves to the cause that is presented.

4. *Didactic Prose.* All Prose is, in a sense, didactic. Its office as distinct from that of Poetry is to teach and explain, to show the meaning or the truth of a given proposition, or conversely, its obscurity and error. Its purpose is to induce new views or to modify or support

one, and rightly called, at times, Expository Prose, thus conforming to Aristotle's statement "that the power of explaining what is inherent in the subject and adapted to it is the peculiar province of the writer." Hence, it is the least impassioned and incitive of all the forms, the least oratorical in type. It relies on the simple presentation of the truth to reach the mind and effect its ends. It has little or nothing to do with the ornate, the imaginative and poetic, or even with the descriptive, save in so far as this may be used to throw increasing light on the subject in hand. It would not be amiss to call it, the Scientific Form of Prose, the scientific element, however, in any technical expression of it, being held so in abeyance as to keep the type well within the province of literature as untechnical and general. It is an Educational, Academic order of Prose, both because it magnifies the subject-matter over the style and seeks to present it in apprehensible forms. All that is involved in clear and full Definition is here included. It sets the bounds to a subject; marks it off from all related topics with which it might be confounded, and thus it may be said to condition all successful expressions. It is known as Philosophic Prose, the term, philosophic, not being used in any speculative or scholastic sense but in its wider meaning of that which is intellectual and reflective, evincing that meditative character which is so germane to all mental activity, whether in literature or philosophy. As thus interpreted, Philosophic Prose is dispassionate, thorough and deliberate, that species to which Bacon referred when he said that "Studies serve for ability." It is studious, weighty, stable and thoughtful, reducing literary form to the lowest terms and exalting the idea to its highest plane. It is the most sedate and dignified type, its Senecan sobriety amounting almost to a moral quality and corresponding to sublimity in poetry. Gravity supersedes pleasantry, and maturity of conception, method and expression marks the type. It is thus that Bacon wrote his "Advancement of Learning"; Pascal, his "Thoughts"; Hooker, his "Polity"; Draper, his "Intellectual Development of Europe"; Schlegel, his "Dramatic Literature"; Longinus, his Treatise "On the Sublime"; Fenelon, his "Dialogues on Eloquence," and Emerson, his "Essays," and thus have all those authors written who have felt that they had a high message to communicate to men and must take earnest heed that they deliver it as it stands.

There is a sense in which Philosophic Prose, tho mainly didactic, is to some extent, awakening. It is of interest to notice the various subordinate forms which it has historically assumed. Its close relation to Narrative Prose on its higher plane is seen in the Philosophy of History, as in Grote, Buckle and Guizot. In such a novelist as George Eliot, we see an example of Philosophic Description, the serious study of character and motive as represented in "Romola" and "Daniel Deronda." In Lessing, Saint Beuve and Coleridge, we have Philosophic Miscellany; in Choate and Webster, Juristic Prose on the philosophic side; in Whitney, the Philosophy of Language; in Bacon and Bain, the Philosophy of Style. Bentham has thus written on Jurisprudence; Kames, on Criticism; Walpole, on Government; Alison and Burke, on Taste; Clarendon, on English History; John Foster, on Character; and Emerson, on Plato, each seeking, in his own way, to reach the foundations of the subject in hand and to present it in its fulness. Not the most common form, it is sufficiently current to keep literature well established on safe foundations and successfully oppose all tendencies to the superficial. In fine, there is a place in Letters for Didactic Prose, a Teaching Type, disciplinary and corrective, nor is there any better test of a literary era as high or low than the presence or absence of this educational form. All Golden Ages have evinced it, as ages of inferiority have been notable for its absence. Light literature has its place and mission, but can not possibly subsist alone and be contributive to the general good. There must be a body of literature, a substratum on which to build and abide, nor is English Literature second to any in this particular feature. If asked—What is the End and Final Effect of this Order of Prose, we would answer—Mental Stimulus, a quickening of all the powers, the invigoration and enlargement of the mind. There is such a thing as Mental Movement or Impulse, a something much higher than mere emotional impulse, a movement in the region of the Faculties and all the more effective by reason of its rareness.

5. *Periodicat Prose.* In so far as English Prose is concerned this particular name has been used to designate this type since the days of De Foe and the regularly appearing publications of the time in dailies, weeklies, monthlies and annuals. The term, Miscellaneous Prose, is also used as indicative of its character, as confined to no one province or method, to no one class of themes or phase of style, enjoying within the area of prose a kind of license as free as that allowed in verse. Nor is it to be accepted that Miscellany, as such, is an inferior form of prose expression, or is called Miscellany, because it defies classification and is marked by no distinctive merit. On the contrary, there is no domain of prose

that it does not enter. It may illustrate in turn the highest forms of each, and if it lacks in definiteness of area and topic, gains immensely in compass and variety and diversity of method. So wide is its province, that we may be said to have Narrative, Descriptive, Oratorical and Didactic Prose all expressed, when needed, in the form of Miscellany, the author in each case not feeling bound to restrict himself to the specific type in hand, save in a general way. Its special danger, therefore, lies in the line of the discursive and desultory, assuming, at times, the phase of the capricious. It is to the lasting credit of Dr. Johnson that, tho he called two of his General Collections of Essays, respectively, *The Rambler* and *The Idler*, he held himself, in the main, strictly to the topic in hand, and was, at the same time, versatile and thorough. It is safely within the truth to say, that the best Miscellaneous authors of English Letters are entitled to similar praise, such an essayist as Bacon presenting a model in this respect to all succeeding writers.

It is a noteworthy fact that Brevity is as much a feature of the highest Miscellany as is Variety. Just because the Periodical is necessarily limited in scope as compared with the book or extended treatise, the author is obliged to hold himself well in hand and make a study of the art of condensation. So anxious have some essayists been to keep within the law of literary economy, that they have passed to the extreme of terseness and given us an order of style so laconic as to be epigrammatic. Thomas Carlyle is proof in point. Lord Bacon specifically tells us that what he gives in his Miscellaneous Essays, he gives "in certain brief notes," aiming as he did toward such terseness that he must compact his thoughts into the restricted compass of the Apothegm.

Just here is one of the most difficult problems that the Miscellaneous author has to solve—to be brief and, yet, comprehensive; to be interesting and, yet, suggestive; to secure, at the same time, specific and general ends; logical unity and logical breadth. The increasing demand for this order of Prose is sufficient evidence that it is a standard form and that its best exponents are succeeding in meeting its demands. Its attractiveness as a type, is, also, seen in the fact that most of the best prose writers of every standard literature have attempted and accomplished something substantial in this direction. So true is this that a study of the history of European Prose would involve the study of European Miscellany. In such an English Era as the Augustan it is seen to be the prevailing form so that all other literary developments must be interpreted in the light of it. One great reason for its currency is, that it is an eminently natural form, "coming home," as Bacon states it, "to men's business and bosoms . . . handling things wherein the lives of men are most conversant." Nor is it to be forgotten by the English student that the Periodical is essentially of English origin. *The Tatler* of 1709, was, according to Drake, "the first legitimate model." Preceding *The Tatler* were the Essays of Bacon, in 1597; those of Temple, in 1672; of Collier, in 1697; and of Cowley. Especially noticeable is De Foe's *Review* of 1704, several years in advance of *The Tatler*. So, in Continental Europe, La Bruyère and Montague and others had written. Be this as it may, Miscellany is a characteristic British type, nor need we go outside of English Letters for the best examples it has given us. Of the different Divisions of Miscellaneous Prose it may be said that Journalism, Letters, Essays and Reviews are the chief, Travels and Tales being, also, assigned a place therein.

In so far as Journalism is concerned, the reference is to its higher forms as seen in the wide department of magazine production, as distinct from the Daily Newspaper Press, and may best be examined under the caption of Essays and Reviews. As to Letters, suffice it to say, that the reference is exclusively to the literary side of epistolary writing, as seen in the correspondence of Goethe and Schiller; of Fenelon and Madame Guyon; of Carlyle and Emerson. There is such an admissible phrase as, Literary Letters, as the "Paston Letters" of the fifteenth century; or those of "Junius" in the Age of George the Third. Those of Swift, Temple, Walpole, Lamb, Cowper, Sara Coleridge, Lockhart, Macaulay, Ruskin, Matthew Arnold, Lowell and Stevenson are of this order, in which literature and life often come to their best expression; where all artifice and imitation disappear in the presence of nature; where soul reveals itself to soul, and, for the time at least, the author is lost in the man. By far the most common and typical expression of Miscellaneous Prose is the Essay, whatever the form may be—Descriptive or Critical. The first represents the lighter, freer, more popular order. The latter is best seen in Literary Criticism, as in the columns of the *Edinburg Review* and similar organs. Of these, the first is the more normal, characteristic and frequent, the readable essay of Modern Letters, just substantial enough to be called good literature, and, yet, racy and informal enough to appeal to the average reading public. It is, in fact, the ideal literary type, presenting truth and knowledge in acceptable form, clear, vital and in good taste,—the great literary staple of the reading world. Of the higher form, the Critical, it is enough to say that it occupies a field of its own, tho comparatively a narrow one ; is demanded in order that literary standards may be preserved ; finds its illustration in such notable manner in Lessing, Saint Beuve and Lowell, and is miscellaneous only in the sense that it deals with all literary themes and times. From this wide subject, as thus discussed, we notice a few suggestions of interest.

A. As to the Relative Value of Prose Types. Here it may be urged that it is as unliterary as it is useless to draw close distinctions among these forms that are all Primary. Each in its place is best at the time, and, when one is emphasized, it is understood to be on the principle of convenience and temporary conditions. While, if necessary, all of them could be reduced to the Narrative and Descriptive as most fundamental, no such necessity exists, the author and critic alike seeking to magnify their unity of spirit and purpose. Literature is a comprehensive and catholic art.

B. As to the Relation of Prose Forms to Prose Periods. Here, we mark a connection so evident that it must be something more than accidental. Elizabethan and Augustan Prose can not be conceived of as properly interchanging places. The *Spectator* and Dryden's "Critical Prefaces" are not looked for as contemporary with the Essays of Bacon, as these are not sought in the more expansive era of Macaulay and Carlyle. The stirring forensic prose of the Commonwealth came to its excellence in the fulness of time, and was not needed prior to the days of Milton. Hooker's "Polity" would be a strange volume, indeed, in the Victorian age, as the finished pages of Newman and Pater would have been in the Elizabethan. The great Historical Prose of Hume and Gibbon; the Prose Fiction of Fielding and Richardson; the Philosophic Prose of Coleridge, each arose when needed, while the Modern Era is what it is because it is when it is and not earlier or later. Here, again, Literature adjusts itself to Life.

C. As to the Relation of Prose Forms to the Ideas behind them. Here we open the vexed question of the true relation of Form to Thought, of what is called Style to Subject-Matter. Is the relation conventional or vital? To this it may be answered, that there is no such thing in authorship as mere form; that all true literature, in prose or verse, and especially in prose, is the expression of a substantive something beneath it. It is an embodiment of thought. Irreparable injury has been done by the Esthetic School, in their unwarranted emphasis of the formal side of literature, as an end in itself and for purely artistic effect. Literature, in its last analysis, is the expression of thought, and tho, as distinct from Science and Philosophy, that expression must have due regard to the claims of art and taste, it must, also, be so embodied and conveyed as to give to the thought its well-deserved primacy. Literature, it can not be too strongly urged, is one of the Intellectual Arts. Its various forms are, therefore, mental and not merely verbal.

D. Hence, the Final Suggestion, as to the Relation of the Type and the Man. Here, we need not be in doubt. Literature has no place in and of itself. It is nothing if not the open expression of the author behind it. Personality is its prime essential. We speak of the man and the book. More correctly, it is the man in the book, and Literature is but the free spirit of man for the time circumscribed by human limitations. That literature is the best and most potent in the world's mental history which gives to this conscious and semi-divine spirit in man the fullest freedom and function. Literature, it is said, is the expression of thought in written form. More than this, it is the expression of soul and life, of human personality, of a man's essential self, of his deepest experiences and highest ideals. Tho a Science and an Art, it is, more distinctively still, a Revelation and a Vision.

Literary Forms be they this or that, be they in Prose or Verse, are of value only as they serve to receive and convey to men in unmistakable terms and ways this Vision and this Revelation.

CHAPTER FIVE

THE HISTORICAL DEVELOPMENT OF EPIC VERSE

LITERARY critics have practically agreed on the classification of the primary types of verse as three, Epic, Dramatic and Lyric, with two subordinate types, the Descriptive and the Didactic, the last one of these being the least essentially poetic of all, while Descriptive Verse is in reality a miscellaneous or composite type, expressing in combination many of the features belonging to the three primary orders. It is with the first of these three generic types, the Epic, that we now have to do, it being our special purpose to follow what may be called its Historical Development and to explain some of its leading characteristics.

First, as to the Definition of the Epic, the Greek word —Ἔπος—meaning, a word or tale, and in the plural, a discourse in metrical form, points, primarily, to the idea of a narrative. It involves a statement in poetical form, of an event or a series of events, historical or semi-historical; possibly, purely mythical. Hence, it is often called, Narrative Verse, as dealing solely with the actual or imagined past. As has been said, "It is based on what has happened or on what men think has happened," on history, or myth, the epoist holding himself strictly within the region of fact or what he conceives to be fact. When it is said—"that the epic must rely solely on the memory and imagination," the imagination to which reference is made is the historic imagination in its retrospective function, as distinct from the philosophic or poetic imagination. The eye of the mind is turned backward upon the antecedent centuries, historic and prehistoric, in order to gather necessary literary or epic material. The Epic, moreover, is known as, Heroic Verse, by which it is meant not only that the particular poem in question should have a hero, or that the theme should be heroic, but that the epic throughout, as a poetic product, in its inception, unfolding, governing aim and final effect should illustrate this feature. It is with this fact in view that Epic Verse might be defined to be—The Presentation in Metrical Narrative of Actions and Events Heroic in their nature.

As to the Origin of the Epic, we are carried back, in tracing it, to the origin of poetry itself, to that primitive, precivilized period when men were little more nor less than children of nature, living out under the open sky, in constant communion with heaven and earth and sea, receiving, in their own way, the multiform impressions that came to them through mind and sense, and communicating, in their own way, such impressions in myth and song and saga. The origin of Epic Verse is thus natural and ancient, antedating prose expression, and taking us back to that simplicity of thought and life which may be said to have disappeared from history as civilization appeared and developed. Bards and minstrels composed these ballads and sang them to listening courts with the joyful accompaniment of harp and lyre. More than this, poetry claims a sacred and even a divine character. It is supernatural as well as natural in origin, intimately allied to all religious life and worship. It is most at home in temples and at altars. It is an inspiration and a divine endowment, a vatic gift for holy uses, whereby the poet and the priest become one in function, and the finite is brought into closest affinity with the infinite. It is "the vision and the faculty divine" in its earliest manifestation. It is this twofold origin of verse that so invests the study of it with interest and makes it incumbent on the student to coordinate all the complex elements that compose it. Epic Verse, most of all, exhibits this suggestive combination. On its narrative or historic side, it is a thoroughly natural, secular form of verse, while, on its symbolic side, it carries us aloft to the highest phases of the supersensible. If it is true, as Professor Gummere states it, "that belief in the impressions of sense is the foundation of the early epic," it is equally true that belief in the impressions of the supersensible is a valid foundation, the distance, in these primitive eras, between the natural and supernatural being reduced to the minimum, if not, indeed, to the vanishing point. It is thus that Tyler, in his "Primitive Culture," teaches us that epic poetry goes back "to that actual experience of nature and life which is the ultimate source of human fancy" which is the same as saying that the original source of the epic is found in the era of legend, as being an essentially poetic era and as marking the inseparable union of the actual and mythical. Tacitus, in his "Germania," acquaints us with the characteristics of these old Germanic legends in which the heroic deeds of gods and men were completely blended, when man was deified and the divinities incarnated and all the processes of nature personified and spiritualized. That these myths and mythologies were a fruitful source of poetic and epic literature it is needless to state. The very word, legend, is synonymous with the word, narrative, while such narration of necessity and by natural process expressed itself in verse rather than in prose and mainly through the medium of sign and symbol. Whether originating in Scandinavia or Germany or Celtic Britain or in the Orient, these unwritten sagas of the oldest life of the race were the real materia epica of the world's literature. In fact, we are now treating of a time which by way of eminence may be called, the Golden Age of the heroic, the Epic Age of man. What a fascination there is in the era, as we study it—when all conventionality, social and literary, was made impossible by the very temper of the time; when the world was young and fresh and daring and far more the subject of romance than of reason or reality; when poetry was the expression of the ideal as it has never been since and can not possibly be; when the people at large were poets, and contributed, as such, to their tribal and national verse; when literature itself was unlettered, in any highly esthetic sense, and simply sought, as Stevenson states it, to express "the eternal life of man spent under sun and rain." Such was the epic age, the source and inspiration of all later epics, the age of popular verse, which should be read by us, as Herder tells us, as if its authors were singing in our streets and quite unconscious of the conditions and restrictions of what we call our cultured modern life. Hence, it is noteworthy that the epic in its earliest and most highly elaborated form is a growth, and not a mere collection or compilation fortuitously gathered and in process of time unified by some guiding and masterful hand. It is "the spontaneous growth of a whole people," rising to its first expression in the earliest childhood of the race, and assuming more and more modified form and function as the race develops toward a vigorous and aggressive manhood,—first expressed and best expressed in oral form, in the unstudied minstrelsy of the bards. Once originated, however, what may be called, The Historical Development of the Epic, may be said to be partly in keeping with general historical and literary development but, mainly, an independent development, following its own instinctive leadings and seeking to preserve, as far as possible, its original spontaneity. The teaching of Macaulay "that the most wonderful proof of genius is a great poem produced in a civilized age" has a special application to epic verse, and emphasizes the fact that this independent epic expansion is serionsly impeded by the necessary conditions of highly civilized life.

The possible forms which the Epic may assume or has historically assumed is a subject of critical interest. Various classifications have been adopted and may be said to possess their respective merits. Thus, we speak of a fourfold Division. It is as follows:

The Epic proper, as seen in the "Iliad" and "Odyssey"; the Metrical Romance, as seen in Chaucer's "Roman de la Rose," a kind of semi-epic, midway between the epic and specifically romantic verse; the Metrical Chronicle, as in Robert of Gloucester's "History of England," essentially narrative as history, and containing, withal, the substantive epic feature; Ballads and Tales, of the heroic order, as seen in Macaulay's "Lays of Ancient Rome," in which the epic borders closely on the lyric and descriptive and in which brevity is a conspicuous feature. What is called, The Heroic Ode, as seen in Keat's "Ode to Liberty," would illustrate it, it still being an open question just where the ballad is of the lyric order and where of the epic. So, we might classify into the Higher and the Subordinate Epic. We hear of the Earlier and the Later Epics.

What Taylor calls, The Medieval Epics, the epics of the Dark Ages, lie midway between the primitive and the modern. A simple twofold order will suffice :

A. Primary Forms, embracing the Popular or Folk Epic, and The Courtly or Art Epic.

B. The Secondary Forms, embracing The Allegorical or Symbolic Epic, and Ballads.

"In examining the German Epics of the Middle Ages," says Taylor, "and tracing the sources of their material as well as the tastes or fashions of thought which have had an influence in determining their character, we soon discover the presence of two very clearly separated elements. One has a racy flavor of the native soil, the other betrays the presence of foreign ingredients," and he adds, "I should call the first the Epic Poetry of the People, and the second, The Epic Poetry of The Courts." A brief examination of each of these classes will serve to throw light on a subject invested with difficulty and as to which there is ample room for individual judgment.

First in time and, indeed, in importance is The Popular or Folk Epic, the genuine Volkslied of German Letters, one of the most significant poetic expressions of that Primitive Culture of which Taylor speaks. It may justly be called, The Primitive Epic, as compared with other and later forms. Burger would term it "the epic of nature," as distinct from the epic of art, the most unstudied and original form in which the epic genius of any race or nation seeks to embody and perpetuate itself. The appellation given it by critics, "the communal epic" points to its origin as popular or general, as distinct from those later, subordinate forms whose production may be traced to some individual bard. This communal, racial or national origin of the Folk-Epic, by reason of which it is so called, is one of its fundamental features and pervades the poetic criticism of all medieval verse, the primal question being whether it is the unconscious evolution of the people's poetic life, gradu ally consolidating into what we call a poem, or whether it is the specific product of a specific poet. Hence, we read of a poetry "which belongs to no one poet, which appeals to the ear rather than to the eye, which once came from the people as a whole and represents the sentiment neither of individuals nor of a class."

Students of German Literature and the history of poetic criticism are well aware of the almost passionate enthusiasm with which the poet Herder contended for this Folk-Epic or the popular principle as constituting the essence of all true poetic life. He has been followed in Germany and elsewhere by a goodly number of sincere disciples. He insisted, in the language of Goethe, "that Poetry is the mother tongue of man"; that it is coterminous in its origin with language itself; that when the people speak unconsciously; they speak poetically; their oldest legends and traditions "of themselves taking on poetic form" quite unaided by any rubric of the schools. He thus calls Homer "a singer of the people" and the Iliad and Odyssey may in a sense be said to have composed themselves, so fully were they the spontaneous outflow of the language and life of the ancient Greek. Thus it is in fullest sympathy with Herder that Jacob Grimm, the great philologist, insists that it is useless to seek after the author of "The Nibelungen Lied" as, indeed, must be the case with all national poems because they belong to the folk as a whole." "Every epic," he adds, "must compose itself" as the poetry of nature pure and simple. "Epic poetry," he reiterates, "can no more be made than history can be made." It is the folk, in its composite, communal character which for the time becomes the bard. The Popular Epic as thus described is distinctly the epic of growth rather than the epic of composition, illustrated in the "Iliad" and "Odyssey," in "The Nibelungen Lied" and "The Lay of Hildebrand," in the "Æneid" and "Beowulf" and "The Cid," each of which poems sprang, it is said, spontaneously out of the racial life of their respective peoples and answers fully to all the conditions of the folk-epic.

The second form of the Primary Epic is, The Courtly or Art Epic, later by necessity than the Communal Epic and, in some respects, inferior by reason of its relation to the canons of art and the conditions of advancing civilization. It is the epic of modern culture rather than of primitive culture; the epic of literature proper rather than of unliterary and preliterary periods; of specific personal origin rather than of general origin; the expression of esthetic study rather than of nature. In fine, it is the epic of the schools, and suggestive in its historic forms of the various eras and tendencies under whose influence it is produced. Reference has been made to Herder's enthusiastic defense of the Popular Epic as the only legitimate type and in full accord with the natural origin of all verse as distinct from prose. This second form, also, has found able advocates, the controversy as to origin, whether popular or scholastic, almost equally dividing the earlier critics. Schlegel, Wolf, Müllenhoff, Scherer, Paul and Böhme stoutly contend for the principle of individual authorship, decry the idea that epics produce themselves, and, while admitting the popular factor, refuse to consider it in itself a sufficient explanation of the epic proper.

These old mythologies, they concede, existed and furnished epic material for the earliest bards, but they also submit that a poem argues a poet, an epic an epoist, and that "Beowulf" and the "Iliad" must finally be assigned to a definite origin in the person of one or several authors. These advocates of the Courtly Epic speak of "the nebulous poet-aggregate called Folk," deny "that a whole people ever made songs," and plead for what they call "the theory of artistry." There is truth in each of these positions and a foundation for each of these typical forms, the Art Epic of the later age being as natural to the advancing stages of modern civilized life as the Folk-Epic is to the cruder conditions of primitive periods. Moreover, it may be added, that, as in the Popular Epic, a certain measure of artistic skill must be present, so, in the Courtly Epic, there must be found a certain measure of the popular element to constitute it a genuine poem.

Hence, it is suggestive to note, as Taylor tells us, that in the latter part of the twelfth century, "The Nibelungen Lied," a strictly Folk-Epic, was reproduced in two distinct versions, the popular, under the title, The "Vulgata" and the formal. It was a popular poem to be recited at courts. Be this as it may and despite the fact that the courtly version soon fell into abeyance and disappeared, it may be justly urged that there is room in literature for these two epic types and that historically they are found to exist. Thus, it might be argued, that the "Iliad" and "Odyssey" are both communal and courtly, classical epics of a preclassical period, the materia epica, as found in the Greek Mythology, being partly natural in origin, their adjustment into epic form being, in every sense, artistic. The same suggestion applies to "The Æneid" and, to a limited extent, at least, to the Old English "Beowulf." So, of the epics adduced as Courtly, such as Tasso's "Jerusalem Delivered" or "The Lusiad" or "The Messiah" or Cædmon's "Paraphrase," impartial criticism must allege that a certain measure of the natural and racial exists in them, even tho the artistic element may control. The "Paradise Lost" is as scholarly an epic as literature contains and, yet, no one would be so bold as to contend that it was exclusively scholarly or artistic, the basis of its myth and mythology taking us back not only to the Old Testament History, but to those ancient traditions that lie back of the biblical narrative itself and furnish material alike for poet and chronicler.

These are the two cardinal epic types, nor is it a matter of material moment to the literary student that they should be too sharply differentiated, it being often impossible to assign any given epic to one of these classes exclusive of the other. Suffice is to say, that to the one or the other and to both as related all the great epics may safely be assigned.

There is a second order of Epics which may be called—Subordinate Epics or Secondary.

Of these, the first is The Allegorical or Symbolic Epic, the Epic of Romance, an order of Epic less marked by sublimity and majestic movement than the primary forms, and more fully characterized by the presence of fancy and adventure and chivalrous sentiment. It is a kind of romantic narrative midway between history and legend, as seen in Chaucer's "Legende of Good Women," in Scott's "Marmion," in "Enoch Arden" and "Hiawatha" and in "Piers the Plowman." Malory's "King Arthur" has thus been called—"An Epical Romance." We might call it, by inversion, a romantic epic. What is known as, The Romance of Chivalry, so current in the Middle Ages as seen in the Charlemagne and Arthurian and Classical Cycles, is of this secondary order, the romance often taking the form of religious legend, as allegorically representing some Christian virtue, as embodied in the lives of the saints. The cycle of poems centering about the Legend of The Holy Grail is of this particular type, as are "Judith" and "Elene" and "Christ." Tennyson's "Saint Simon Stylites" or Arnold's "Saint Brandan" would be classified here. The "Færie Queene," lying closely on the border-line of the Courtly Epic, is the most signal example in English of the Allegorical Epic, being, from first to last, of this symbolic order, in structure and imagery and poetic purpose, while the "Divina Commedia" "the supreme allegory of the world," partakes as well of the courtly and artistic character of the epic proper. What is called, The Fable, expressed, at times, in the well-known Beast Epic of Literature, falls properly under this romantic category. In the "Rape of the Lock," there is seen the Epic Parody, a real Mock-Heroic poem, exhibiting, in burlesque form, many of the features of epic allegory.

Another form of the Secondary Epic is seen in Ballads and Tales, a poetic title that evinces the close relation of epic and lyric verse, and, at times, the epic and dramatic, the Epic Ballad, however, being distinctive enough to have a separate place and function. Such are some of Macaulay's "Lays of Ancient Rome," Longfellow's "Wreck of the Hesperus," Kingsley's "Three Fishers,"

Schiller's "Diver," some of Thackeray's Ballads, and Byron's "Corsair." The Old English "Battle of Maldon" and of "Brunanburh" are thus epic in character, the term, Ballad, as Childs has shown us, taking on a large variety of form, sacred and secular, historical and fanciful, and not infrequently exhibiting the genuine marks of the primitive folk-epic of prehistoric times. In fact, the Ballad is the Folk-Song, the old Epic of the people in miniature, the heroic ode of later European verse. It is one of the forms of communal song, losing more and more of its original freshness as civilization advanced.

When we are told "that the ballad must give us the sense of tradition and a flavor of spontaneity," this is as much as to say that the ballad and the popular epic are essentially the same, historically expressed under a wide variety of form.

We are now prepared to state and discuss the Leading Characteristics of the Epic.

In so far as Structure is concerned, logical and literary, Unity must be preserved, as to theme, thought, method and purpose, involving, according to Aristotle, the completeness of the epic, its opening progress and close. The action must be one. Whatever the details may be, the central thought must be clear and all incidental matter made dependent on it. The Epic as a narrative poem insists on this historical unity, the events occurring in regular order and with reference to some leading personage or principle. Episodes are admissible only as related to the main topic and indirectly contributing to its development, it being clearly discernible by the observing student whether such episodes are forcibly introduced or in obedience to the natural demands of the subject. Properly interpreted, the hero of the epic is sufficient in himself to preserve its unity.

Further, as to Structure, there is something of the Dramatic Element involved, tho incidental and exceptional. In Homer, this feature is expressed, as elsewhere, in the external form of the dialog. Hence, there is a sense in which the phrase "poetry of action" as applied to the epic is a proper one, it being carefully noted that such action is narrated or recited, in regular historic order, rather than being represented as in the Play for scenic effect upon the stage. Apart from these two laws of structure, there are some distinctive epic elements. The first is Scope, vastness of outlook, an unlimited range over which the historic imagination is to wander. It takes in the entire past of human events and, in so far as the epic involves the semi-historical or legendary is not confined to the region of reality.

Sustained Power, is a further element; the possession of an order of mental ability able, in current phrase, to hold its own, from first to last, throughout the unfolding of the narrative. More is meant here than mere historical continuity, the revelation of the sequence of events. The continuity is mental. There must be evidence of ability to compass the scheme proposed, so that there shall not be abrupt transitions from mastery to mediocrity. It is a power in poetry corresponding to that of the athlete in the long and trying ordeal of the actual contest, to that of the eagle on the wing in mid-heaven from dawn to dawn. It is here that creative genius enters into the epic as a mental product, the requirement that this expression of genius shall be so pronounced as to hold the poet steadily to his work until it is completed. It is, indeed, the most crucial test to which he is subjected.

Exaltation, is another element, applicable to the theme as heroic and to the entire content of the poem. The thought, diction, method, spirit and final aim must be, in the language of Longinus, sublime. As the word etymologically means, it must be elevated. Whatever may or may not be true of prose writing or of the other forms of verse, Sublimity is the first essential of the Epic, assuming, at times, an almost supernatural cast as dependent on the special theme in hand. The great religious epics of literature are of this special order. Critics speak of "the stately and formal" character of the epic, a kind of imposing movement which the epic as an exalted production naturally assumes. There is a loftiness of conception and execution without the presence of which it can not exist, a high decorum and demeanor in keeping with the spacious historic background on which the epic rests and the exalted purpose which it has in view. It might be called, the dignity of the epic, a something worthy of its origin and aim.

Simplicity is essential, an element of literary product common to prose and verse, applicable alike to form and content, to method and purpose, to the author and authorship, an indefinable something without which literature can not exist, in any substantive excellence. It is first in importance and last of attainment, the complete triumph of the natural over the artificial, in keeping with the highest art, and, yet, immeasurably above it, especially essential to the epic because of its exalted type.

A final feature is, Impressiveness, mental, moral and literary, as embodied in the gradual unfolding of the narrative, and, most of all, in the sum total of its effect on the mind of the reader. It is that "high seriousness" which is germane to the sublime, in nature, art and literature. It is sublimity itself. Tho the epic enforces no ostensible moral, it is, after all, morally sublime and, hence, impressive, demanding of the reader a kind of deference amounting to reverence, as he attempts to compass "the height of that great argument" to which it summons him.

Such, in brief, are the cardinal elements of the Epic, it being always understood that the human factor in the epic, despite all myth and symbol, must be sufficiently present to keep it well within the conditions of narrative verse and enable it to awaken and sustain a valid human interest. Hence, it is almost needless to state, that the epic, in its highest forms, is a type of verse difficult of production, and, as a matter of fact, rare in literature. Not more than ten or twelve such masterpieces can be found, it being especially notable when any literature, such as that of Greece, possesses more than one undoubted example. The conditions are too exacting to meet with frequent fulfilment, while it is to the high credit of general letters to note that a goodly number of poems exist illustrative of the second epic order, and a larger number yet of poems that are epical in tone and aim.

It would be an interesting study to trace the history of the English Epic, to discover, if possible, the presence of some historical nexus, as we find it in the English Drama and in English Prose. Such a survey would open with Cædmon's Paraphrase, "The Epic of the Fall of Man," the great Bible Epic of Old English, and with "Beowulf," the still greater Battle Epic of the time, and with the Legends of the Saints, as found in "Elene" and "Judith" and "Guthlac" and "Christ."

In the Norman Era, "the golden age of romantic narrative," as seen in chronicle and allegory, we note, the "Brut," the "Vision of Piers the Plowman" and Chaucer's Legendary Tales. In the Modern Period, are the "Faerie Queene," the epics of Milton, Southey, Scott, Keats, Byron, Browning, Morris, Swinburne and Tennyson and Longfellow, a list sufficiently large to constitute a history and awaken the interest of the student of letters.

There is one aspect of the subject that needs emphasis. It is the Reproduction of the old Germanic Epics in Modern English, the racial relation of the two countries making them common heirs of that original epic material which is found in the old Gothic and Scandinavian legends. Thus Taylor, himself an Anglo-German, writes —"If we, as Americans, have an equal share in Shakespeare, Spenser and Chaucer with our English brethren, so the Gothic and Saxon blood in our veins claims the inheritance of the 'Hildebrandslied' and the early Nibelungen legends as fully as the German people." It is a kind of epic dowry to each of the races as Teutonic, so that the reappearance of these old Germanic myths in the latest English Verse is directly in the line of national unity and historic sequence. Thus, the "Lay of Hildebrand," reappears in Arnold's "Sohrab and Rustum"; the Arthurian Cycle of legends, in Bulwer and in Southey's "King Arthur" and in Tennyson's "Idylls of the King." The legend of "Der arme Heinrich" is reproduced in Tennyson's "Enid" and Longfellow's "Golden Legend." In Arnold's "Tristram and Iseult" as in Tennyson's "Last Tournament" the old "Tristram" of Gottfried von Strasburg is seen. In Morris' "Lovers of Gudrun" and "Sigurd the Volsung" there is the same reproduction. In Tennyson's "Sir Galahad" Wolfram von Eschenbach's "Parzival" is seen, as the "Nibelungen Trilogy" and "Lohengrin" carry us back to the earliest folk-epic in central Germany. The Golden Age of the Teutonic epic under the Hohenstaufens corresponds, in duration, with the Golden Age of the English Drama. Thus poetry repeats itself and the popular myths of the Middle Ages reappear in vital form.

A final question of interest emerges—What is the Epic Outlook? Is the Heroic Age in the past only? "Balladry of the best Kind," it is said, "is a closed account." Is it so with the epic ballad? The answer reopens the prior question of classification as Primary and Secondary Epics, and it may be said, that the Age of the Primary Folk-Epic has passed, while even the Courtly Epic in its highest form has apparently passed, the later expression of epic being, either translations of the older epics, as Southey's "Cid," or such modifications of them as we have found in "The Idylls of the King."

This is not to argue that modern verse marks a decadence, if so be that other poetic forms have advanced. The decline may be epic only. Suffice it to say, that contemporary European Literature is non-epical, nor is there any visible promise on the literary horizon of the near approach of an epic day.

CHAPTER SIX

POETRY

A LIVING American critic in discussing the subject of Poetry, opens his volume with a chapter entitled—"Oracles Old and New." We may similarly open our discussion by stating that this fruitful theme before us is ever old and ever new, bidding fair to maintain its attractiveness as a topic of unfailing literary interest. Every new investigation of it but serves to show that there are phases of it yet unstudied or but partially revealed, the ever increasing complexity of modern civilization so modifying its characteristics and expression as to make it a practically new subject to every generation of literary students. Especially of late has this interest revived, so that there has never been a time when this particular theme has been more closely and fully examined than during the closing decade of the Victorian Era. New phases of the discussion that were presented so ably by Matthew Arnold and Shairp have been reexamined and enlarged by later critics, both on the sides of theory and of praxis. Of these recent and most noteworthy contributions, two or three lie before us as we write - Courthope's "Life in Poetry and Law in Taste" and Gummere's "The Beginnings of Poetry," each of them connecting the earliest and the latest results of poetic criticism, each of them marked by independent research, and each alike especially anxious to get down, if possible, to the deepest foundations of the subject and settle some of the questions that have hitherto been in debate. Some of these questions are as follows: What are the

Earliest Expressions of Verse and when did they appear; how shall Poetry be defined as to content and form; what are its relations to Prose, to rhythm, meter, thought, feeling, taste, art and morals; how far is it Realistic, and how far Romantic and Mythical; the Vocabulary of Verse, what are its primary features and how secured; what are its Uses and Aims; what is the relation of poetic conception to poetic composition; how is Poetry enriched, and how are its best interests retarded or advanced. Such are the queries that arise at once and open up a province of investigation as interesting as it is promising and difficult. In the study before us we shall present the topic under two related captions—Poetry and Poetics, representing, respectively, the Content and the Form, poetry as a mental conception and an esthetic composition, as a product of what Dowden has called, Mind and Art. Using the words, Poetry and Verse, as synonymous, the word, Poetics, would be tantamount to versification, the mechanism of verse, the poem in its external appearance on the page. Poetry must have Subject-matter and Structure, an inner something, call it what we will, that makes it Poetry, and an outer something that makes it Poetry. As we study them thus interpreted, their diversity and unity will alike appear.

POETRY

As we take up the first and more fundamental of these two sections of the general subject, we inquire, at the outset, as to

I. The Essentials of Poetry, what Stedman calls, The Nature and Elements of Poetry, and what, in his treatise, he specifically discusses, under the caption—What is Poetry, a subject, it must be conceded, which will baffle and elude us, in some of its phases, and which we can hope to compass but approximately at the best. As we conceive it, it is made up of four distinct and, yet, related factors, each contributing its share toward the unified result and by their cooperative action making poetry what it is.

1. The first and most important factor is, Thought. Upon this, despite all opinions to the contrary, insistence must be made, not that Thought is to appear in poetic composition to the same extent as in prose or in the same way, but that it is substantially to appear; that, first and last, the poet must be a man of ideas; a thinker as well as a seer. He must have sense as well as sensibility and sentiment, and never be even suspected of making verse a covert for ignorance or even for an inferior order of mental ability. The Nonsense Verses of the English Schools were prescribed for the pedagogic purposes of the classroom, but surely were never meant to furnish the model for the author as a poet. "No work of art," we are told, "has real import; none endures unless the maker has something to say, some thought which he must express imaginatively." The poet is a maker, and therefore comes under the law of ideas as a necessity. Hence, we speak of him as creative, an original producer. Poetry is the product of invention as well as of imitation. When Aristotle teaches us that "Poetry is an imitative art, imitative of the passions and manners of men," he is speaking of dramatic verse as represented in comedy and tragedy on the stage and not of the inherent quality of verse as dependent on mental life. When Mill speaks of it as "the influence of our feelings over our thoughts" this mental

feature is included. As Devey well expresses it—"It is an art both imitative and inventive, of which truth is the object."

This is not to say that Poetry is to be intellectual in the didactic, technical sense of the term ; that the thought is to be so prominent as to make it scholastic or speculative or even philosophic in its type, and thus unadapted to the general mind; but that thought shall be sufficiently present to give a mental type and basis to the poetry and save it from the reproach of being superficial ; that mind shall superintend the whole productive process tho not arbitrarily imposing itself upon it ; that Poetry shall be, in a word, as it ought to be, one of the varied forms of intellectual activity. It scarcely need be said that this mental process is more pronounced in certain forms of poetry than in others, in epic verse and in the tragic drama more than in lyric and descriptive verse ; in the masterpieces of Homer, Shakespeare, Goethe and Racine more than in the verse of Sappho, Burns, Goldsmith and Heine.

Moreover, in poetry as distinct from prose, the thought is to be presented indirectly, mediated through the agency of some other faculty or function. As stated by Stedman—"It is the exclusive presentation of thought that makes poetry didactic and hence untrue in the artistic sense." By this he would say that the thought must be conveyed through other agencies and poetry thus be made to differ from the sciences and philosophies in which thought is presented, as such, exclusive of all merely artistic ends, and with no purpose save that of enunciating and enforcing the truth as truth.

2. The second factor is Imagination. We speak of

the imagination under various points of view and as having different functions, as exercised in different ways and spheres. Thus, we note the Philosophic Imagination, within the province of speculative study, dealing with problems that involve the immaterial and invisible; the Historic Imagination, taking all past time for its domain, making it live again as if in actual presence before us; the Scientific Imagination, as exercised among the infinities of Mathematics and the immeasurable spaces and durations of Astronomy. In Poetry, however, we have to do but incidentally with these exceptional modes of imaginative action, save, indeed, as the historic element is involved in Narrative Verse. We deal here with the Poetic Imagination proper, a form and function of it so peculiar to verse that it has but modified illustration in general literature or in the wide department of Prose. Hence it is that poets and critics not a few have satisfied themselves with a theory of verse that either makes this faculty the most prominent one or the exclusive one. Thus Bacon speaks of poetry as "feigned history." "By poetry," says Macaulay, "we mean the art of employing words in such a manner as to produce an illusion in the imagination." Shelley opens his famous "Defense of Poetry" with a comparison of Reason and Imagination as related to verse, insisting upon the superiority of the latter faculty and stating conclusively "that Poetry may be defined to be the expression of the Imagination." So, Shakespeare:

> "The poet's eye. in a fine frenzy rolling,
> Doth glance from heaven to earth,
> From earth to heaven;
> And as imagination bodies forth
> The forms of things unknown, the poet's pen
> Turns them to shapes, and gives to airy nothing
> A local habitation and a name."

We speak of the office of the imagination as constructive, combinative, plastic and pictorial, while it is significant that in the varied forms of poetic activity all these offices are exercised, that of the pictorial being as prominent as any. Here, also, as in the case of the Intellectual Element, the measure and power of the imaginative function differ in different grades of verse—that type of it seen in the "Divina Commedia," or "Faust," or "Hamlet," being of an incomparably higher order than that displayed in Schiller's "Diver" and in Milton's "L'Allegro." In the "Idylls of the King" it is one thing; in "Enoch Arden," quite another; while in the great Epics of literature there is a reach and amplitude about it altogether unique. The current distinction between the Imagination and the Fancy is here in place, as marking the difference between the exalted and serious expression of the one and the light and often sportive action of the other. It is, moreover, to be suggested that in no one of the offices of this faculty, not even in poetry, where the error is more natural, is there to be a trespass beyond the bounds of the credible and rational. "Beyond the actual works of nature," says Hobbes, "a poet may go; beyond its possibilities, never." He must keep within the limits of the probable. Tho he pass out freely into the region of the supernatural, he can not pass into that of the unnatural. The most distant flight of the poet must have a limit somewhere and his very reveries be under the regulation of reason. His "fine frenzy" must be under control, so that mere grotesqueness and caprice shall not usurp the place of judgment, and poetic license degenerate into poetic lawlessness.

3. Feeling is an additional element of Poetry. It may be expressed under various terms, as passion, sentiment, emotion, sensibility, fervor. Poetry is an expression of heart as well as of head, and more, indeed, that of the heart than of the head. If pressed to a preference, the emotive element must be given the precedence. Thus Wordsworth speaks of Poetry as "the spontaneous outflow of powerful feelings." Milton calls it "passionate." It is imitative, says Aristotle, of the "passions" of men. It is, says Elliott, "impassioned truth," while Stedman connects feeling and imagination in the statement "that the poetic utterance that lacks passion is seldom imaginative." Thus essentially and as a matter of literary criticism and experience Poetry is emotive and takes its place as such among those great historic agencies through which the soul of man finds outlet and enjoyment. "The poetry of a poet," says Mill, "is Feeling itself." This is but another way of saying that Poetry must be intense and vital, must have a throb of life in it, revealing a distinct heart action, sending the blood through and through the body of a nation's verse. Here, as before, the different forms of verse require and evince Feeling in different degrees and phases, the Epic and Descriptive naturally involving less of it than the Dramatic and the Lyric, it being, most of all, in the sphere of tragedy and lyric that Feeling rises to its mastery, as in "Athalie" and "King Lear," in "Comus" and "The Blessed Damozel." Within the domain of the Lyric itself, Feeling may range from the comparatively modified measures of it, as in Pope's "Pastorals" or Macaulay's "Lays" or Vergil's "Eclogues" to its most impassioned outbursts, as in Milton's Sonnets or the National Songs of Modern

Europe. In the world's great Elegies, as "In Memoriam" and "Thyrsis," the passion tho less pronounced and visible is equally vital and potent. So spacious is the poetic province here, embracing all possible phases of human sentiment,—love, hate, friendship, patriotism, ambition, hope, fear, joy and sorrow, that poetry, as an expression of feeling, would seem well-nigh to cover the whole ground of verse. It is probable that at no other point of view and in no other aspect of it is poetry as a literary form so potent as it is here, touches the world's life so closely and makes itself so indispensable a medium for the necessary experiences of the human heart. If "one touch of nature makes the world akin," poetry, under this phase of it, possesses and expresses that sympathetic touch as Prose can not possibly do.

The Fourth Factor is Taste, in all the wide variety of its relations and applications. It is a term difficult to define and describe, as to which literary critics are still in doubt. Applicable in all the divisions of prose and verse, it is in Poetry that it has primary and special application.

Some of the theories historically held regarding it may here be stated. According to Cousin, it expresses the union of all faculties and feelings. Hutcheson and Akenside regard it as a separate faculty having its own separate sphere and function. Hume and Ruskin emphasize it on the side of sensibility, while Burke, in his notable "Essay," coordinates these differing opinions by conceding its twofold action, as, at times, a single faculty, and, at times, a union of faculties working to a common end. As far as our present purpose is concerned, Taste may be defined to be—that Faculty and Sensibility through which we come to the knowledge and appreciation of the beautiful. It thus combines knowledge and feeling, one of these being, at times, more prominent than the other, but neither of them ever absent in any comprehensive study of literature. In what is known as Literary or Poetic Criticism, its function as a faculty of discernment is the more apparent, while, in the reading of literature for purposes of pleasure or general culture, its function as a sensibility on the side of appreciation is the more prominent. It is further noticeable, on the basis of the submitted definition, that the entire department, included in the term Beauty, is essentially involved, and here a field of inquiry is opened full of literary interest, as to the Nature and possible Manifestation of Beauty, its exact place in literature, and the conditions of its expression. At this point, theories greatly differ. With Leibnitz, Beauty consists in perfection. Plato views it as mental and spiritual. With Diderot, it consists in Relations. With Goethe, it has to do with Expression. Socrates viewed Beauty and Utility as one. Augustine regarded it as Order and Design. In the light of our purpose, it may be said to be—that Quality whose presence is discovered and appreciated by the Taste. It is at this point, in the joint relations of Taste and Beauty, as involved in Poetry, that the spacious subject of Esthetics is suggested, the Science of the Beautiful.

More especially, what is known as Sublimity is also involved, so closely connected with Beauty that we think of them as one, and, yet, so different in the character and occasions of its expression that they must be separately examined. If we inquire as to the agencies by which Taste may be cultivated, the answer is a twofold one.

First, by a careful study of the laws and principles of

Beauty as deduced by the masters of the art; secondly, by a close and sympathetic study of Poetry itself as seen in the world's greatest poems, it being noteworthy that Taste, in its best expression, is a gift of nature and not a product of the schools. It is an expression of heredity, an innate faculty, as independent in its origin as it is in its manifestation. If it be further asked, How it embodies itself in general literature and in verse, we answer—in unity and symmetry, in fitting diction and structure, in all that wide variety of written expression that passes under the name of Style. It appears in the theme of the poem and its unfolding, in its adaptation as a product to the occasion that evoked it and the purpose it contemplates. Such are the elements of Poetry—Thought, Imagination, Feeling and Taste—each essential in its place, each contributing its measure to the final product, and the action of each involving, in a sense, that of all the others. Poetry may thus be defined—as, The Expression of Thought, in metrical form, through the Imagination, Feelings and Taste as media, and with the primary purpose to please. Hence, we speak correctly of an author's Poetic Personality, of his Genius, as a poet. It is the content or sum total of his power, that which makes him what he is as a man and a man of letters. Herein appear the High Demands of Verse, in that it brings into full activity the whole man, in the complete compass of his ability as an originating agent, a maker and creator. The poets are thus producers. Their work is their own. It is here that Poetry, so often underrated, rises to its highest plane, allies itself to all that is highest and best, and, when conjoined with conscience and character and beneficent intent, completes the circle of the arts.

II. THE CHARACTERISTICS OF POETRY

1. The first of these is, Scope. It must have outlook, and uplook, latitude and longitude, the range of all space and time, as Dante and Milton and Shakespeare had epical reach and function, dramatic range. It must have extension. Lyric Verse, as we have noticed, runs up and down the gamut of human life, while even descriptive verse embraces all that is natural and supernatural. If Imagination in its varied offices is an essential faculty in poetry, this is the same as saying that poetry has all the immensities and infinities for its field, an unimpeded approach to all being and all truth, the right of way across the universe of all known existences and far afield into the region of the unknown. Every poet of high endeavor must attempt, as Milton did, "an adventurous song" and make no "middle flight" into the upper air of imaginative soaring. Poetry in its original idea is spacious and supernal, ignoring at will the local and the temporal, scorning the imposition of any limit applicable to other forms of human activity. Heaven, earth and hell are conjoined. The past, present and future are conjoined. All distances and durations are eliminated. Poetry must have an open road through earth and air and sea and sky. It must have what Emerson calls "atmosphere and amplitude." It is here that the principle of freedom enters as one of the conceded prerogatives of the poet, an absolute liberty of action under the well-defined conditions of reason and literary law, a license as a poet and because he is a poet to go where he may and do as he may quite irrespective of the canons of the schools or the accepted limits of prose literature. This is not to say, with Macaulay, that such freedom may take so extreme a form as to indicate a certain unsoundness

of mind, or that poetic freedom is synonymous with the capricious freaks of fancy in childhood and in the infancy of a semi-savage people, but that all ordinary barriers are removed; all technical statute outlawed; that it is understood, the literary world over, that the poet is an author at large with special concessions and franchises to his credit. It is all the more essential, therefore, that the poet in the substantive character of his mind and in his views of literary art shall be a sound man, conspicuous for sanity and balance, so as to avoid the reducing of law to license or abusing a privilege freely accorded him. It is here that the poets may be classified into the masters and the mere imitators; into poets and poetasters; into authors to whom scope may be safely given and those into whose hands it is perilous to entrust it.

2. Rhythmic Quality is a second feature. We have already noticed the fact that Poetry must have subject-matter as well as form, must have the poetic essence, idea and sentiment, imagery and taste, a fundamental poetic content. We may advance a step further and add that it must have an inner harmony or melody, an inner movement or measure that is characteristic of poetry as such, clearly discernible by the poetic eye, a something that can not be counterfeited by the most adroit adventurer and that makes the lines superior by its presence. The Thought, Imagery, Sentiment and Taste must be rhythmic. The American poet Poe exalted this feature to the highest level, and defined Poetry to be—The Rhythmical Expression of Beauty. In the "Raven" and "Bells" he illustrated it. Gummere, in his "Beginnings of Poetry," thus writes—"Poetry is rhythmic utteranec—that form of art which uses rhythm to attain

its ends." It is a vital part of poetry, without which it is not poetry in the sense in which the masters have written it and interpreted it. An American critic, in writing of Browning, speaks of "the ebb and flow" of his verse. It is an inner tidal movement that marks the composition as poetic. So, the elder Schlegel writes—"Rhythm is born with Poetry and, whether by the Ontario or the Ganges, where Poetry is there is rhythm," "that uniform recurrence of syllables" of which Shelley speaks in his "Defense of Poetry." Rhythm means this regularity of movement, the recurrence of stress at regular intervals, a definite succession based on accent and producing by its uniformity special poetic effects. This is "the essential fact of Poetry," constituting a composition poetic by its presence and in proportion to its presence, its utter absence making it unpoetic. Even Prose evinces, at times, enough of its presence to make it deviate from the nominal type and assume the name of Poetic Prose, a kind of semi-rhythmic order this side the domain of poetry proper. One of the points of close connection between Poetry and Music is seen here in that each is essentially rhythmic, tho the rhythm is present in each in different measure and manner. Poetic Masterpieces may be tested here. Have they this internal and pervasive rhythmic quality, this distinctive movement toward poetic form before such form actually assumes visible expression? The exact relation of this inner rhythm to that external type of it as seen in Metre or Metrical Structure will be noticed in the sequel when we examine the subject of Poetics as connected with that of Poetry.

III. We may now inquire as to the Uses and Recompenses of Poetry, its offices, immediate and remote.

What are its aims and functions and how does it minister by way of reward and practical benefit to him who surrenders himself to its fullest influences. That it possesses any useful end is strictly denied by those unpoetic natures who pass through life upon the prose side of it only. Poetry as a Fine Art is disowned by them and it is the Useful Arts alone that appeal to their judgment and interest.

1. We note, as the first Recompense of Poetry, that it is a Revealer, an Interpreter of Life and Nature, of the world within and without, in their relations to each other; entering, often where no other agency known to man has access and audience, bringing to light the things that are hidden. Professor Shairp has given us a volume on "The Poetic Interpretation of Nature," applying the principle in one of its provinces, "The grand power of Poetry," says Arnold, "is its interpretative power"; that power, he would teach us, by which the poet through the combined activity of thought, feeling, imagination and taste can see deeper and farther than the ordinary observer, can better examine and unfold that which he sees, and, for the first time, disclose the real man to himself. We see it in any of the forms that Poetry may assume—epic, dramatic, descriptive and idyllic; at times, as in the epic and descriptive, interpreting human history and the natural world; and, again, as in the dramatic and lyric, interpreting the human heart at its deepest depths and highest aspirations.

Chaucer, Burns, Thomson and Crabbe and such out-of-door naturalistic bards teach us one set of truths as suggested by the endless diversity of physical phenomena, while Æschylus, Shakespeare, Racine and Schiller teach us another class of truths suggested by the equally endless diversity of mental and spiritual phenomena. It is the poet who has this vatic and prophetic power, this insight and outsight developed to the fullest, so that he deals at first hand with fundamental facts whether inside or outside the area of the visible and material. What an interpreter of the heart the poet is in comedy and tragedy, as he depicts the manners and passions of men; their faults and follies; their disappointments and sorrows; or in the more subdued expressions of the lyric dwells upon the pastoral simplicity of primitive life! The poet is the Seer. His work is penetrative and interpenetrative, and as he gives us in fitting form the results of his study he does for us a work reserved for him alone to do.

2. A further recompense is seen in the Elevating and Refining Influence of Verse. This is what Longinus, the Greek Critic, means when, in his treatise "On the Sublime," he dwells upon Elevation of Thought, Feeling and Expression as its principle element. "Anything is sublime," says Ruskin, "which elevates the mind." According to Kant, "it is the attempt to express the infinite in the finite." This is the sphere in which the poet by his vocation and preference must dwell; in which he must do his noblest and most lasting work, and when out of which he descends to the level of the merest rhymester. Poetry is the language of the ideal, the expression of that which finds no voice through the ordinary channels of communication. "All truth," says Devey, "which awakens within us the feeling of the infinite is poetic." When the poet or the student of

poetry surrenders himself to this divine afflatus, the inevitable result is mental and moral uplift, the raising of the whole man, if we might so express it, to the ninth power, to an upper plane of outlook and experience where there is no horizon visible or no language at command duly to express the ideas that are dominant. Hence it is, that Moral Sublimity is the first characteristic of poetry, and, hence, the accepted superiority of the epic and the tragic as the forms that best embody and reveal it, where the imagination and all the creative faculties must rise to their best endeavor, and the poet, in the sum total of his power, allies himself with all that is supreme and, for the time, at least, forgets his earthly origin.

There is here, also, a decided Refining Influence, a cleansing and sanative effect, as the true poet prosecutes with "high seriousness" his chosen work. Aristotle speaks of this in reference to the drama, as "purifying the passions." We have spoken of Taste as an element of Poetry. This is simply saying that it involves all that properly belongs to the beautiful. It is, preeminently, the artistic order of composition, involving a sense of form and fitness not so essential to prose. Poetry, as a Fine Art, is a Refining Art, giving tone and color to all that it touches. The much debated word, culture, means this, at least, that it ennobles and purifies the possessor of it, and culture is vitally included in the very conception of poetry. To make the best poetry popular, interesting to the average reader, is a matter of no little difficulty, in that the uncultured classes, so called, are outside the sphere of literary privilege, and must be, in a sense, educated beforehand to appreciate a type of literary product that is specifically esthetic. It is here, also, that the beneficent function of the actor and the stage enters to popularize through scenic effect and the oral arts dramatic verse as a written product, and, thus, unwittingly to the public, to refine the general taste and give a kind of note of dignity to the people in the aggregate. Here, also, lyric verse, through the special medium of the song and ode, secures, in a different way, the same popular effect. In noting, thus, these special effects of poetry, a question "ill to solve" emerges, as to the presence in some of the greatest poets of the lower and coarser type of mind—a type so signally illustrated in the Elizabethan dramatists and in such later poets as Dryden and Byron and Shelley and Goethe. The best explanation of this anomaly is that it exists in spite of poetic gift; that human nature has "the defects of its virtues"; that the imagination, so prominent in verse, is of all the faculties, the least amenable to law, and that a corrupt court or a corrupt public taste has often forced a poet to pander to its behests or suffer for lack of bread. Nor should it be forgotten that this lower type finds its illustration mainly in the second and third orders of poets and not among the masters. English and American Letters have an enviable record here

3. Personal Pleasure is, also, a recompense. This, by many critics, is made the final aim of poetry as an art. This is the recreative side of verse to the poet and the reader, in epic and drama and ode and song, in humor and satire and sorious reflection. Poetry, in this view of it, is a satisfaction, ministering to us when we stand in need of comfort and cheer and hopeful impulse. So true is this that he to whom high poetry makes no ap-

peal and in whom it meets no need may well be concerned as to the constitution of his nature. Poetry is as old as man himself and makes appeal to his deepest instincts, to savage and civilized, to old and young, to lettered and unlettered alike, and, presumably, at least, has something to say of value and interest to every man as a man. Such are the Elements, Characteristics and Uses of Poetry, and such the claims which it has upon every lover of literature and all who are interested in general culture. A suggestion of interest arises as to what is called, The Poetic Spirit. Altho presumably found wherever the literary character is found, its absence is often marked. Some authors and some literary peoples and periods are signally devoid of it, authors who purposely or by necessity confine themselves to prose, the historians and essayists, having but little need in their didactic work for imaginative literature. The Eastern peoples are more poetic than the Western; the Southern, than the Northern. In Northern Europe, the Scandinavian races are more poetic than the Slavonic. In the Elizabethan Age, the poetic spirit was dominant; in the Augustan, it was in abeyance, while the Victorian is notable for its presence in common with a general literary tone and taste. We do not look for it in the troublous days of the Commonwealth, nor during the Thirty Years' War in Germany, nor in the latter part of the eighteenth century in France. Present in all the great imaginative prose writers, and, especially, the novelists, and in the great exponents of descriptive miscellany, it comes to prominence, at times, in such descriptive authors as Macaulay and Prescott and Guizot; in such philosophic authors as Cousin and Descartes. Even in Literary Criticism, its presence is revealed, as in Saint Beuve and

Lessing. The literary man should be in sympathy as such with all poetic expression, while the poet, also, should enlarge his vision so as to include the most outlying horizon of literary endeavor.

Literature, broadly interpreted, is a general term. It does not stop to inquire whether its product is in verse or prose, but only whether it is in keeping with literary taste and the highest canons of the art of expression.

CHAPTER SEVEN

POETICS

We have already discussed Poetry in its essential content and characteristics, its internal quality and subject-matter, as the mental product of the poet. We are now brought in logical order to the examination of poetry in its external, visible form upon the page, to the technique of poetry. It might be called, the more literary side of poetry as distinct from the intellectual side, its strictly architectural feature. At the outset of the discussion it is to be noticed that, in poetry as contrasted with prose, Form is an indispensable characteristic. Tho important in all literary work, in poetry it is essential, so that no such product as poetry can exist without it. According to the Greek etymology of the term, the poet is a maker, or, in the more expressive Old English, a shaper, this formative process being a necessary one. There must be the molding and arranging of the poetic material at hand into proper form for the final purpose of poetry, as designed to gratify taste and minister to pleasure. Hence, when we call it a Fine Art, we emphasize the word, art, in that poetry must have this excellence of technique, as a statue or a painting or an attractive building is supposed to have it. A poem to be such must have structural beauty, must have unity, symmetry grace and finish—in a word, style. The Component parts of Poetic Structure may be said to be three:

I. Verbal Structure—the vocabulary of the poet. There is such an order of diction as the poetic, included, of course, in the general diction of authors, but having its own type. It is what might be called, the linguistic side of poetry, and must be taken into account by the author, the reader, and the critic of verse. Some of the chief features of Poetic Diction may be examined.

1. It is first of all, Figurative, known under varied names, as symbolic, pictorial, descriptive or graphic, an order of diction largely induced by the presence of the imagination in poetry, in conjunction with the elements of taste and beauty. Hence, all writers on Poetics include a full discussion of Figures, this tropical vocabulary being necessitated by the fact that in poetry we are outside the region of the literal and ordinary and must seek a diction appropriate thereto. It is thus that Addison, in *The Spectator*, discusses Words under the caption of the Imagination. They are the imaging agents. When Fenelon tells us, in speaking of French, that depicting is one of the leading offices of style, it is the poetic style that is meant, where Word-Painting, the portraiture of thought, is essential. Poetic Diction is photographic. When Aristotle says, "that beauty of words consists in the image they present," he is referring, primarily, to poetic beauty on the side of symbolism, the symbol or picture making the word that contains it beautiful. This is the explanation of the fitness of Suggestive Words in poetry, meaning more than they state, leaving something for the imagination to discover and enjoy. "The marvel of Shakespeare's diction," says Whipple, "is its immense suggestiveness, his power of radiating through single expressions a life and meaning which they do not retain in their removal to dictionaries." In a word, the critic would say, Shakespeare's

diction is poetic because of its suggestiveness. It intimates much that is not and can not be literally embodied on the page. This is the explanation, also, of the frequent presence in poetry, especially in its earlier eras and forms, of the Etymological Uses of words, in that in the root of the word the symbol is found which constitutes the word poetic. This is the explanation of the Poetry and Poetic Prose of the Old Testament, the Hebrew in its alphabetic characters being simply a series of pictures treasured up in words. It should also be emphasized here that Figurative Language is more adapted to some orders of verse than others—to the dramatic and the descriptive more than to the epic and the lyric. What is known as Romantic or Naturalistic Verse abounds in the simple imagery of the woods, the streams and the fields.

2. An Antique Diction is poetic. Not that this is a prevailing type of the vocabulary of verse, but that it is a valid and an allowable part of it—its antiquity being an element of its beauty, as is true in painting and architecture, even where the more modern word might be clearer to the average reader. In these earlier words there are often found those elements of suggestiveness and etymological metaphor to which we have referred. Hence, the revival of old words and the uses of these in novel senses, by which a certain attractive quaintness is given to the style, so as to awaken at once the curiosity and interest of the student. It will not be misinterpreted when it is said that there is a kind of obscurity permissible in poetry, a partial and purposely half-concealed revelation of meaning in order to stimulate the fancy and quicken all the poetic instincts and faculties. In such a

use of the older terms, moreover, Poetry seems to come nearer to its sources in the earliest eras of history; when men were but children of a larger growth; when civilization, if it could be so called, was unconventional, and the language of the bard was the language of the heart, a natural utterance, unaffected by current criticism. Just here, in so far as our vernacular poetry is concerned, is seen the literary importance of Old and Middle English, of Alfred and Chaucer, the Old Style of Elizabethan Days, so happily revived by Tennyson, not only in the distinctive Old English poem, "The Northern Farmer," but in his poetry as a whole. The "Idylls of the King" signally evinces it. Hence, the importance of Native Words, in that they preserve the character and flavor of the olden time, and impart to the diction a something that can not be counterfeited or improved. It gives tone and dignity, a sort of aristocratic note to the verse that marks it as eminently English. So, in the German, Scandinavian and South European languages, the same principle prevails, the old ballads and folk-songs of these people finding much of their charm in their age and consequent appeal to the poetic imagination. The increasing interest in Dialect or Provincial Poetry is largely due to the fact that this dialectic diction is antique and peculiarly impressive. Just because it is a variation from the standard language, it at once elicits interest and study. English Poetry is especially rich in this department of local verse, while the old Castilian and Provençal songs of Southern Europe, as those of the great Teutonic nations, exemplify the same unusual law.

II. A second expression of Structure is found in The Sentence as distinct from the separate word. It is the arrangement or adjustment of words, their proper placing. This is Structure Proper, or, in different phrase, the Textual as distinct from the Verbal Structure. There is such a thing as Poetic Sentence Structure, having its own character and credentials and easily discernible wherever expressed in appropriate form. It includes the grammatical and all that is meant by the syntactical in language, correct construction, the right word in the right place, what the earlier writers called, Propriety. It is the Syntax of Poetry. Of the Characteristics of Poetic Structure as Textual, the most important and, in a sense, all inclusive, is Flexibility or Variety, not that there is no standard of sentence arrangement, as in prose, but that, under the principle of poetic license, there is an allowable liberty in departing from it. Thus it is that we find in the best poetry of all nations an almost endless variety of clause and phrase and paragraph ; inversion and transition, gradual and abrupt; frequent antithesis and paraphrase ; sentences reduced to the limit of the laconic and expanded to the limit of enlargement. Circumlocution is expected in poetry, so that the reader is disappointed when not finding it. If we speak of a Poetic Period, the very word means, a Circuit. As Bacon would state it, we reach our purpose by indirection, and not, as in Prose, as the word Prose means, by directness. Even redundancy is not always an error here, as in Euphemism and similar constructions. Pleasure is one of the purposes of Poetry and, to secure this, exceptional methods are in vogue. Here and there, standard poets have violated this principle by pushing their liberty into lawlessness, right athwart the accepted canons of syntax. Robert Browning is in error here, and not infrequently ; an error from which Tennyson is signally free. Old English Poetry is marked by this apparant Irregularity, so as to impair the essential nature of the verse. This is partly due, indeed, to the mutilated manuscripts of the older verse, but, also, due, in part, to the limitations of the poets themselves. Here is a test of the master and the poetic masterpiece in that variety will be present without unrestrained diffuseness; flexibility without abruptness; paraphrase without unmeaning digression; the use and not the abuse of privilege. Two such poets as Longfellow and Whitman will evince the difference between poetic freedom and mere poetic caprice.

III. The third expression which Structure may assume is, The Metrical, as distinct from the Verbal and Textual. So important is it in relation to the subject before us that it has often been regarded as synonymous with it, Poetics being thus differentiated from Prose. As we have seen, Poetry must have Content and Form. By Poetic Form, Metrical Structure is meant. A clear understanding of the terms here involved is first in order.

The word, Verse, as used to express what we mean by Poetry, expresses this distinctively metrical view of it. The word, Verse, however, as synonymous with Stanza, meaning, etymologically, the turning of the line at the close of it to begin another, is the more correct use of it. The word applied to poetry as metrical has, however, become permanently current. Hence, the word, *Versification*, the making of verse, is used to mean, the external construction of the poem, on artistic principles, its body or technique. It involves, thus, the theory of verse, the study of those scientific laws which have generally obtained among poets when embodying their poetic conceptions in written form. Versification, therefore, is the arrangement of words and syllables on the basis of quantity or accent; the first order, the syllabic, existing in classical poetry, and the second, or accentual, in modern literatures, as the English. It is what De Quincey would call, the Mechanism of poetry as distinct from its Organism. It has nothing to do with the quality of the poetry as good or bad, but simply with its mechanism as a question of feet and syllables, of line and stanza, of accent and quantity.

Rhythm, is another essential word, one which we have already found in the content of poetry before it comes to external expression. The point of interest lies in this fact of the presence of rhythm both in the subject-matter and form. Poetry must have rhythmic quality, an inward poetic movement or impulse, and it must, also, have rhythmic structure, an outer movement correspondent to that within and based upon it. The one demands the other. Rhythm is thus the arrangement of syllables with reference to sound. It is based on accent and implies an easy and a pleasant succession of sounds, occurring at regular intervals, the regularity of the recurrence being itself rhythmic. It is a wider term than Meter or Rhyme, and passes, at times, beyond the limits of poetry into the province of prose.

The word, Meter, tho, at times, used as synonymous with Rhythm, is to be carefully distinguished from it. In its Greek origin, the word means, a measurement, and signifies the measuring of the verse. It is the marking off of the rhythmic movement in sections, longer or shorter; the arrangement of rhythmical language in lines that correspond with one another. Meter is measured Rhythm, the particular name of the Meter varying, according to the length of the line—Monometer, Dimeter, and so on. From the days of Sidney, a somewhat strange discussion has obtained as to whether Meter is essential to Verse, its strictly external type making it appear, in the eyes of some critics, as a mere adjunct of verse, to be accepted or rejected at pleasure. Thus Sidney himself and Shelley and Johnson and Coleridge contended. Suffice it to say, that the great majority of the great critics of verse, as well as of literary students at large, regard meter as an essential in poetic construction, as rhythm is to poetic content; that in poetry the rhythm must be measured or metrically adjusted. No aggregation of theories, it is held, can controvert the fact established by Aristotle and others. that just as soon as the written language is constructed on the principle of accent or quantity, of stress and time and relation of feet and syllables, the structure becomes thereby metrical as well as rhythmical, becomes that which, for want of a better term, we call, Poetry. Hence, no production that is unmetrical, in the sense explained, can be poetry. It may be poetical; it is not poetry proper.

Rhyme refers, simply, to the similarity of vowel sounds and, generally, at the end of the lines. This is final as distinct from sectional rhyme. Etymologically, the word means, a counting of the syllables. It is not essential to poetry as Meter is. Hence, Blank Verse is a kind of middle ground between prose and poetry, the preference of the masters of verse for this rhymeless meter being clearly seen in the great epics and dramas of literature. In the study of poetry on its structural side, other and less important terms are found, as Alliteration, a similarity of initial letters; Assonance, a similarity of vowel sounds in the middle of the line; Foot, the unit of measurement; Cadence, Harmony, Melody, Elision and Euphony, all having mainly to do with poetry on the side of Versification. Such is the Technique of Poetry, as Schipper, Ten Brink and others have discussed it. It is what Poe has called, The Rationale of Verse, and Lanier, The Science of Verse. It is the framework or scaffolding of poetry and, yet, a something more, in that its absence makes the product non-poetic. We might change the figure and say that as language is the incarnation of thought, versification is the incarnation of verse, its body and its indispensable form tho not its essential being, a something, therefore, which the student of literature must examine, if he is to compass the province of poetry. Moreover, so delicate and invisible is the dividing line which separates the subject-matter from the external expression of it, and so essential is it that this dividing line, as narrow as it is, should be so maintained and not arbitrarily enlarged that the student of Poetry should be, thereby, a student of Poetics, as he, in turn, must study Poetry in its essential content. Hence, we are led by our discussion thus far of the Content and the Structure of Poetry to note that these two are and ever should be inseparable—so conceived and so applied by the author as a poet and by the critic. This combination is happily effected, in part, by the fact already stated, that Rhythm is found alike in the subject-matter and the form, and, in part, by the personality of the poet who, in his poetic work, proceeds upon the assumption of their unity and acknowledges no abruptly dividing line between them. It is the Poetic Spirit that mediates between the two and secures their cooperation and practical fusion. The poet, in the zeal of poetic composition, never stops to inquire as to the precise relation between the inner and the outer; as to which, if either, is the more important, but silmpy originating and arranging in one and the same personal activity, being as every author should be, the thinker and the artist in one. A signal confirmation of the correctness of this view is found in the fact that poets may be classified at this point as primary and secondary. The examples of great poets who are great in violation of this law of unity between the internal and the external are so rare as to constitute an exception. In English and American Verse, this unity is singularly observed, Browning and Emerson with all their errors scarcely transgressing enough to invalidate the principle. In a recent book on "The Principles of Criticism," by Worsfold, of Oxford, we read: "Genius is a quick and an unerring perception of the just proportion in which the form and the thought ought to be united. This union is the perfection of art," and, he adds, "on these terms the masterpieces are produced." If this is true in general literature, it is signally so in poetry, where the conditions are more delicately adjusted and where the neglect or violation of literary statute is attended with greater evils. It is in this connection that we read, and properly, so much of late as to the way in which different poets have illustrated in their verse the various Meters open to authors—whether they have used them in consonance with the thought beneath the structure and supposed to give it character and influence, or whether simply as verse-builders, on the architectural side, they have been artists first and poets afterward.

No English author has met with higher eulogy at this point than Milton, whose versification has always commanded the interest of critics and is in itself a literary study. "Milton's diction is called poetic," writes Raleigh, "because it was absolutely fitted to his purpose," and his purpose, we may add, was so to select and develop his Meters as to make them the natural vehicle for the expression of his poetic ideas. When he decided to embody "Paradise Lost" in Blank Verse, he did so contrary to the custom of all non-dramatic poets of any note preceding him, the rhyming couplet of Chaucer and the nine-line rhyming stanza of Spenser being the accepted models. Even in the drama, crities were questioning the propriety of Blank Verse, so acute a critic as Dryden later contending that while it might be allowable in Comedy, the rhyming couplet was better in Tragedy. Milton adopted Blank Verse, therefore, for his Epics just as he adopted the Couplet for his Lyrics, only because he deemed these measures best adapted to the respective purposes of narrative and idyllic verse and that neither would have done in the place of the other. So, in the composition of "Comus," which is, in part, lyric and, in part, dramatic, he uses both types of Meter with equal skill and felicity, as the interests and ideas of the poem respectively demanded them. Moreover, in the variation of feet and line and stress and pause, he always reveals the hand of a master bent on adjusting the structure to the sense, so that tho using, theoretically, the Iambic foot as the prevailing one and best suited to Heroic English Verse, he never hesitates, when the sense and the melody demand it, to use other primary feet, the dactyl, anapest and trochee, and even such secondary feet as the Spondee, the Pyrrhic and Amphibrach, this deviation, as Symonds says, "constituting the beauty of Blank Verse." It is for this reason, among others, that the first book of "Paradise Lost" has been said to be "the most perfect production of metrical art" and the praise might be extended to the epic as a whole. If we pass to his shorter poems, this deviation of form to suit the sense assumes still wider illustration so as to secure, at the same time, verbal and mental melody. His poetic style has thus been called "a close-wrought mosaic," so nicely fitted is the word to the idea. So, Keats, Longfellow, Schiller and Racine adapted their Meters. Here it is, once again, that the discussion as to Shakespeare arises and we are plausibly told that he had poetic genius but no artistic sense; that he wrote his Sonnets and Plays with an eye on the subject-matter only, with but little or no regard to structural method and effect. Professor Moulton, in his volume entitled "Shakespeare as a Dramatic Artist," writes in his Preface, and as stating the occasion of the book: "An impression is not uncommonly to be found, especially among English readers, that Shakespeare's greatness lies mainly in his deep knowledge of human nature, while, as to technicalities of dramatic art, he is at once careless of them and too great to need them." To this allegation the volume in question is a sufficient answer, while the ever increasing study of these marvelous dramas but serves to confirm the conclusion that it was just because of his consummate poetic genius that the thought and the form are found in such fusion. Hence it is, that what are known as Schools of Poetry, representing different poetic theories, are but the different ways in which poets and critics represent Poetry and Poetics as related. Wordsworth, in the Preface to his "Lyrical Ballads," gives us his Theory of Verse. When examined, it is found so to subordinate the technique of the verse in order to express common life in common language that he may be said to come dangerously near to robbing Poetry of much of its artistic merit. So, we speak of Whitman's Theory of Poetry, which we find to be but another name for Prose, so deficient is it in that technique which is of right expected in all genuine poetic expression. Thus the Alexandrine Poets represent in Keats and Shelley the emphasis of the esthetic side of Poetics. So, the Art School of Tennyson, while the Realistic School of Crabbe and Browning gives the emphasis to Poetry. So, the Poets of the Affections magnify the content of verse. Such a poet as Lowell may be said to carry the esthetic principle to the extreme of academic, conventional verse. It is, in fact, only the poetic genius who is best endowed to unify the matter and the form and thus escape each extreme—that of the unduly artistic and the unduly didactic. Every great literature has had its Romantic and Classical School of Verse, and it is in these respective types that these extremes are apt to be found. Especially is it true of the classical poets, the poets of correctness and style, that they are exposed to special peril in the emphasis of the formal at the expense of the natural. 'Twas so with Pope, and, later, with Matthew Arnold, these poets not always succeeding in concealing their hands as mere artists in the province of poetic language. The secondary poets of literature are largely such because they have neither original genius enough nor artistic taste enough to exemplify them in their literary unity and kinship. There is such a province, therefore, as Poetics within the wider province of Poetry. Poetic Ideas are not Poetry till reduced to the terms of written, metrical expression, nor is the mere arrangement of words in a certain rhythmical order Poetry till such words are seen to be the embodiment of poetic thought. They are the masters who best understand and exemplify these literary relations.

SUGGESTIONS

From the foregoing discussion we note as follows:

First, as to the Relations of Poetry, both in material and structure, to Esthetics, or the Science of the Beautiful. The Study of Poetry, as Matthew Arnold uses the phrase, touches, it is conceded, the subject of Esthetics. As to just how it does so, is the open question, the current and even critical opinion being that it touches it on the side of Poetics only, that of external form, beauty of diction and sentence and metrical composition, beauty of presentation or representation. It is at this point, therefore, that the question must be decided. If Esthetics, as the Science of Beauty, is such on the understanding that Beauty is mere external ornateness quite independent of the character of the subject-matter and is an end in itself, then the current view has the evidence in its favor. If, however, as some of the great estheticians teach us, such as Plato, Cousin, Lessing, De Quincey, Ruskin and Herder, Beauty is a quality as well as a manifestation, a something inherent and indestructible as well as outward and transient, then the current view needs modification and Poetry and Esthetics touch each other subjectively. The view taken by Kant is, thus, correct, that as Beauty pertains both to the content and structure, Esthetics touches Poetry in each of these sections, the structure itself taking its character from the poetic content beneath it. Immense harm has been done in the name of Esthetics and by the unduly free use of celebrated names in criticism by interpreting the science superficially and then by necessity connecting it with Poetry on the side of Poetics only. Baumgarten, by whom the name Esthetics was first given to the Science in 1750, is adduced in confirmation. The controversy is as old as Plato and Aristotle, the more superficial view of Aristotle being given the precedence, until the very name Estheticism must needs be explained and defended lest it be accepted without debate as indicative of formal embellishment only. We are now dealing with Poetry in its most comprehensive sense, and in this sense but one opinion can be held, and that is that Poetry is related to Esthetics vitally and internally as Poetry proper and, also, structurally and externally as Poetics, no attempt being made to draw an arbitrary line between them, as, indeed, no such dividing line exists. The English critic Burke effaced all such distinctions, as he held that Matter itself is beautiful. Even on the esthetic side, therefore, the poem must be essentially poetic. A second Suggestion arises—As to the Desirability of Poetic Composition and Criticism as a literary exercise. The reference here is not to the custom in the English Schools of translating classical verse into English, partly, for the classical and, partly, for the English instruction and purely for educational ends. There is, indeed, some benefit in this by way of comparing native and foreign meters, or contrasting the accentual and the syllabic methods of versification, but the exercise is so strictly perfunctory and pedagogic that it loses, thereby, a large part of its value and is, in a valid sense, totally foreign to the idea of Poetry as involving freedom and scope and voluntary action. Our reference, here, is to the free and spontaneous function of the student for purely poetic and literary purposes, quite independent of any such thing as linguistic examination of poetic diction and structure or the exercise of the art of versifying as a praxis only, beginning and ending in theory. We are emphasizing the production of poetry by the amateur to test any poetic ability that he may possess and to develop it to fuller function, the composition of verse on the side of poetic content as well as on that of formal correctness. Moreover, it is important to note that we are to place the emphasis upon the content; bringing thought and imagination and feeling and taste to bear in their combined activity, and as expressed in the sphere of rhythmical and metrical product. Thus interpreted, Poetic Praxis is to be encouraged, nor are the benefits far to find. It serves experimentally to prove just what Poetry is as distinct from Prose and just where and how they approach and touch each other; it disciplines the taste and all the esthetic sensibilities; develops poetic conception as distinct from general mental conception; disciplines the poetic spirit and the poetic imagination; elevates and refines the whole intellectual nature and reveals to the student in his work his merits and defects in poetic composition and construction. The accepted theory that literary effort on the part of any outside the circle of accredited poets should be confined to prose production, is as unwarranted as it is prevalent and should be discarded. So, as to Poetic Criticism as a literary exercise, a delicate and difficult field indeed, and, yet, there is no law by which such territory should be a high-walled enclosure, accessible only to the specially initiated. The critical examination, on the part of an advancing student, of a poem or a body of verse to discover its governing features, its conformity or non-conformity to established poetic principles, if properly conceived and conducted, can have but one result and that a helpful one. There is a commendable poetic criticism that is purely experimental.

A final suggestion emerges, As to the Poetic Outlook. Is it promising? Mr. Courthope inclines to a hopeful view. Matthew Arnold tells us, "The future of Poetry is immense"—immense, he seems to mean, as a possibility. He felt that Poetry has in it an enormous potentiality, if it only can be evoked and applied. Just here the question hinges, Can this "immense future" be realized in Modern Europe? Is it now realizing in any substantive sense as the new century opens, and the great masters of verse are in their graves? The answer opens a spacious region of inquiry, philosophic and social as well as literary, in that Poetry is now viewed as related to all other great departments of human effort and to the life of the world at large. When we ask the apparently simple question—Is the immediate Future of Poetry promising? a score of related questions must first be settled. What is the existing political and social status of Europe? Is it friendly to the poetic spirit and to the poet as a man? What is the dominant philosophy and how does it affect the poet? What is the type of the age on its merely material side and is it provocative or repressive of poetic effort? What is the general literary type of the time and is it auxiliary to verse? Is the spirit of the old masters still controlling or is it weakened by alien influences? In fine, the answer is conditioned by place and time, by mental and social environment, by tendencies and movements, as literary and unliterary. On the contrary, perchance the mysterious law of Periodicity may be verified and Poetry come round, once again, by regular recurrence, after an era of depression, to supremacy and all the critics be silenced.

Suffice it to say, that, as we survey the outlook, the "immense future" of Poetry is a distant future and not immediate. He must have special gifts of vision and prophecy who can see far enough along the line of developing history to cheer our hearts by the valid promise of anything like a genuine poetic revival. Possibly, the near future may reveal a decided advance in one direction—in a revival of poetic genius or of poetic art. "Deficiency of construction," according to Arnold, "is a characteristic of contemporary poetry" due, as he thinks, "to the absorption of the age in scientific pursuits." At another time, he tells us, that the present age is one in which any great manifestation of poetic genius is not to be rejected, it being an age of "industrial development and social amelioration only and not one of moral grandeur." Of the two orders "the famous men of genius" and "the famous men of ability" he sees no promise of the first, tho, even as he was writing this, the superb development of Victorian Verse was at hand. So may it be again. "For one, I believe," writes Stedman, "that the best age of imaginative production is not past; that poetry is to retain, as of old, its literary import and from time to time to prove itself a force in national life." As Emerson says: "Sooner or later that which is now life shall be Poetry, and every fair and manly trait shall add a richer strain to the song." This optimism is, at least, our privilege. In the sphere of Letters, it may, indeed, be our duty.

CHAPTER EIGHT

PROSE FICTION, AS A FORM OF LITERATURE

WHENEVER any literary product assumes the popular prominence that is now held and has, for the last decade, been held by what is known as Prose Fiction, it becomes a matter of obligation as well as of interest on the part of students of letters to investigate the causes of such a widespread currency. As Crawford, the eminent American novelist expresses it, "Of making novels there is no end, in these times of latter-day literature," and he gives a sufficient reason for such production, when he adds "that there is a demand for them and a profit in producing them." Mr. Crawford is himself a notable illustration of the truth of these statements, both as to the continuous production of novels and the pecuniary profit resulting therefrom. Be the cause as it may, Fiction, in one form or another, is the existing dominant literary type, more prevalent than any form of verse, and more so than such popular forms of prose as history, biography, and the higher miscellany. It is the literary staple of the modern reading public. In submitting it, therefore, as a form to analysis and study, we notice, first, its Origin and Development. This we shall find to be both Natural and Historical, a matter of innate, inevitable tendency and a matter of gradual sequence along the lines of general development. When Dunlop, in his "History of Fiction," tells us "that the art of fictitious narrative appears to have its origin in the same principle of selection by which the fine arts in general are created and perfected," he means to say substantially that it has its origin in the nature of things, in obedience to the laws of the human mind and the primitive constitution of human society, and such we find to be the case. As far back as we go in the recorded facts of history, we find some phase and measure of its presence. We find it indeed in the prehistoric periods of legend and tradition where we are wont to look for the crude beginnings of other forms of literature, such as epic and dramatic verse and the simplest types of narrative and descriptive prose. When we are told by Crawford "that the novel is a distinctly modern invention, satisfying a modern want, not finding it in existence till late in the last century," his reference is to the fully developed novel of the nineteenth century in its ultimate artistic and literary form, and it in no sense contradicts the assertion as to its early historic and prehistoric beginning. If literature, properly interpreted, is a portraiture or expression of life, there is no type of it more characteristic of this function than Fiction, so that it may be said to begin when the life of the race begins, with all its multiform phases of experience awaiting the pen of the narrator.

So there is a sense in which its rise and growth may be said to be Historical, following what is called, Social Development, a chronological course in keeping with the Progress of Civilization, its expressions at different periods being characterized by the respective conditions of particular eras and peoples. In this sense, we have a History of Fiction, the record of its accredited beginning and its diversified development. In the favorite phrase of the day, we have the Evolution of the novel, in the successive stages of its literary growth. Hence, we speak of Ancient and Modern Fiction; of Oriental and Western Fiction ; of Continental and British Fiction, the classification being mainly historical, with but incidental reference to the rise of Fiction as natural, or to its quality as superior or inferior.

If now we descend to particulars and inquire as to the exact historical origin of Fiction, its day and date and first exponents, we find that approximate results must suffice. Whether first existent in Scandinavia, Arabia, Brittany, Greece or Rome ; in prose or verse ; prior to the Middle Ages or not till then, and whether first as Romance or Fable, as song or story, these are questions beyond the province of exact solution. As Saintsbury states it, "The exact times and seasons of literary births no man knoweth, at any rate, the first appearance of full-blown, full-fledged Romance." He goes on to show the folly of those oversagacious students who are sure that they have shown that Romance is of Teutonic or Celtic origin, and that its beginnings belong to this or that century of the Christian Era. Accepting, then, the principle of comparative results, it is of interest to state, that the Rise of Fictitious Literature, historically viewed, is probably in the Medieval Era, and, more specifically, in the twelfth and thirteenth centuries ; that its four great Cycles are those of Arthur and Charlemagne, and the Greek and the Roman, as expressed, respectively, in the Book of Alexander the Great and the Book of Troy ; that the medium of its expression is both prose and verse, the poetic form being the older ; that its early authorship is mainly anonymous, and that the French were especially prominent in its production and diffusion. These are conclusions of approximate certainty, and afford a fairly substantial basis on which something like an intelligent study of Fiction may be pursued.

The more specific question of the exact Historical Genesis and Growth of the English Novel, were it in place to examine it here, is full of literary interest, and well within the region of safe historical inquiry. The recent researches of Jusserand and Raleigh and others have thrown increasing light on this attractive subject and have done much to elucidate the general question as to the origin of Fiction. Suffice it to say, that the work of Malory, author of "L'Morte D'Arthur, 1470;" of Caxton, the first English printer and the editor of Malory's treatise in 1485, and the work of Lord Berners, the translator of Froissart, marks the beginning of English Fiction, as these respective writers gave to the Arthurian and Charlemagne traditions their first embodiment in English Prose. The literary type thus established found later expression in the Elizabethan Age in Lyly's "Euphues" and Sidney's "Arcadia," as in the various translations of Italian Romances. After some transitional work, in the seventeenth century, especially in the line of epic romance, the Modern English Novel Proper took form, in the opening years of the eighteenth century, in the graphic delineations of De Foe, followed by Richardson and Fielding and Smollett and Sterne and Sheridan on to the days of Sir Walter Scott and that superb succession of English novelists that from that day to this has represented English Literature and may be said favorably to compare with any succession of romance writers which any European Literature adduces.

The inquiry now in order has reference to the Characteristics of Fiction.

1. To this, it may be answered that Fiction is primarily Idealistic. Whatever it is or is not, it is, as the word

signifies, a something feigned or invented, a something supposed for the time to be and thus described as a present entity. It would not be aside from truth to say, that Fiction is Ideality reduced to verbal form. Hence, the functions of Fancy and Imagination in the conception and production of fiction whereby the novelist makes his own world, irrespective of all actual existences; peoples it as it pleases him, and in Shakespearean phrase "bodies forth the forms of things unknown, and gives to airy nothing a local habitation and a name." Hence, the various terms that are used as synonymous with Fiction, all of them indicative of that which is feigned or imagined. Such are fable, allegory, apologue, legend, myth and romance, by the use of which terms the primary quality and purpose of all fictitious literature is seen.

2. There is, however, an element of Reality in Fiction. This visible and practical side of Prose Fiction is, at present, more emphasized than ever. Hence, the twofold classification of Fiction as Idealistic and Realistic. The division of all fiction into Romances and Novels Proper is due to the same literary theory, the Romance being the more idealistic as the product of the Fancy, and the latter, the more realistic as the product of the creative imagination, illustrated, respectively, in such works as "Don Quixote" and the "Arcadia," "Henry Esmond" and Bulwer's "Pompeii." What is called, The Tale or Story, occupies a kind of Borderland with special tendency toward the more fanciful form, as the Tales of Poe and Stevenson. If we turn to one of our latest English lexicons, we read as to the Novel—"A Prose Work in narrative form in which the incidents, characters and scenes are partly or wholly imagined."

Hence, the original conception of Fiction as wholly feigned must be somewhat modified in obedience to later criticism and, in fact, to the demands of literary law, so as to state that it is the union of the Idealistic and Realistic in verbal form ; the union of fact and fancy, the imaginative element being, however, the dominant and determining one. The reversal of this relation would produce an order of literature which, whatever it might be, would not properly belong to the category of fiction.

3. A further Feature of Fiction is seen in the fact that Pleasure is its primary object. "No one denies," writes Crawford, "that the first object of the novel is to amuse and interest the reader," and he uses the word novel in its widest sense as embracing all forms of fictitious writing, whether romantic or realistic. He calls it a "luxury," tho "an intellectual and artistic luxury," . . . "not contributing directly," as he says, "to the support of life or the maintenance of health," but rather, as he would intimate, to the general entertainment of the reader, in those hours of comparative leisure when he is off regularly assigned duty and seeking mere enjoyment. The novel must amuse, but must amuse us "reasonably." In this respect, Fiction, tho strangely called, Prose Fiction, is closely allied to poetry as a literary form, each of them seeking mental and artistic pleasure as the controlling end. "Novelists are nothing more," adds Crawford, "than public amusers" whose sole business is to cater to the public taste, follow the rapidly changing phases of public sentiment, take the people into their confidence, and give to them when they open their pages precisely what they have a right to expect at the hands of those who have made a special study of the art of

pleasing. So current is this theory that any other conception is regarded as literary heresy, and the offering of any other kind of product a gross violation of the assumed contract between author and reader. Hence, the important question here arises—Has Fiction any other end than Pleasure? Into the discussion of this vexed question Modern Criticism has entered with a good degree of warmth, nor is the temper yet abated. Critics such as Howells and Stedman stoutly contend that there is no room either in the Romance or Novel for didacticism in any form, much less for anything at all of the nature of ethical or educational sentiment; that "the novel of purpose," so called, is a contradiction in terms. On the other hand, such critics as Selkirk and Thompson and Devey and Masson are as earnest in maintaining that, the primary end of fiction being pleasure, there is no good reason why some form of instructive appeal should not be made a secondary end, nor is there any reason, it is urged, why the novelist should ever be on his guard lest he inculcate some wholesome moral lesson and make the reader better as well as wiser by his teaching. They insist that the other forms of literature should not have the monopoly of educational value,—"In art of all kinds," says Crawford, "the moral lesson is a mistake," while in the special art of novel-writing he would make such a lesson-giving doubly offensive, yet, it is Mr. Crawford himself who in the same treatise, tells us, unwittingly, perhaps, "that the foundation of good fiction and good poetry seems to be ethic rather than esthetic. Everything in ethics which appeals to the taste may ultimately perish, but that which speaks to man as man must live and have a hearing with humanity so long as humanity is human." This is the same as saying that, in the last analysis, Fiction and Poetry, in order to be effective and vital, must do what all other literary products that aim at durable influence must do—address the primary human convictions and minister to the primary needs ; must, in fine, address the Will and Reason and Conscience as well as the Taste or the mere passion for pleasure. On this higher theory, there need be, as we think, no irreconcilable difference of view between contending schools, it being understood that the best fiction, while primarily produced for literary pleasure, is and should be incidentally wholesome and educating, these factors being so concealed that their influence may be felt rather than seen. This is, indeed, the true theory of all art, and, while maintaining Fiction in its proper province as mainly ministrant to human interest, also insists that such interest rightfully excludes all that appeals to the lowest and basest human instincts. Tho the novelist is not a preacher, he is a teacher of truth and human life, and as such responsible for the ultimate ends he is seeking.

The question now arises as to the various Types which Fiction may assume. These are found to be of marked diversity and compass, thereby indicating a high degree of vitality and flexibility, such diversity being at present more marked than at any preceding period of modern literary criticism. Attention has already been called to the fact that Fiction may assume idealistic and realistic type, as seen in Romance and Novel. These may, however, assume many subordinate forms as seen in Historical, Descriptive, Philosophic and Sentimental Fiction. In Historical Fiction, we have the best illustration of that union of reality and ideality on which we have insisted, the fact, however, being for the sake of the fiction and thus differentiating the novel from history proper. Scott, Cooper, Bulwer, James and Kingsley are pertinent examples of this order. "It is doubtful," writes Crawford, "whether any genuine historical novel has ever yet been written for the sake of the history it contained." He regrets the fact that, despite this principle, not a few readers insist on learning French History from Alexander Dumas and Victor Hugo, and British History from Scott and Bulwer. Historical Fiction is thus realistic and by reason of this element it is all the more difficult for the novelist to execute it with skill. Descriptive Fiction, as the name implies, because it is graphic and pictorial, may be said to be the leading type. It is, also, the most common form, the Novel of Life and Manners, its primary purpose being to give a vivid and truthful picture of men and things. It is the picturesque or scenic form, in which delineation or word-painting is an essential factor.

What is known as the Domestic Novel, the simple portraiture of the daily life of the home and village, is of this scenic character, having just enough of the historical to give it credibility. Jane Austen's Novels are of this order, as is Macdonald's "Annals of a Quiet Neighborhood." Hence, this is the poetic form, one in which the great novelists, Thackeray, Hawthorne, Dickens and Reade have done their notable work, a form in which romance and reality happily combine to the production of the best literary effect.

Philosophic Fiction is, in a sense, a contradiction, being too thoughtful, too intellectual to meet the conditions of successful fiction. Its groundwork, however, is imaginative. In its symbolic dress it has the features of fictitious literature and is developed on pictorial lines.

Of all the forms, however, it is the least imaginative, and borders most closely on ordinary prose. By reason of its solidity and serious interest, it often starts the question as to whether the final purpose of fiction is, after all, that of pleasure. The Psychological Novel is here included. Manifestly, it is the most difficult to produce and to enjoy, while it is not strange to note that this is the form which of late has assumed so significantly the specifically religious character, as seen, especially, in the work of George Eliot and George Meredith. Religious Romance, it is true, may be expressed, as by Bunyan, in the simplest verbal forms, but, as a matter of fact, is generally expressed in connection with theological and ethical questions, in a somewhat dispassionate and reflective form. This kind of novel is not frequent in literature, as it requires a high order of mind to produce it, and the protest we are now hearing against it will lead to its more decided diminution. It is sometimes called, the Novel of Philosophic Realism, as seen in Mrs. Ward. It is noteworthy that this distinct philosophic tendency of the novel is but another evidence of the fact that, despite all the theories of the schools, as to the absolute divorce of fiction from the educational element, such an element has perforce entered and will always to some extent exist. This modern meditative novel is largely the product of female authors whose nature and ideals, it would seem, would lead them into regions wholly idealistic.

Sentimental Fiction has two distinct types, the higher and lower. The one is Sensuous; the other, Sensual. They are alike, however, in their common emphasis of the impassioned element. Here, again, the romantic and the realistic meet and blend, the higher type of the

Sentimental Fiction being generally expressed in the form of Romance and the lower in that of Realism. The modern Experimental Novel of Zola and Tolstoi is, thus, realistic, portraying in a defiant and, often, revolting manner, the innermost nature of man. So pronounced is this form that it has usurped the title, Sentimental, and makes it all the more important to insist on the two species and to show that sentiment may be pure and sweet, as in Maclaren's "Kate Carnegie," and Connor's "Sky Pilot" and "Black Rock."

In addition to these leading forms of fiction, various other types are seen, such as Political Romance, as More's "Utopia" and Disraeli's "Lothair"; Pastoral Romance, as Sidney's "Arcadia"; the Epic Romance of the seventeenth century in France and England, and the Chansons de Geste of Northern and Central Europe. So, we have Fairy Tales and Fabliaux: Novels of Satire and Humor, as in Rabelais and Cervantes, and, last of all, the Dialect Novel, as seen in Barrie and Caine and Cable and Harte, concerning which the important question is raised, whether it really conforms to the conditions of Fiction, as general and not local, as a popular and not a technical type of literature. Despite the critics, however, it has made its place and holds it with success. The Relation of Fiction to other Literary Forms is a question of standing interest. What, in particular, is its Relation to Poetry. As a matter of fact, Fiction has been expressed both in prose and verse, the early Celtic Romances being characteristically prose as the early Norman and English Romances were verse, much of the work of the early translators consisting in rendering these Romances out of one form into the other. Thus, we have the famous Metrical Romances of French and

Anglo-Norman origin, such as Chaucer's "Roman de la Rose," Layamon's "Brut," "Sir Tristram," and "Sir Havelok," and the almost limitless list of medieval examples, classical and British. Such critics as Minto and Moir assign Fiction to Poetry. So Masson classifies it with poetry, as "containing matter of imagination." The majority of critics, however, assign it to Prose, as being presented in unmetrical form. History, however, may repeat itself, and romance, as of old, be given in the form of verse. Whatever the relation, Fiction has a decided dramatic element, especially, on its descriptive side. Here, again, it manifests its poetic tendency and spirit and inclines to poetic form. "A novel," writes Crawford, "is, after all, a play." The best answer to the question, What is a Novel? he adds "is that it is a pocket-stage," a novel being excellent according to the degree in which it produces the illusion of a good play. The modern dramatization of the novel is proof in point of this relation, a tendency rapidly increasing tho partly induced by pecuniary profit. The close relation of the Novel to the Epic, as seen in Historical Fiction, is, at once, apparent, while Narrative and Descriptive Prose may be said to be the accepted media in which Fiction best embodies and expresses itself. From the discussion thus presented, some suggestions arise—and we inquire, first, As to the Essentials of Success in the production of Fiction. The most important is Imagination, sufficient in its scope and vigor to meet the conditions of such an order of authorship. We are now using the term Imagination, as the faculty of imagining, of presentation and re-presentation, as the symbolic function of man's mental nature, possessed of high creative power, of a specific constructive agency, plastic and pictorial, that organ of the mind by which it communicates with the invisible world of spirit and makes it real and visible. It is, eminently, the faculty of idealization and of realization, "the eye of the soul glancing from heaven to earth and earth to heaven," including within the spacious sweep of its observation all worlds and all orders of beings. It is, also, the faculty of combination; presenting in ever varied forms the manifold objects of human knowledge. It is the picturing power of the mind, ever engaged in the formation of mental images and the reproduction of images lying latent in the soul. It is thus closely allied to memory and to the vital law of mental association. Something of the area of its action may be seen when we note the variety of forms and functions it may assume, as creative or artistic; as historical or scientific; touching in its action the confines of all departments of knowledge and all types of mental and moral being. Distinct from the other powers of the mind, it stands in vital relation to them all, affecting them and affected by them, and subject for its cultivation to the same great laws and agencies. This is the faculty which, first and last, is essential to the Novelist, seen in its reproductive function, in Historical Fiction; in its pictorial function, in Descriptive Fiction; in its constructive and reflective function, in Philosophic Fiction; seen, indeed, wherever symbolism and fantasy enter in any appreciative measure. It might be called, the Faculty of Characterization, assuming its more intellectual form in the Novel Proper, and its higher form in the Romance. It is here also that Fiction and the Drama are seen to be related, in that characterization is fundamental in each. Each has this historic, scenic element, and each is alike successful to the degree in which it represents the imaginary as real and, for the time, produces upon the reader or spectator the impression of lifelike reality. Here, also, is seen the close relation of Fiction to Poetry, in that in each Imagination is a vital faculty, so that here the old discussion as to the place of Fiction is revived, as to whether it belongs to prose or verse.

Here also emerges the larger question, as to the Place of Imagination in Literature, especially in Prose, and to what degree Prose License rightfully exists. The more we examine it, the more certain it appears that the Imagination has a wider function in literature than has hitherto been conceded, in that apart from bare narrative and technical discussion this power enters and controls or affects the process. The growth of symbolism in literature and life is a matter that must arrest the attention of all thoughtful students of either; the widening of the world of unreality; the ever larger interaction of the pictorial and the practical—in a word, the imperative demand for some kind of imaginative outlook and exercise.

A second Essential is the Knowledge of Human Nature, profound and broad; an intimate acquaintance with man and men; with the human mind and heart; with human motives, ideals and impulses, and thus with the best methods of reaching men. The novelist must know men better than books, must be at home on the street and in the shop and caucus. Such a knowledge must be psychological and social, must include the human environment, social, civil, industrial and ethical.

Realistic Fiction is in special need of this as it purports to deal with life at first hand and as it actually is. Fiction is thus a photographic art in literature, the art of verbal verisimilitude, demanding in the artist a full acquaintance with the subject with which he is dealing.

A third Essential is Style, in all the complex elements that it involves. The Novelist and Romancer must be, in the best sense, Stylists; exponents of literary art, emphasizing, as such, the value of literary form, of technique in prose expression.

We have spoken of Fiction in its relation to the Imagination as a faculty of representation. It is, also, the faculty of presentation, a specifically literary function. In no department of prose is what may be called, literary manner or method, more essential. The primal purpose of the writer of Fiction is to make his readers spectators; to make them see the object he is depicting precisely as he sees it; a result all the more difficult to reach in fiction, in that the author has not, as in the drama, the important aid of the actor and the scenery, but must rely for his effect absolutely upon himself and his ability to set the truth before the reader in such wise as to make it a reality. If it be asked, what are the principal features or Principles of Style which the novelist should exemplify, we answer, that there are three of these which any literary product whatsoever should illustrate,—Clearness, Vigor and Taste, while, in Fiction, Style must be Delineative. Delineation is a specific quality of Prose Fiction, drawing the lines about a subject, a scene, a person or a principle, mapping them out before the eye of the world in a bold and graphic manner. The novelist must be a Limner, an Illustrator, a literary draughtsman with pencil in hand, a verbal portrait-painter. In this sense, all fiction is descriptive, even tho the product be historical, philosophic or sentimental, so that no marked or permanent success can be secured without it. In a word, Style in Fiction must be Scenic, Spectacular, and, here, again, we come to the dramatic element in romantic literature.

The question is sometimes pressed—What is the Ideal Novel? Is it at all realized or is it realizable? "It has always seemed to me," writes Crawford, "that the perfect novel exists somewhere in the state of Platonic idea, waiting to be set down on paper by the first man of genius who receives a direct literary inspiration," and, he adds, more definitely, "it must be clean and sweet; it must have the magic to fascinate and the power to hold its reader from first to last; it must deal chiefly with love; its realism must be real, and its romance must be truly human, and its religion must be of such universal span as to hold all worthy religions in itself." Here, indeed, is a lofty aim, given by one who is himself a master in the art and seeking ever to approximate more and more closely to the ideal he has drawn. If the ideal novelist must have these characteristics, then must the essentials stated be present—a high order of imagination, a full knowledge of human nature and an order of literary art, alike clear, urgent, chaste and impressive. What, we are asked, is the Probable Permanence of the present dominance of Fiction? The novel is said to be "a marketable commodity," and we hear "of the still growing taste for fiction," and the question is raised by Crawford "whether this expresses an enduring want of educated men and women." Apparently, it does. More authors are now writing it than ever, while there is no visible sign of declension. If, moreover, the novel must deal chiefly with love, and if in that passion, all men and women share, we are warranted in asserting that the conditions of permanence are present. What is all literature, after all, but Romance or Realism, and what is all life but these? Inasmuch as Fiction exemplifies these as no other form of literature does, it is clear that it will ever have a controlling influence and hold the patronage of the people. Hence the necessity of its production in its highest and best forms. To the effecting of this result every novelist should be committed as a protest against the dominance of the modern novel of revolting realism. Careful observers of the literary signs of the times are speaking of the Revival of Romance and of Realism, a Revival, we hope, of the Romance of Scott and the Realism of Thackeray. If this be so, the increasing currency of imaginative literature need not disturb us, as in the long working-day of this matter-of-fact world it will serve to afford us many a needed hour of hope and happiness and cheer.

CHAPTER NINE

OPEN QUESTIONS IN LITERATURE—I

IN literature, as in other departments of intellectual inquiry, there may be said to be some elements that are stable and finally adjusted, and others that are more or less variable, tho working gradually toward a finally established and permanent form. No sooner are problems that have long been agitated brought to settlement than new problems are seen to emerge demanding similar study and adjudication, it being presumable that the area of settled questions is constantly enlarging as that of unsettled questions is diminishing. There is no prospect, however, that the discussion of such questions will ever be finally closed. There is, indeed, in the agitation itself a sign of life, one of the best indications possible that literature, as all other valid sciences, is progressive, in touch with the advance of kindred sciences, and as such coordinated with every form of mental activity and with the ever-changing phases of life itself. It is in view of this fact that the study of literature, in its highest and best expressions and on rational methods, is a specific mental stimulus as well as pleasure, ever inviting the student to the investigation of new phenomena, and ever repaying his researches by their better understanding and adjustment. Some of the more important of these questions may now be discussed.

I. *The Relation of Prose and Verse as Literary Forms.* At first sight it might seem as if the lines of difference between these two types were so marked as to make it impossible to confound them. The one we have been inclined to regard as the embodiment of reason and intellect proper, and the other, of imagination and taste; and yet, on examination, we are at once aware how fully and easily prose expression, as in De Quincey's "Opium Eater," takes on an imaginative cast, and poetry, as in Browning's "Ring and the Book," takes on the reflective and mental cast. The object of the one, we are wont to say, is instruction, and that of the other, pleasure, while, here again, each of these provinces is invaded by the other; prose, as in Lamb and Irving, being made specifically entertaining, and poetry, as in Goethe and Milton, enlightening and stimulating. Even when we emphasize the most essential difference between the two, and say that the one is unmetrical and the other metrical, we are confronted with the fact, as in the semi-metrical prose of Ruskin and Hawthorne and the semi-unmetrical poetry of Akenside and Whitman, that the boundary line is often scarcely discernible. In fact, the writer passes almost imperceptibly from one to the other, the suggestive statement of Dryden being here in place when he speaks of poetry "as the other harmony of prose," each of them being but a varied form of some one generic literary principle. It is a striking fact that in so far as the derivation of the terms—prose and verse—is concerned, there is practical identity of meaning, the Latin etymology of the word, prose, from proversus, giving us the very word, verse itself, the present difference of the words being a matter of later variation and usage. Prose is direct verse. Hence, the well-known middle area of what is called, Poetical Prose, as in Prescott, and Prose Poetry, as in Pope. That immense field which, for want of a better term, is known as Prose Fiction, illustrates it, the very phrase so involving the combination of prose proper with some other element more or less poetic that such critics as Minto and Masson place it under verse. Thus we read of "prose rhythm" as well as of "poetic rhythm." Saintsbury gives us, in his "Specimens of English Prose," the characteristics of each of them. As a notable example of this English "prose rhythm" he adduces a portion of the Canticles of Scripture, and while referring to Ruskin, as an exponent of it, adds, "that it has invaded history, permeated social writing and affected criticism." "To draw the line between the domain of prose and verse," says Corson, "is not easy." In referring to Shakespeare "as the first to mingle organically, in dramatic composition, blank verse and rhyme and prose," he admits that, even in Shakespeare, "verse constantly encroaches upon the domain of prose." So it was in the plays of Ben Jonson and Lyly and other Elizabethan dramatists. Much of the English Comedy of the seventeenth and eighteenth centuries is presented in this exceptional form. Dryden himself illustrates it as he reduces to prose the "Canterbury Tales." So we have "The Vision of Piers Plowman" in prose by Armour, as we have a prose Beowulf by Hall and Tinker. Thus it is that while some of the historical periods of English may be classified as prose periods or poetry periods, there are other eras in which the two types are so interrelated that they are best studied together. While authors such as Chaucer, Spenser and Longfellow are mainly poets, and such as Macaulay and Emerson mainly prose-writers, there are others as Scott and Holmes and Swinburne who have so illustrated each form that their prose and verse mutually affect each other. In fine, prose and verse, tho distinct types of literature, are yet closely enough allied to be studied in unison, it being quite conceivable that in the highest forms of human thinking and experience the special type of embodiment is immaterial, and the two are blended with unconscious ease and effect. Blank Verse is thus seen to be an accepted and effective compromise between prose and verse.

II. *The Relative Rank of Epic, Dramatic and Lyric Verse.* We touch here upon a topic which serves to illustrate the principle that a question once regarded as finally closed may be, at length, reopened for discussion, new evidence calling for reconsideration. Hitherto, Epic Poetry has been accepted by the critics and the general literary public as the primary form; partly, by reason of its alleged antiquity as a form and, partly, on account of its intrinsic character and final poetic purpose. The element of Sublimity being accepted, theoretically, as the first element of standard verse, and the epic poem being, also, accepted as best illustrating this essential condition of sublimity as laid down by Longinus, the conclusion has naturally followed as to the leading place of the epic in the poetic trio. Later investigation has, however, started the question as to the validity of this reasoning and the conclusion reached, whether, indeed, if the premises themselves be accepted, we are shut up to the inference that is given. If it be conceded that sublimity is the highest element of verse, valid objection may be made to the opinion that attributes to the epic the fullest possession of this quality, the inquiry properly arising, whether in such a tragedy as "Hamlet" or "The Medea" moral sublimity does not reach its maximum expression. Moreover, sublimity tho the highest, is by no means the only element of verse, it being possible that such other important elements are found to such a degree within the domain of the dramatic and lyric as to make them fair competitors with the epic for poetic primacy. Even as to antiquity, it must be conceded that the lyric takes precedence, while it might be a matter of serious difficulty to show conclusively that the legends and traditions which form the groundwork of epic verse are any more ancient than what we may call the beginnings of the drama. If to these considerations, we add that of scope or province, it is quite conceivable that either in lyric or play the argument is against the epic, there being, indeed, no human experience that is foreign to the tragic and the comic and to the emotional element of the lyric. In so far, therefore, as modern poetic criticism is concerned, it may be said that the manifest trend of opinion is away from the epic toward the dramatic, as a kind of verse in which epical sublimity and lyric sentiment alike come to their full expression, and which possesses features additional to those that are peculiarly its own and that make it adaptable to wider needs. National and popular in its origin, and arising out of the life of the people and not of a class and out of the deepest moral instincts of the race, with human history as its field, and the representation of character its final purpose, comprehensive in its range and diversified in its expression, we may say of dramatic verse as a whole what Walpole said of comedy, "that it is the perfection of human composition."

It is to be, moreover, remembered that the epic verse of the world is limited while we have a body of dramatic composition characteristically large and inviting.

III. *The Relation of the Drama to the Stage.* It is the relation of the written product to its oral presentation.

We notice, at the outset, that the word, drama, in its Greek origin, means, action, the manifestation of life, the natural tendency of the written composition to assume the oral, actable form being thus involved in the terms themselves. The English actor, Irving, in a recent work on the "Drama," uses the word throughout as involving both dramatic literature and dramatic representation, the acting of the Play being, as he holds, an essential part of its conception and construction. The Stage, as he teaches us, is best viewed as an interpreter of the poem, so that the poem, as a literary product, can not be said to come to its fulfilment this side the stage. Action in scenic form is involved in the dramatic idea. Saintsbury, in speaking of the nineteenth-century English Drama, tells us "that it has displayed one curious and disastrous characteristic, namely, that the Plays which have been good literature have either never been acted or have seldom succeeded as Plays, and that the Plays that have been acted and have been successful have seldom been good literature." The critic in calling this "a curious and disastrous characteristic" is eminently right in that it runs directly counter to the best literary theory, as it does, also, as a matter of fact, to the most notable dramatic periods in literary history. It would seem to be a thoroughly abnormal relation of the drama and the stage, widely sundering them in ideal and spirit, when both on a priori and experimental grounds they should work together for the same high ends. As it is a sure proof of general literary decadence and of special dramatic decadence when literature and the drama are divorced, so is it an equally sure proof of such decadence when the drama and the stage are divorced. Herein lies one of the unfailing tests of the dramatic character of any particular period or people, the ideal drama being alike representable and conformable to the best literary models. This is not to say that all Plays are alike actable, nor that what is called, The Closet Drama, or The Melodrama, as in Browning and Byron, may not have a good degree of dramatic and literary merit. There is, indeed, a valid difference between the terms, dramatic and theatric; the first referring to the internal quality of the poem, and the second, to its scenic adaptability to the stage. There is such a form of literature as dramatic prose and poetry that is not marked by the theatric cast. Not a little of the seventeenth and eighteenth century English Drama was of this particular type, this being one of the marks of its inferiority as compared with the Elizabethan Drama. Herein lies much of the weakness of the dramatic verse of Tennyson, in that, with all its literary vigor and charm, it evinces a notable lack of the stage features, the masterly genius of Mr. Irving being put to its severest test to make the best examples of it, such as Becket, at all acceptable to an English audience. The great actor elicited unmerited praise just because he partially succeeded in presenting with scenic effect those English Plays that lack some of the fundamental elements of a Play. As the French state it, he succeeded "in creating a part," and thus has somewhat atoned for the absence of histrionic features. It may further be noted that the highest ideal of dramatic art is found when the author and the actor are one and the same personality, as in the case of Sophocles, Æschylus, Molière and Shakespeare, it being an interesting historical fact that the Prologue to the Play was often spoken through courtesy by the author himself and then the Play was committed to the players. Here we have Impersonation in a double form and a corresponding increase in the effect. Dramatic critics have gone so far as to say "that no one who has not practical knowledge of the stage can write a good acting play." So, Saintsbury writes, and so Irving has taught us. Who can tell how much of the success of Shakespeare was due to the fact that he knew experimentally every detail of the actor's work and appeared in the representation of his own characters! It is here, as nowhere else, that the Baconian theory of the authorship of these Plays finds its refutation. It is not strange, therefore, that Mr. Irving, in his book on "The Drama," devotes a portion of it to the history of four great actors, Burbage, Betterton, Garrick and Kean, whereby he shows the intimate connection between the actor and the acting, so that, even where the actor is not himself the author, his main object as an actor is to minimize the distance between himself and the author. We speak of representing Shakespeare, by which we mean the reproduction of his characters in living presence on the stage as if they were veritably in person before us. Garrick, whose special glory it was "to make the Shakesperian Drama once more popular," must have been heard with unwonted interest, as in "The Lying Valet" and "The Clandestine Marriage" he was alike actor and author.

IV. *The Relation of the Drama to the Novel.* A priori, it might be argued that such a relation of intimacy exists, in that each of them might be defined to be—A Representation of Life. This is true alike of tragedy and comedy, and true of every form of the novel, narrative, descriptive, or philosophic. When we say that one of the main features of Fiction is that of delineation, we state, also, one of the chief features of the drama, and when, conversely, we describe the purpose of the drama, in Shakespearian phrase, "to hold the mirror up to nature," we equally aptly describe therein one of the prime purposes of the novel as such. Hence, many of the definitions applicable to the one may justly be applied to the other, much of their difference lying in different forms of applying the same generic principles. Thus, Macready, the actor, as quoted by Irving, defines the object of the drama to be "to fathom the depths of character, to trace its latent motives, to feel its finest quiverings of emotion, to comprehend the thoughts that are hidden under words and thus possess one's self of the actual mind of the individual men," all of which language would well set forth the ultimate ideal of the novel. So, Mr. Irving himself, in describing the drama as "the Art of Human Nature in picturesque or characteristic action," gives us the essential feature of fiction. When Sidney Lanier states, that the principle of the development of the novel is the exhibition of the idea of personality in its progressive growth, we have the drama essentially described, while the accepted division of Fiction might be applied substantially to Plays. Thus, we have drama, as "The Midsummer Night's Dream," written in specifically fictitious form, and novels, such as Victor Hugo's "Les Miserables" and "Ninety-Three," written in dramatic form, so as to lessen more and more the distance and the difference between the two, and require, on the part of any author who would be a master in either, to possess the evidences of a good degree of ability in the other. If the historical beginning of The English Novel is correctly assigned to the Age of Sidney, in his "Arcadia," then we have the origin of the Modern English Drama and the Modern English Novel as contemporary. Jusserand's treatise, "The English Novel In the Time of Shakespeare," affords us, in its very title, this same historical relation. Mr. Ward, in his "History of The English Drama," traces the same historical and literary connection from the Age of Elizabeth to the death of Queen Anne. There are special proofs of the closeness of this connection. The one is found in the increasing interest that is now taken in The Dramatization of Novels as recently applied with good effect to the fiction of Maclaren and Caine and Hope and Barrie and Wallace and others, the double object being sought of making the novel itself more realistic and presenting the dramatic poem from every possible point of view. Indeed, in the widest meaning of the word—realistic—applicable alike to the Novel and the Play, we discover still another evidence of their common characteristics and the literary value of emphasizing them. Mrs. Stowe's "Uncle Tom's Cabin; or, Life Among the Lowly," so successfully dramatized on the stage, is a pertinent illustration of this common realism in literature. A further evidence of this relation is seen in the combination of the dramatist and novelist in one personality. We need not go outside the province of English Letters to substantiate this view, as in Bulwer, author alike of "Rienzi" and "Harold" and of "Richelieu" and "The Lady of Lyons"; or in Goldsmith, as the author of "The Good-natured Man" and "The Vicar of Wakefield." So, Smollett wrote "The Regicide," and Scott, his semi-dramatic poems; Longfellow, his "Spanish Student," and Taylor, his "Prince Deukalion." So, Goethe wrote "The Sorrows of Werther" and "Goetz von Berlichingen," the wonder being that literature, ancient and modern, is not fuller than it is of this double form of literary product from the same authors. A study of interest emerges here as we investigate the common causes of these two types, the common ground on which they stand, the common ideals they have in view, the dialog of the drama, hitherto so strictly confined to it, being now a common part of fictitious narrative. In the unacted novel there is simply wanting the regular succession of act and scene, and the writer, instead of representing truth as external to himself, is supposed to present it as it appears to his own mind.

This conceded, with other points of difference, it still remains true that their relationships are so pronounced as to confirm the fact of increasing unity in literary types. "The end of philosophy," says Bacon, "is the intuition of unity." This is, also, one of the ends of the philosophy of literature.

V. *Generalization and Specialization in Literature.* The question is as to their comparative importance, being in literature what the A Priori and A Posteriori methods are in logic and philosophy. It is the mooted question of the Deductive and Inductive in Letters. At the outset, it may be noted, that in such a discussion we have a tangible proof of the fact that literature is no exception to the application of scientific modes of reasoning, that it is thus proved to be a science and philosophy, subject to the same great laws of logical process and conclusion, and thus thoroughly coordinated with all the great departments of human thought. As soon as we pass from the domain of philosophy or science to literature we find a province in which all these processes have an application, it being competent for the literary student to begin deductively with a principle or set of principles or inductively to collate sufficient facts on any given book, author, period or movement to justify the inference of a general law. Which of these methods, the critics ask, shall dominate, it being in place to say, that the nature of the literary topic in hand, the specific purpose of the student at the time, and his own best judgment will prove a sufficiently accurate guide to a proper choice of methods. There are some subjects that are abstract in nature, in regard to which there are but a few facts to collate and which are thus in themselves fitting subjects for deductive process. Other topics are mainly concrete, open to personal observation and experience, are within the well-understood area of testimony and, as such, are naturally of the inductive type. It can not be too strongly urged that in literature, as in other spheres, these two methods may be appropriately applied in conjunction, the very principles from which we argue deductively being first reached through the slower process of induction. Hence, it is unwise to widen the distance too greatly between these accepted methods, or to press the inquiry too strongly as to which should have the precedence in literature. Professor Moulton, in his volume, "Shakespeare as a Dramatic Artist," carries this controversy, as we believe, to an unnecessary and harmful extreme. The treatise is a plea for the inductive method in the study of Shakespeare and thus, by inference, in all dramatic, poetic and literary study. His object, as he states it, is "to present Dramatic Criticism as a regular Inductive Science." He speaks of it as a new departure in literary criticism, as if, indeed, it were not as old as literary criticism itself, tho becoming more and more pronounced as the history of such criticism advanced. It is seen in all the great critics of literature, in Goethe, Lessing, Saint Beuve, Cousin, De Quincey and Coleridge, and developed conjointly with the deductive process. When he tells us "that induction is the most universal of scientific methods and may be presumed to apply wherever there is a subject-matter reducible to the form of fact," we need not demur, but must add that it is not the only important scientific method and that deduction may be presumed to apply equally well, in literature or elsewhere, wherever there is a subject-matter reducible to the form of principle. When he adds "that inductive criticism will examine literature in the spirit of pure investigation" the same may be said of deduction. In fine, there is room and need for both methods, while there is no error in making the statement that, in accordance with the trend of modern science, philosophy and literature, criticism is becoming, and rightly so, more and more inductive, "the whole progress of science consisting," as Professor Moulton urges, "in winning fresh fields of thought to the inductive method." Even here, however, students of literature must be on their guard, and heed the note of warning that is sounded in these days against the tendency to undue specialization. Otherwise, Literature may become a mere collation of facts, a tabulation of data, and the student's energies be absorbed in the mere classification of material.

It is possible thus to devote months of study to the poetry of Pope or the Prose of Dryden without touching on those great generic principles which these authors represented. In literature, as elsewhere, there is such a thing as the sense of perspective, the need of good sense and good taste. There is manifest need, just now, in literature of the severer application of Generalization. A great result is reached when a fundamental principle is secured.

VI. *The Question of Literary Standards.* The usage of the best writers, we are wont to say, is the final standard of taste: What, we may ask, is the law of classifying writers as good? What is the standard of good literature itself? To this it is answered: It is The Accepted Principles of Literary Art, such principles having been reached by long and patient study and ratified by a consensus of opinion, the literary world over. This conceded, it is important to state, that tho the standard of literature remains from age to age in its substantial character as such, there is still within the province of literature a wide variety of feature, partly induced by external influence of time and place and race and, partly, by an inherent and ever active tendency to variation. We speak of the historic development of prose and verse, which is the same as saying that the prose and verse of different periods, while practically conforming to a common standard, also reveal marked differences of type. The prose of Bacon and that of Macaulay are alike standard, and, yet, dissimilar, as revealing the respective personalities of the author and the epochs in which they lived. So the epics of Homer and Milton, the Plays of Shakespeare and Racine, and the Lyrics of Schiller and Burns, reveal decided variation while conforming to poetic law. It is thus that Saintsbury writes of nineteenth-century prose "that the change of style therein is as much the leading feature of the century as in poetry the change of thought and outlook." So, Moulton, speaking of standards as settled or variable, refutes the idea "that the foundations of literary form have reached their final settlement," and confirms the dictum "that literature is a thing of development." These two facts, therefore, conceded, that there is such a thing as a fixed standard in literature and that within the limitations of such a standard there is much literary liberty and consequent variety of type, it remains to utter a word of warning against the increasing tendency in modern times to depreciate or modify such a standard in the interest of some temporary literary movement or leader, until, at length, the question arises, whether we have left us any standard whatsoever, literature being "boxed about" in obedience to the whims of this or that disturber of the peace of the literary world. Literary fashions there may be, legitimate changes of the dress which literature from age to age assumes, in obedience to a healthy critical and general sentiment. Style itself is but the fashion of a people or an author, and may change under normal conditions. The danger lies in the direction of a merely capricious and an unwarranted change in the line of the grotesque and eccentric. There is such a thing in literature as foppery and mere finery, an element of cockneyism and coquetry, a mere display of literary wares for the sake of the display. Careful observers of the signs of the times speak of a manifest "unrest of style," while the varied expressions of such unrest are almost endless, appearing, at times, as at the close of Elizabeth's reign, in the guise of affectation and studied ornament or in the form of extreme literary vagaries and heresies. Exaggeration of some sort they all are, departures from a norm or law, experiments in which the veriest literary novices may figure conspicuously as leaders. When we are told by a competent observer that now in England we are "too literary," write too much and read too much, the anomalous statement finds its force in the fact that the original standard of literature has become so modified and lowered that the veriest tyro may easily conform to it, so that we have quantity rather than quality, imitation instead of originality, artifice in the place of nature, and mere books in the place of literature proper. Genuine literary fashions are one thing; literary facts are another; even tho great names seem to support and justify them.

Whether this decadence of standard is due, as Saintsbury suggests, to the dominance of the modern society novel, or as Collins suggests, to that of the modern sensational press, it is a tendency demanding immediate check. There is a normal standard in literature which must at all cost be maintained. Authors and readers alike are committed to its maintenance. Scholars at large and, especially, literary scholars, are committed to it, while literary institutions have a mission at this point second to no other, and have it in their power thus to transmit to those who follow them an uncorrupted body of letters.

CHAPTER TEN

OPEN QUESTIONS IN LITERATURE—II

In addition to those already examined, we note the following, some of them of a general nature applicable to literature in its widest sense, and some pertaining to special forms and phases of literary expression. We notice

I. The Relation of Literature as a Written Form or Product to the Oral Presentation of it. These are not the same. Literature in its specific sense is the embodiment of thought in written form. To be literature at all, it must be reduced to writing. When presented orally, it ceases, then and there, to be literature, and becomes a something different by whatever name we may designate it. This difference is further seen in the fact that literary ability is neither necessarily nor historically coincident with the ability to express it in oral form. In fact, they often seem to exist in the inverse ratio. Certainly, the presence of the one does not argue that of the other, nor are the methods by which the one is secured or taught the same as those obtaining in the other, so that we are forced to the conclusion, that they are in some valid sense different; assume different conditions, are dependent on different faculties, proceed by different agencies, and contemplate differect ends. Thus Matthews, in his volume, "The Historical Novel," in writing of the relation of the drama to literature, remarks: "Nothing ought to be clearer than the distinction between the written word and the spoken, between the literature addressed to the eye alone and that which is intended primarily for the ear." He quotes from Jebb to the effect: "Much of the ancient criticism of oratory is tainted by a radical vice, confounding literary merit with oratorical merit." Insistence is made by critics on the point that the writer appeals to posterity, and the speaker, to a present audience, and aims at an immediate impression, so that the great orations of history must be tested, first of all, as to the effect produced at the time of their delivery and not by their intrinsic literary quality. It is indeed the oratorical quality in an oration that gives it power as spoken, so that critics are misled who test it merely or mainly on literary grounds. Some of Burke's best orations from a literary point of view were failures when delivered. So as to Isocrates, the Greek orator, while the speeches of Sheridan were effective tho void of special literary merit. So as to the sermons of Whitefield and the Wesleys. This is not to say that there is not a valid connection between the written and the oral product, but that there is a valid difference, also, even tho in the ideal literary and oratorical production this difference is reduced to the minimum. Hence it is pertinent to state, that the various forms of Prose and Verse may be classified as being more or less adapted to oral presentation. As a rule and naturally, Prose possesses more of this adaptability than Poetry. If we speak of Prose as narrative, descriptive and forensic, it is clear that the forensic is adapted to oral expression, as histories, sketches and essays are not. So, if we classify verse as Epic, Dramatic, Descriptive and Lyric, it is equally clear that the form most adapted to oral embodiment is the dramatic, while the lyric, in so far as it includes

Songs, has something of this pronounceable quality. It is because Prose Fiction has much of the dramatic element in it that it is seen to possess something of this oral adaptability and is more and more presented in public scenic form. In fine, there is such a type of literature as the oratorical, and to the degree in which it is such it may be made to assume the definite oral form. If we now inquire as to what these Specific Forms are in which literature easily assumes oral expression, two or three of prominence are found.

1. The Oration as it appears in manuscript form, as a purely written product. Of all possible types of oratorical literature, the oration is the most so. It is from this fact that it takes its name. It may take the type of the Public Address, at the behest of great civic and social interests; or it may assume Argumentative Form, as in the Debate; or Parliamentary form, as on the floor of Congress; or, in Sacred Discourse, that of the Sermon. In all these classes of Oration, so essential is the oratorical quality, that the writer, in their preparation as literature, before they are delivered must ever keep in mind the fact of their prospective delivery and elaborate them with the audience in view. That Addresses, Debates and Sermons are often heard without the least impression is largely due to the fact that their author had ignored the vital relation of literature to oratory. They are composed, presumably, not so much as literature proper for some far distant effect and as such to be recorded and preserved for the reference of the reader, as mainly, if not wholly, for present results, and fail of their mission if they do not accomplish them. Tho, as with the orations of Cicero and Webster, a pronounced liter-

ary quality coexists with the oratorical, it is this latter and not the former that is the dominant feature. When the American critic Whipple writes as he does of Webster as a master of English Style, it is, after all, the oratorical style that he is emphasizing, the close relation of literature in some of its forms to oral expression. If we go further than this and interpret the word, oratorical, in its widest meaning, as that which is impassioned and impressive, there is a correct sense in which all prose literature that is not miscellaneous and didactic should be to some degree oratorical, written for effect. "Thoughts that breathe and words that burn" are, as such, oratorical, tho not assuming specific forensic form, while the most signal example of this principle is seen in those orations and debates which were never delivered and thus stand upon the page as specimens of oratorical literature.

2. The Play. Here we enter a most inviting field, in the careful survey of which many questions of interest arise as to the relation of verse and prose, of the dramatist and actor, and of the scenic in general. The matter of interest that first engages us is the fact that dramatic verse is of all the Forms the most presentable and pronouncable, has in it most of the actable qualities, and is composed with primary reference to its public presentation. It is the most representable form of verse. There are, indeed, unacted and unactable Plays, the Closet Dramas of literature, as in Browning and Byron. They are mere Dramatic Monologues, written more from the view-point of literary art than from that of oral exhibition. There are also dramas written for the stage which, however, never reach it, or, reaching it, are soon recalled because they have not the histrionic quality. 'Tis thus

with some of the Plays of Tennyson. As, in prose, the Oration must have something more than mere literary quality to make it successful orally, so, in poetry, the Play must have dramatic or scenic quality as well as literary quality, to make it successful orally. It must have theatric quality, that something which adapts it to public recital. The first question with the dramatic composer is, How can his conceptions be embodied in such written form as to make them representable? And this requires distinctive genius. The mere division of a Play into Acts and Scenes will not do it. The mere development of a Plot on toward a Catastrophe will not do it. There is a unique something below the text and behind all acts and plots that gives tone to the composition, that differentiates it at once from the epic as a narrative and the lyric as a sentiment, and demands the stage, the actor, costume and scenery properly to present it. Such a composition may or may not be expressed in the best literary form. This is what Brunetiere must mean when he says in apparently extreme manner, "that a Play is under no obligation to be literary." Even Shakespeare and Moliere wrote their Plays as Plays and not as mere literature, for the auditor and not for the reader only, and did not seem to care how they read if they succeeded on the stage. So true is this that the general literary critic is not always competent to the judging of a Play. He must possess the dramaturgic faculty, as in judging an Oration he must possess the forensic faculty. When we are told by Brunetiere "that a comedy has no more call to be literary than a sermon has," we are told, in effect, that the comedy and the sermon depend for their main effect on other than literary features, on the faculty of oral representation. One of the prime factors, explanatory of all this, is the actor or the orator in his personality, gesture, voice and general manner, a factor so potential as often seeming to act in defiance of all relations and making a comparatively inferior Speech or Play impressive. Hence we must acknowledge the presence and power of the Oral Arts. There are oratorical Poets and Prose writers, and to be judged as such. It has been justly said—"tho the survival of a Play depends on its literary quality, its success depends on its dramatic quality." There are two other forms of literature that in a modified way reveal this relation between the written and the oral.

3. The one is the Novel, in so far as dramatized. The Novel becomes susceptible of oral embodiment and expression just to the degree in which it possesses the inherent dramatic element, while here, again, the close relations of prose and verse are seen. It is in Prose Fiction, so called, that we are now finding more and more of the dramatic quality, and, hence, a poetic quality.

4. The other form revealing this relation to oral type is Lyric Verse in the Song or Ode, primarily prepared for public recital. The Song is distinct from other lyrics in that it possesses the musical quality, a something that fits it for singing. Here we touch the borders at least of the difficult problem started by Poe and discussed by Lanier and others as to the exact relation of music as an art to literature. In the Songs of the Shakespearian and European Drama, we find a practical illustration of the dramatic and lyric combined, or, in such a dramatic lyric as "Comus," the Play or Masque and the Songs are alike adapted to stage recital.

Thus, in Oration and Play and Novel and Song we note the literary or written forms that have in them an oral tendency and adaptability. If we widen the subject to its utmost limit, it may be said that this interaction of the written and oral may be seen in all that is properly included under the terms—Prose and Poetic Recital. The Recited Selections given us by the elocutionist or public reader, gathered from the open province of general literature, serve in their place to reveal this same connection.

II. The True Relation of Literature and Style. This is a question naturally confined to the sphere of Prose. Literature is the written product, the content or subject-matter of the author's work. Style is the form or manner of its expression, the mode of its presentation. From the time of Quintilian down to the modern school of Bain and Spencer, the question has been agitated—What is the real relation of the Product we call, Literature, to the Presentation of it we call, Style. What is the relation of Thought to Language is the philological form of this same question. The answer which historical criticism has given has been a twofold one, represented, respectively, by some of the ablest minds, and including not only literary but rhetorical and linguistic suggestion. These two divergent views may be called, The External and Internal or the Esthetic and the Intellectual. De Quincey, in his notable papers on "Language," "Rhetoric" and "Style" speaks of literature under the twofold order of "Mechanology" and "Organology." In its application to our present purpose, this would mean, the Superficial and the Essential. The one school holds that the relation is purely formal and unimportant, and the other, that it is vital. On the one side, are ranged the esthetic critics of literature who approach and examine it through the medium of the poetic imagination and as a fine art ministrant to pleasure and artistic culture. With such minds, Style is a more emphatic word than Literature itself, the manner in which such literature is presented being all-important. They interpret the word, literary, as the Belles-Lettres or Polite Literature of the South European School, the expression of ideas in attractive forms. This is the position of such a critic as Hugh Blair of Edinburgh. In Macaulay, as a literary critic, this method is much too prominent, while Matthew Arnold and the later school are too often found on this side of the critical line. Most of the secondary critics of literature are of this order, while a large part of the hasty and misleading criticisms of modern times gives evidence of a tendency in this direction.

On the other side, are the philosophic and thorough students of literature, as De Quincey, Coleridge, Spencer, Lessing, Cousin and Theremin. Herbert Spencer, in his notable essay—"The Philosophy of Style," assumes this high position. "Form is not form only," says Cousin, the French critic, "it is the form of something, it unfolds something inward." "Beauty is not mere expression; it is the expression of ideas." These authors hold that there is such a thing in literature as Intellectual Form; that the mind of the writer should control his method; that there is an inner as well as an outer form, the form in which the author presents the subject to himself before he presents it on the page to the reader. It is what Lathrop has called, "a sense of form." "The words which a man of genius selects," says Mathews, "are as much his own as his thoughts." They are his own just because the ideas are his own. Language is thus more than the dress of thought or the atmosphere of thought or the medium of thought. It is its incarnation, its flesh and blood, its body. With these critics, the word, Literature, is always emphasized above that of style, which is but the avenue of its expression. It is not so much Literature and Style of which they speak as it is Literature, the one comprehensive and sufficient word which properly interpreted includes all that is meant by Style at its best. Between these two theories and their respective exponents there can be, it would seem, no serious difficulty in choosing the latter, insisting that the relation between authorship as a content and an expression should be so intimate that the one would be found always to involve the other.

If it be asked,—What is the vital bond that connects the two, we answer—The Personality of the author, expressing itself continuously in the act of authorship and in the specific external form which such authorship at the time assumes. If, as Buffon tells us, "The Style is the Man himself," we might reverse the statement and affirm that the Man is the Style itself, the one proposition being as tenable as the other. It is this cardinal doctrine of Literary Personality that goes far to furnish the needed solution of this problem and relegate this Open Question to the sphere of settled opinions. Literature is the product of the author's mind, and style is the expression of the author's art, and they must thereby condition and control each other. One of the best proofs of the correctness of this conclusion is found in the fact that the best literary eras and the greatest literary names best evince it. It is in Golden Ages and among the Masterpieces that we best see its exemplification, in the Age of Pericles, Augustus and Elizabeth and in the persons of

Herodotus, Cicero and Milton, at which eras and in which authors Literature and Style are so conjoined that no dividing line is discernible. It is this principle, also, that brings literature into harmony with all other great departments of human thought and activity, where the product and the poem are not sharply differentiated, but are rightly viewed as a twofold expression of one causative agency. As to what is meant precisely by style in Literature two elements are noteworthy:

(*a*) The one pertains to an author's vocabulary, the words he uses, their number and character, their sources and appropriateness. Good Diction lies at the basis of good literature on the side of style, so that the aspiring author must make a study of it in the light of his constant needs, emphasizing native words above foreign; standard words above local or provincial; making clearness, vigor and good taste in the use of language a matter of conscience. This is the verbal side of literature and all literary work.

(*b*) The other element of Style is found in the author's Sentences—their structure and use. Swift's definition of Style, "the right word in the right place" is in point here. The sentence must be clear, concise, vigorous and chaste, stating what and only what the author has to say, and stating it with force. Simplicity, Brevity and Vigor are essential features. This is the structural side of literature, that which presents it in good external form. At these two points, of Vocabulary and Sentence, Literature and Style meet and unite and can not properly be divorced.

III. The Literary Spirit—its nature, forms of expression, methods of cultivation and value, a subject second to none in its interest and varied relations, forced upon the attention of the student of letters, and a subject through the full interpretation of which we compass, in a sense, the entire content of literary history.

As to its Elements or Characteristics, these may be substantially expressed in the statement, that the phrase, The Literary Spirit is in sharp antithesis to Literary Technique, to the exact verbal statute as laid down by the schools, from which no departure is supposed to be allowable. Tho the word, literature, in its Latin origin, refers to that which pertains to the letter, this current use of the term is well understood and, in no wise, contravenes the statement, that, in literature itself, the letter may be magnified above the spirit and the very life of literature be imperilled. Here, as in morals, "the letter killeth." Hence, in all those authors and eras in which the word or form is exalted above the idea, and style is made an end in itself, this antithesis is seen and the result in authorship is always evil. Hence, in periods of general literary decline, the Dark Ages of Literature, the spirit is always in abeyance to the letter, Literary criticism is in special danger here just because it is criticism. The literary judge sits down to a work that is presumably technical and, at times, purely professional, so that it is manifestly easy for him to magnify the analytical side of literature and justify himself in so doing. It is his vocation as a censor. One of the surest tests of the critic is just here, whether he is able or not to recognize and exalt the essential influence of the spirit in literature and subordinate to it all that is merely verbal and technical; whether he understands the difference between literary appreciation or mere literary exposition; between the interpretation of literature in its catholicity and generic elements and mere literary comment and exegesis. There is another province in which this error is particularly easy and prevalent, in what may be called, Educational Literature, in Literary Manuals and Theses, in which the author as an educator is so intent upon the purely pedagogic side of his work as to exalt it above all due limits and present a product to the student which is not, in any valid sense, literature at all. We speak of a body of literature. From this point of view, it is all body, absolutely soulless and lifeless. It is needless to say that here lies the perilous temptation of the university class-room, as a place for literary study and teaching, lest literature be conceived of and taught as a purely scholastic subject, amenable to the most formal exactions of the curriculum. It required all the courage of a Longfellow and a Lowell as professional educators to escape this pedagogic peril and teach literature in a literary way as they themselves understood and applied it. If it be asked, more specifically, just what is the main Element or characteristic of the Literary Spirit, the answer would best be expressed in the word, Spontaneity, as it appears in thought and language, in word and sentence, in method and product, in all that pertains to the author's preparation and presentation of his subject. This means a sane and normal liberty of action, personal freedom within the well understood conditions and limitations of literary law. It is what Emerson calls, atmosphere and amplitude, space in which to think and write at pleasure, absolutely unhampered by any of the artificial canons of the schools. Not only is there such a principle as Poetic License, well understood by the poet and in no sense conflicting with well established poetic statute, there is a Prose License, also, a general Literary License, conceding to the man of letters as such a larger share of freedom than would be accorded the scientific or technical student. He is to have "ample room and verge enough" for the proper exercise of imagination and feeling, as distinct from the exercise of the logical and critical faculties, where narrower limits are supposed to exist. It is clear that anything like Genius in literature must have such scope, in order to effect the ends of high endowment. Spontaneity of mental action is indeed but another name for inspiration in authorship.

As to the expression of this Literary Spirit historically in authorship and the reasons for its growth or decline, various conditions are seen to exist. There are authors not a few in whose personality and work it is but incidentally present, or in whom it but rarely, if at all, comes to any special prominence. This fact alone would assign them to the list of the secondary writers. There are other authors whose work is marked by its presence and in communion with whom we are never inclined to think of the mere letter and the statute, and these are the masters, old and modern. There are also entire peoples who as clearly evince its presence or absence. In the one case, literature seems to be a natural instinct or habit, and, in the other, an exotic, transplanted and superinduced, partaking of all the features of a foreign growth. It is an after-thought. A contrast between European and Oriental Literature would sufficiently confirm this fact, as within the limits of Europe itself it is illustrated. So, within the limits of any separate nation, there are special periods of authorship which evince, respectively, its presence or absence. Occasionally, a distinctively literary era, marked by freshness, vitality and vigor and a large amount of original production is closely followed by one as clearly marked by literary servility and the reign of mediocrity. This is on the principle of action and reaction. Still again, there are Institutions that are specifically literary and so designated, while not a few belie their name by the conspicuous absence of any such feature. It is scarcely too much to expect that in all institutions of liberal learning in the Modern European world, this Literary Spirit should be present in some substantive measure. In the very word, Liberal, Spontaneity and Scope are essentially involved. In so far, therefore, as in these centers of learning, literature is made a subject of study, it should be such in its most vigorous forms and impart life and character to the entire university curriculum. Literary Institutions should be pervaded by a profound literary impulse; should be centers of literary influence; aflame with literary zeal, and, thus, be potent factors in preserving and perpetuating the literary repute of peoples or languages.

As to the means by which such a spirit may best be secured, developed and maintained, there are two that are peculiarly essential—Absorption in Literary Work, and Contact with Literary Influences. The litarary man must keep in touch with literature, with its production and those who produce it, with literary scenes and surroundings, with the leaders and the landmarks of literature, with the best books and the best literary ideals. There is a philosophic principle that is here involved—that of mental affinity, induced and increased by contact. We speak of Literary Influence. It is this influence which is the direct result of literary activity and association, strengthening and deepening with the years, and in which there is a mutual giving and receiving. All this is true, and yet it can not be concealed that the literary spirit in its best elements and expression is a gift of the gods, an inheritance, innate and connate, and thus an organic part of the author's personality as a man, his personality itself. Tho in a sense and to a degree it may be cultivated, even here the primal factors of it must already exist, if there is to be any pronounced development of it. It is the very last literary product or characteristic that can be procured at call or made to appear by any prescribed process. It requires but the casual glance of him who possesses it to note in any book, author, period or people whether it exist as a natural endowment or whether it exist as a product of education. Here, as everywhere, it is seen that nature is the best guide, while, in so far as nature may be supplemented by other agencies, such agencies must be marked by naturalness. Any forced process is out of place.

As to the value of such a Spirit, individual or national, but little need be said, for it is the spirit that giveth life, and where the spirit is there is also liberty. What Courthope calls, The Liberal Movement in English Letters, is this movement of the spirit, an unmistakable sign of life. What modern critics are so fond of calling, Literature and Life, is but another name for its manifest presence. There is a spirit in man and there is a spirit in literature, shaping and controlling all that is embodied and making it effective over men. Whatever we name it, genius, inspiration, "the union and the faculty divine," originality, instinct, creative power, it is a subconscious something beneath the letter, which makes the letter what it is, and apart from which it lies inert upon the page. So indispensable is it that all high literature may be said to postulate it. It is a prerequisite to its being,—its soul and sustenance. By this test as by no other may the present status and the promise of literature be determined among modern states and peoples.

CHAPTER ELEVEN

HEBRAISM AND HELLENISM IN LITERATURE

IN a very interesting book entitled, "Social Ideals in English Letters," the accomplished authoress writes as follows:—"With that instinct for large historical views which Matthew Arnold probably inherited from his father, he sought in the past for a great expression of the attitude he admired. He found it in the spirit of Greece, and, following a hint of Heine's, he adopted the distinction between Hellenism and Hebraism and made of it the center and pivot in his interpretation of English life. It was, of course, Hellenism which he sought to foster; Hellenism, with its stress on intelligence and gentleness, its demand for sincerity of thought rather than of heart. The uppermost idea with Hellenism is to see things as they really are; the uppermost idea with Hebraism is conduct and obedience. Energy driving at practise is not lacking in the English people, but the intelligence driving at those ideas which are, after all, the basis of right practise is wofully absent among them." Thus has Matthew Arnold developed Heine's suggestion and carried it much farther than his German original did or intended to do, and in the elaboration of it has evinced much of that very prejudice, narrowness of view, and mental and literary dogmatism which he considers essentially Hebraic in origin and type. One queries, at the outset, by what right Mr. Arnold is empowered to attribute the monopoly of "intelligence and gentleness and sincerity of thought" to the Hellenic race; to insist that in Hellenism alone one sees things really as they are. With equal surprise the question may be raised why to Hellenism itself there should not be credited, to some extent, that gravity of character and practical energy which the English critic attributes to Hebraism only. It is strange enough that an accomplished Greek scholar could rise from the reading of the great Greek epics and tragedies and underrate that essential seriousness of narrative and scene which is inseparably connected with the highest Greek poetry. Despite all inconsistency, however, the contrast has become historic and pervades the content of modern English criticism. Literature, Mr. Arnold teaches us, is Hebraic in its type or it is Hellenic. Emphasizing, therefore, the specific sense which the great English essayist attached to these respective terms, it is in place to mark, first of all, the Distinguishing Features of Hebraism and Hellenism in literature as thus interpreted, so as to secure a correct understanding of the theory in question. In the one, Character, we are told, is the dominant idea; in the other, Culture. In the one, "strictness of conscience" is the phrase; in the other, "spontaneity of consciousness." In the one, we hear of "Energy"; in the other, of "Intelligence." So, on the one hand, are such terms as—Feeling, Force, Conduct and Gravity; on the other, Thought, Art, Grace, Aspiration and Cheerfulness. The one is theological and biblical; the other, classical and secular, and, indeed, as Mr. Arnold would urge, the one is uninteresting and undesirable, while the other is attractive and inspiring. These are some of the contrasts of the English author's favorite theory on which he sounds the note unceasingly, nor does he allow us to forget that the Hebraic element in literature is out of good form among the literary elite, the property of the Philistines, a literary cult out of which an ambitious student should seduously educate himself by sitting at the feet of the Grecian oracles to learn what wisdom really is. Hence it is that in such works as "God and the Bible," "Saint Paul and Protestantism," this anti-Hebraic bias is kept prominent, as it is, also, in such treatises as "Literature and Dogma," and "Last Essays on the Church and Religion." The American Poe held a somewhat similar theory in what he called, "The Heresy of the Didactic," insisting that poetry, as such, had nothing whatever to do with duty or truth. Truth, he insisted, belongs to the intellect; duty, to the conscience; and beauty, to the taste; the only difference between Arnold and Poe being that the British critic applied his principle to all departments of authorship. It requires but a cursory examination of this theory of literature to discover that it is superficial and untenable, representing but one side of a very important and many-sided question and shutting the student up to an alternative to which he should not be confined. It is the central imperfection of Arnold's work as a critic that he has thus insisted on an antithesis where none in reality exists, and has started many a question which it is as impossible to solve as it is useless to attempt to solve. Hence, we are forced to such an extreme inquiry as this—What is the final purpose of literature—character or culture; feeling or intelligence; action or art—a question as irrational as it is insoluble. The literary student is not to be placed in any such attitude, but may have a wider outlook and a broader theory. It is significant to note that in the study of Arnold's mind and method he had abundant opportunity to correct this one-sided view of letters, had he been so inclined. In England and America, some of his warmest admirers were not slow in exposing the error of his position and intimating to him the need of its substantial modification. Such suggestion, however, seemed but to deepen his hold upon his accepted views. Students of Arnold who have insisted upon his intellectual narrowness and bigotry have been justified, at this point, in their position. It did not seem, indeed, to lie within the scope of his ken as a thinker to rise above or break away from this restricted view of literature in which he had but little company. It was in the sphere of education only that he seemed to be free from this dogmatic temper and to display catholicity of reasoning.

The saner and broader view of literature combines the Hebraic and the Hellenic and insists upon their unity and interaction as fundamental, while in no sense failing to attribute to each element that which properly belongs thereto. The question, now, is not—the Hebraic or the Hellenic—the ethical or the esthetic. The only legitimate question is—How, in any given school, or style or period or writer each is present in vital form, as contributing to the same great end, the expression of the truth for the best effects. It is this fusion of the two types that the poet Keats, himself an accomplished Hellenist, has in mind when he says,—"Beauty is Truth and Truth is Beanty." Ruskin, an artist on principle and by profession, tells us, that "moral sublimity is essential to the appreciation of beauty." The high theory of Plato "that all beauty is mental or spiritual"; and of Leibnitz, "that beauty consists in perfection"; and of Hegel, "that it consists in character and expression," is in the same direction of this combination of the ethic and esthetic.

To the same effect a recent American critic writes—"There is no necessary connection between literature and righteousness, but literature does not lend itself to the service of evil as readily as other art forms, notably music and painting, do." This is the same as saying that there is no natural or necessary antagonism between good taste and good morals; that the best things should be current alike in Athens and Jerusalem, and that the author who attempts to divorce things that are accordant is unwise therein and goes far out of his way to confirm a preconceived opinion. It would be an interesting study to apply these principles within the domain of English Letters; to note how each of these factors, the Hebraic and the Hellenic, has had its ardent exponents, and how the fusion of the two has, also, had its equally ardent advocates. If we illustrate by a reference to the Schools of English Verse, we note the Oriental and the Greek. The one is biblical in its origin, development and aims, having in it a supernatural element and spirit, and might be included, as a study, among the Divinities. The other is pagan and secular, wherein the natural and earthly obtain, and is included among the Humanities. It is easy to see that the abuse of the Oriental might lead to mysticism, and that of the Greek to sensualism. Each of them seeks perfection; the perfection, however, respectively, of the soul and the taste, and between these two there is a "a great gulf fixed" by the extremists, and by them only.

If we illustrate by a reference to Periods, we are told that the first is the Puritan Era of English Letters, and the second, the Augustan; the eras, respectively, of conscience and taste; the former being regarded by the followers of Arnold as too Hebraic to be interesting. Taine is never weary of drawing this extreme antithesis and of insisting that this Puritanic type is far too pronounced in British authorship. He sees it in the influence of the great English Reformation on Elizabethan Letters; in the early history of the Romantic School when such sober-minded authors as Cowper and Coleridge conserved it; while far on in the Victorian Era he discovers its presence in the Brownings and the lamented Laureate. It is in writing of this Puritan period and type that he says—"No culture here, no philosophy, no sentiment of harmonious and pagan beauty. Conscience only spoke, and its restlessness had become a terror. They steeped themselves in texts of St. Paul, in the thundering menaces of the prophets. The external, natural man is abolished; only the inner and spiritual man survives," and he adds—"That was not a conception of life from which a genuine literature might be expected to issue. The idea of the beautiful is wanting, and what is a literature without it? The natural expression of the heart's emotions is prescribed and what is a literature without it? They abolished as impious the rich poesy which the Renaissance had brought them. They are without style and speak like business men. The Puritan destroys the artist and fetters the writer." This is simply the old fight between the Hebraist and the Hellenist, conducted in a partisan spirit and to effect a specific end on behalf of a one-sided theory. With Taine, as with Arnold and Poe, one-eyed criticism leads to obscure views of truth. Hence, the illustration which they give us of this extreme theory in specific English authors is here in place. First among the Hebraists, of course, and the greatest sinners of them all are Bunyan and Milton. "Strictly speaking," writes Taine, "the Puritans could have but one poet, an involuntary poet, a madman, a martyr, a hero, and a victim of grace; a genuine preacher who attains the beautiful by accident while pursuing the useful on principle. If he had, at ten years of age, a Puritan tutor, the world rejoices that, soon after, he enjoyed the tuition, at Saint Paul's school, of an accomplished classicist." He speaks of him as a "poet buried under a Puritan," the author of "the Protestant epic of damnation and grace, in spite of his Calvinistic dogmas and the vision of Saint John the Divine." Milton, he concedes, was a great poet but in spite of his Hebraic type, and only because of his study of Polite Letters at Cambridge and his familiarity with the classics. It is not a little amusing to see how Mr. Taine grapples with the problem of accounting for such Hebraism and such literary merit in the same personality. He solves the syllogism by begging the question. So, as to Bunyan, he admits, that, Puritan tho he was, he was a poet in prose, but "a poet because he was a child," innocent enough of all classical culture and ignorant enough of the wisdom of the world to be the appropriate subject of over-wrought imagination, credulity, hallucination and special supernatural influence, a child of nature and of grace, the author of a widely current literature in spite of the absence of all literary training, so that "under his simplicity you will find power, and in his personality the vision of sin and grace." From the same point of view, Addison and Cowper are too Hebraic as contrasted with such Hellenic authors as Keats and Landor and Shelley.

According to Arnold, such works as "The Pilgrim's Progress," "Paradise Lost," "The Task," and the Moral Essays of "The Spectator" might have been written in Palestine, but "Endymion," "The Hellenics,"

"The Essays of Elia," "Childe Harold" and "Queen Mab" create a fresher air and belong to the literature of life and modern thought. They are absolutely devoid of the Judaic type and have the genuinely Gentile cast of Attica and the Ægean. "Culture," writes Arnold, "has one great passion—the passion for sweetness and light." This passion, he contends, is mainly, if not wholly, Hellenic. Even so conservative and just a critic as Dowden speaks of Bunyan's great Allegory as "The Prose-Epic of English Hebraism." If, now, we seek for concrete illustrations of the better theory which represents these two types in combination and mutual interaction, the theory of Hebraism and Hellenism in fusion, there is no need that we sharply contrast the Oriental or Biblical School with the Classical or Pagan, or either of these with the Gothic or Northern type, as seen in "Beowulf," but there is need of emphasizing such a literary order as The Lake School of English Poets, marked alike by the Hebraic and the Hellenic, true to the best interests of English character and English culture, in the writings of whose best exponents we are reminded both of the English Church and the English University. It is with this in mind that Devey writes—"In the nineteenth century, the old schools have been found in connection with new combinations; the natural with the philosophic; the romantic with the realistic; the pagan with the Christian; the esthetic with the practical." In a word, types are fused, and the union is conducive to strength. On this better theory, no one would think of placing Keats and Scott, Browning and Tennyson in opposition, but would rather aim to show that as representative poets they all illustrate the fundamental principles of poetic art, and are, also, true to the deepest religious instincts of the race; Hebraic and Hellenic alike, even tho one type, in given cases, and for good reasons, may be more prominent than another. So, as to Periods, we are not obliged to set off the Puritan Age in sharpest contrast with the Augustan and seek to force a literary feud between them, but we are to emphasize the historic place and value of such an age as The Victorian, in which Hebraism and Hellenism alike are found conjoined, each element lending invaluable support to the other, and together effecting results impossible to either alone. The Elizabethan Age was alike the Hebraic Age of the great Protestant Reformation and the Hellenic Age of the Revival of Classical Learning, nor is it necessary for the civil or literary historian to seek to state which of these elements was predominant. It was largely the Golden Age that it was by reason of this cooperative action of types of thought and letters and life. Even in the non-Hebraic and sensuous age of the Restoration, John Milton, a Puritan of the Puritans, lived and wrote epics and lyrics so involving the Hebraic and Hellenic as to defy the keenest analyst to distinguish them. Throughout the Pagan Period of English Letters, a clearly defined line of the Hebraic is visible.

So, as to Authors and Writings, our attention is not now directed to poets and prose writers who represent an exclusive tendency either way, but to those who alike in personality and work represent this dual unity of conscience and culture, of feeling and intelligence, of reality and ideality. Nor have we far to go to find them, inasmuch as most of the greatest names of English Letters are found in this honored list, much of their greatness lying in this natural coordination of things that are accordant. These are Chaucer, Spenser, Coleridge and

De Quincey, Burke and Tennyson and Lowell and Emerson, it being as difficult as it is unnecessary to state which of these types predominates in their work, each of them seeking in his way the interests of truth and the highest ends of art and taste. Still further, and despite the objections of Arnold and the extremists, such representative names as Lamb and Ruskin belong with equal justice to this category, it being as unjust to confine Milton to the Hebraic order as Ruskin to the Hellenic. Strangely enough, there is a true sense in which even Arnold himself illustrates the error of his extreme position, and confirms the true view, his best writings being alike characterized by Hebraic sobriety and Hellenic taste. Certainly, no candid critic would underrate in his writings the presence of classical taste, of Hellenism in its finest form,—a feature which it was the ideal of his life to exhibit and without the acknowledgement of which his works can not be understood. Almost equally prominent, however, is his gravity, so that, by common consent, he has been included among the contemplative poets of England. It is a canon of style on which he insists, that authorship must have "moral fiber," that the flippant and frivolous are unliterary forms of prose and verse and, as such "have no place in literature." He earnestly pleads for the dominance of "intellectual seriousness" in authors, while the careful reader of his works must be impressed with the almost biblical sedateness with which he discusses his theories and pens his productions. So pronounced, indeed, is this Hebraic soberness that we see it pass, at times, from grave to graver forms, until, at length, it takes on a specifically despondent type. Professor Dowden, in his recent volume, "The Puritan and Anglican," thus correctly states it—"Tho Matthew Arnold said hard things of English Protestantism, the son of Thomas Arnold could not escape from an hereditary influence; the Hellenic tendency in his poetry is constantly checked and controlled by the Hebraic tendency." The same continuous influence is manifest in his prose. Were it not that he insists on being classified with the Hellenists only, we should include him in the wider circle.

So, as to Writings, we may cite "The Faerie Queen"; "The Ancient Mariner"; the Essays by De Quincey on "Cæsar" and "Machiavelli"; "The Excursion"; "The Lives of the English Poets"; "The Essay on the Sublime"; "The Ring and The Book"; "The Drama of Exile"; "In Memoriam"; "Evangeline"; "The Cathedral"; "The Scarlet Letter," and "Representative Men," as expressive alike of conscience and culture. Nothing is gained on behalf of either type by widening the distance between them.

If it be asked what is the present tendency in English Letters, we note, that it is toward the Hellenic, as compared with the preceding Georgian type. Stedman calls it,—"the more restrained, scholarly, analytic, artistic period," much of this tendency being due, we may add, to the commanding influence of the late Laureate.

Two or three suggestions of practical moment emerge from this discussion—

(*a*) The first is, that Hebraism and Hellenism must always be found in some substantive sense in every high literature. We need not agree as to the comparative measure of their presence, but that each must, in some well-understood sense, be present, sufficiently so to be influential in the literature. Authorship must have character and culture, conscience and taste. We might assert in biblical terms that every literature, however specifically national and individual, must have room for the Jew and Greek. Even a pagan literature, as the Greek itself, must be, to some degree, an ethical literature, even as the old literatures of the North, the Gothic and the Scandinavian, with all their ruggedness of form and expression, must have a degree of refinement to entitle them to the name, literature. So, every author, whatever his dominant type, must be both Hebraic and Hellenic. "If Hellenism served to broaden, Hebraism served to deepen the national consciousness of England," writes Dowden. This may be said of every literature and every author.

(*b*) Hebraism and Hellenism do not, however, express the sum-total of literature.—Herein Mr. Arnold is at fault, as also, not a few of his forerunners and followers. Character and Culture are not the whole of literature. Intellectual ability enters as a factor. Feeling other than that which is strictly religious or esthetic enters, as embraced in the wide compass of the emotions and passions. Even the Will is an active agent in the execution of motive, while the office work of the imagination is potent and pervasive. Here is a wide province uncovered by the Hebraic and the Hellenic, the province of human nature, in its totality, bordering closely on the confines of the infinite. Literature is far too wide a word for the limitations of the categories and must be used in its fullest meaning. Literature is not the expression of this or that type or school or ideal, but the expression of human thought and personality, of imagination and feeling and conscience and taste, the embodiment of the true and beautiful and good in concrete form, in terms intelligible and attractive to the general mind. There is great danger lest literature may become fractional, divided into types and orders, each with its own insignia, methods and ideals. Sectional literature may be other than geographical and external. Schools of Letters there may be and will be, but not necessarily factions and coteries, begetting divided interests and diverting the attention of authors from the great principles that underlie all literary work. Literature in the Augustan Age, was, at first, political and, then, partisan and, as such, threatened the life of contemporary letters. Even the phrase, Democratic Art and Letters, tho indicative of range, is still a local phrase, the motto of a class or sect. We are speaking far to freely of this or that Literary Cult, as if, for the time being, the current Cult embodied all the wisdom of the time. Hence, the need of Generalization and wider outlook, of the confederation of literatures as of languages and peoples, of the unification of the world's best authorship for common ends. Mr. Courthope has discussed for us, The Liberal Movement in English Letters, and, yet, he has in mind but one historic, national movement. There is a wider use of the term, liberal, and outside the pale of England, applied to what Posnett calls, The World Movement, as far-reaching as literature itself, the common and cooperative movement of the world's great authors toward fuller knowledge and freedom and culture and character, the "disinterested endeavor to learn and propagate the best that is known and thought in the world."

Attention was called, as we opened this discussion, to a volume entitled—"Social Ideals in English Letters," in which this cosmopolitan conception of letters is taken, of literature as a great social force. From the same gifted authoress we have a later volume—"The Life of

The Spirit in Modern English Letters," in which Literature is represented as neither Hebraic nor Hellenic but as the accepted medium for the revelation of the free spirit of man in any of the well nigh limitless forms in which that divinely implanted spirit may embody itself, Literature and Life, the Life of Man and of the Spirit in man. Hereby are the Divinities and the Humanities unified and the study of what we are wont to call Humane Letters is lifted at once to the level of the spiritual.

CHAPTER TWELVE

THE PLACE OF LITERATURE IN LIBERAL STUDIES

THIS is what Mr. Gladden would call one of "The Burning Questions" of the day, agitated, more or less earnestly, for the last two decades, but coming to special issue as the new century opens, an agitation which marks increasing interest both in literature and higher education, and in the practical relations that they sustain to each other. The discussion of what may be called, Educational Literature, or what has recently been called "the academic recognition of the study of literature" is before the educational and literary English Public of to-day as never before, a discussion especially germane to Higher Education and to those who are in process of collegiate training. If the special reasons for such increasing interest in this vital topic be sought, some of them, at least, are at hand. They are seen in a wide and decided revival of zeal in education itself; in the pronounced development of philological study to the possible detriment of purely literary study, and in the reopening of the old and ever new discussion of the comparative merits of the Humanities and the Sciences proper. In England, most especially, and at its university centers, this agitation has become intense and demonstrative, arousing both scholarly and popular interest, and bidding fair, even now, to revolutionize, in the British Empire, all educational conceptions hitherto held. Mr. Collins, in his volume, "A Plea for The Recognition and Organization at The Universities of the Study of (English) Literature" may be said to have reached the high water mark of this revived discussion, as he passionately pleads for more Humanism in Higher Education, against the theory of those who "would reserve the universities as nurseries for specialists and technical scholars" and thus materially impair, as he urges, the usefulness of the universities themselves and the great secondary schools of the country.

In determining, therefore, the specific Place which Literature, as such, should have in a Liberal Curriculum, some prior questions arise for settlement. One of these is as to Literature itself, what it is, what its educational value is, and what its final purpose and ideal. In Part First, Chapter Two, the definition of Literature is discussed. An additional word may here be given.

John Morley is peculiarly significant, as he says: "By Literature I assume you to mean, not merely words and form, but the contents of important writings in their relation to human thought and feeling and the leading facts of human life and society." So, another critic—"Literature is the intellectual product of cultivated nations," or as an American writer states it—"It is that part of recorded human thought which possesses or has possessed a more or less general and abiding human interest." In these deliverances it is noticeable that Literature is allied to all highly intellectual pursuits and made to contribute its share to the mental development of the race. If this be so, the question as to its disciplinary value is at once answered for us, its object being "the building up of the mind in habits of knowledge and thinking." "Ten years experience with the Cambridge University Extension," writes Professor Moulton, "has confirmed my impression that the subject matter of literature, its exposition and analysis from the sides of science, history and art is as good an educational discipline as it is valuable in quickening literary appreciation." It is this higher view of literature that President Eliot is so constantly urging. Literature is thus an educational subject and not a mere avocation for hours of leisure and men of leisure. It is a strictly mental gymnastic for hours of thought and men who think. So as to its final purpose. This is not instruction or information merely, but inspiration, also, a real mental quickening as the great authors of the world come under review.

It is with this in mind that Mr. Balfour recently said at Cambridge—"All education which is not in part, and in considerable part, a literary education is necessarily one-sided" and he adds, "An education which does not make the person educated at home in some great imaginative literature and which does not put him in sympathy with the great literary arsists and thinkers of the past is an education which must leave undeveloped some of the finer sympathies." So, among these Prior Questions, we must ask, as to Liberal Training—What is it, its province and purpose, and what are the best methods by which its legitimate results may best be realized? Here, again, there need be no serious doubt, in that Liberal Education in its very ideal is comprehensive, affecting every faculty of the mental man and including in its range every worthy subject. Literature thus finds its normal place in any scheme of study called, Liberal, its province being as wide as that of any other related subject, its ultimate purpose as high, and the methods of its exposition as varied and effective. It being, therefore, conceeded that Literature should have a place in Liberal Education, the question assumes more definite form and it is asked—What Place—how ample and important; and we answer in the words of President Eliot, relative to English studies—"A place of equal academic value with any subject now most honored." This demand, it will be marked, is not absolute but relative, not for supremacy but equality, as Literature stands related to the other departments of a collegiate curriculum. In that "Renovated Curriculum" of which Professor Bain has spoken, Literature is to be placed at the front, in line with the Sciences and the Philosophies and, thus, in line with all the best conditions of modern educational progress. This is the purpose of the modern literary movement in Great Britain, the healthful influence of which we are already feeling, this side the sea, a movement that has gone too far to be reversed or successfully checked. The notable support which it has received from men of eminence in all departments is itself a sufficient guarantee of its high character and ultimate success.

Mr. Collins has collated such a consensus, the special occasion of his appeal being the increasing need that was felt for an immediate enlargement of the English literary work at Oxford and Cambridge. As we are told—"Almost every eminent authority in education and literature in England" was asked to expresss his unbiased views on the proposition submitted. The proposition in its full form, includes three related suggestions.

(*a*) That systematic instruction in English Literature should be given at the Universities.

(*b*) That English Literary Instruction proper should be discriminated from purely English philological instruction.

(*c*) That the study of Ancient or Classical Literature should receive the place and attention that it inherently deserves in connection with the study of the vernacular itself.

This was the General Proposition, and these the Subordinate Suggestions submitted, as a Plea for Literature. Inasmuch as the authorities adduced were not only authors who might be supposed to have a prejudiced interest, but bishops and justices and statesmen and scientists and, even, men of affairs, the subject is at once lifted from the plane of special pleading or limited academic area to the higher plane of general interest, touching human knowledge on all its sides, and bringing literature into line with every worthy branch of intellectual inquiry. Hence, the practical question arises—How is such a place of equality to be secured? Manifestly, at the outset, there is involved, a readjustment of existing Collegiate Courses, such a modification necessitating the substantive reduction of some established non-literary courses. At this point, the proposition resolves itself into one of educational time and place. Speaking in terms of the modern industrial exposition, the first thing needed is sufficient floor-room for the proposed literary exhibit, an actual standing place for the exhibitor. Down to a very recent date, the area has been a limited one, the space devoted to related studies compassing nearly all the allotted educational room. In the expansion of the modern curriculum the claims of the sciences and philosophies; of art and history and jurisprudence and philology have been pressed and conceded. In the decided sociological trend, the Humanities have had a strenuous struggle for existence. Literature has been so held in abeyance by classical educators to the study of linguistics, that it has been sacrificed in the house of its friends. Not until recently has Literature been given a fair hearing before the bar of Higher Education.

Whether, in the ever more intense rivalry of studies in modern education, Literature shall secure its rightful place, the future only will reveal. In the meantime, the duty of the literary advocate is a plain one, to urge the claims of literary studies to equality with "any subject now most honored."

It may be further noted, that such Equality of Place would involve the more Systematic and Thorough Teaching of Literature, the fact being that it has hitherto been taught superficially, pedagogically, rather than rationally, as an exalted pursuit both for educator and pupil.

One of the main reasons why Humanism has not been holding its historic place and has been so subjected to contesting interests is that the method of the teaching has been erroneous. If, as Collins properly states it, Literature is to be wrongly regarded as one of the lighter subjects for the leisure hours of the drawing-room, and not a mental pursuit for thinking men in their best mental moods, then it is not surprising that it has been left unchallenged on the lower planes of educational work. When properly understood and approached, however, it will be seen to be instinct with life, coordinated with all that is best, and its exposition will be a valid and an effective one.

The literary pedant emphasizing names and dates and the minutest matters of an author's life and work is one type; the literary guide and master, bringing to light great generic principles in literature and illustrating its relation to all high forms of mental discipline is quite another type and the only worthy one. As contrasting these two methods of teaching literature, the pedantic and the philosophic, Mr. Collins has been at pains to summarize a list of questions such as these respective examiners would use, in order to show the immense superiority of the latter.

In the way of specific indication as to how such instruction might be made more systematic, ardent advocates of literary training are contending for the general founding of Schools of Literature, as such a School exists in the University of Virginia, by the agency of which literary instruction might be duly emphasized; placed on a par with Schools of Science, Philosophy and Language; organized under one Faculty of Letters, sovereign in its own domain, jealous of all intrusion, and responsible before the educational public for what it does and fails to do. One of the valid benefits of such a School is seen in that it would attract to it more of the brighter minds among the undergraduates, one of the factors determining the choice of students being the completeness of the organization of a department and the facilities it offers for the best results. Especially would such an organization appeal to those who were looking to Literature as a profession, as authors or educators.

Difference of opinion might be held as to the proper adjustment in such a School of the various studies embraced in Literature—prose and poetry; theory and praxis; history and criticism; of the vernacular literature as related to foreign product, and of language itself as involved in literary study. Whatever their adjustment, they would not vitally affect the issue involved.

A further benefit would accrue in that such a School of Letters would serve to solve many a troublesome question by the increasing unification of studies hitherto conflicting,—such as literature and language, the classical and the continental tongues, as related to each other or to the English. By the proposed Readjustment, Language is assigned to its legitimate area, as Literature is to its area. The linguistic rivalry of ancient and modern literature, or of classical and English Literature, would be largely abated by diverting the discussion to literary channels where each of the great literatures is given its appropriate place and made to contribute to the better interpretation of literature itself. New life would at once be infused, both into classical and modern study, as well as into that of English Literature proper, and the student be enabled to pursue his researches freed from those traditional judgments which have so long served to impede the way of the scholar in letters and make it impossible for him to exhibit anything like catholicity of reasoning. Differences of detail would, of course, arise, as to whether per chance, the Greek or the Latin Literature, the French or the German, should receive the emphasis. Such differences, however, would be slight as compared with the existing confusion.

An additional benefit connected with such an assignment of Literature to academic equality appears in that it would give to Literature for the first time an open field for its best expression. Hitherto, it has been, as a collegiate study, underestimated; largely because the opportunity has not been given it to assert its inherent vitality; to compass its proper province; and to show what it can do in the line of the intellectual quickening of those who properly pursue it. It has sometimes seemed feasible to establish in our Institutions of Learning a Literary Laboratory, a place for literary experiment, observation and result, where teachers and pupils might meet for joint activity, where the actual literary processes might be seen and appreciated, as physical processes are studied in a chemical laboratory. The developing Seminary Work of our Modern Universities is a step in this direction, as is the Preceptorial Method recently instituted at Princeton. In such an environment, manifold questions of interest would arise. The personal difficulties of the pupil would be stated and settled and his interest intelligently guided. In such a literary work-shop, Literature would justify itself, as never before, as a vital educational factor.

From this discussion of the claims of Literature some suggestions of practical interest arise—First, as to the Literary Outlook. It is clear to every careful observer of the signs of the times in educational matters that literary studies are now eliciting an interest more intelligent and intense than at any previous period. Nor is this interest purely professional, but deep-seated and widespread, engaging the attention of the great educational public, and thus of right expected to express itself in safe and permanent forms. The increasing number of liberally educated men now identifying themselves with one form or another of journalistic work is a healthful sign of interaction between our colleges and the more practical side of literary life and work. If we inquire as to these elements of Promise, they are not far to find. One of them is seen, in the new and better status of Literary Study in our Secondary Schools, whereby a close affinity is established between collegiate and pre-collegiate literary instruction, the latter thus preparing the way for the former and unifying all literary courses. Heretofore, no such nexus has been apparent. Each grade of institution, lower and higher, has acted independently of the other, and the results have been correspondingly evil. Through this closer relationship, the colleges and schools will engage in the same great work on common methods and with common interests.

A further element of promise is seen in The Presence of Higher Literary Ideals, especially in bringing students in process of liberal training more and more into direct contact with the best authors, so as to make them thoroughly conversant with their writings and personality and their most intense literary spirit. Above all the theories of the schools and all courses in literary criticism, literature itself as a visible product will be examined by the student on independent grounds. Authors will be studied as far more important than any facts or data relating to them. It is in this way, and this way only, that the right approach to literature is made and its most beneficent recompense secured.

A second suggestion relates to The Existing Needs in Literary Study, in our colleges. One of these is an Enlargement of Literary Courses. While in a few of our colleges and universities these courses are substantially ample, the most of them are herein deficient. Thus, a further need arises as to the Teaching Force, so lamentably meager in most institutions, the literary faculties comparing, most unfavorably, with the philosophic, economic and historical. Those devoted to strictly philological teaching are far more numerous. A further Need is in the line of Library Facilities, whereby the literary student shall have free access to the world's best literature, and, if possible, under the intelligent guidance of an accredited bibliographer, competent to counsel students as to the choice and use of books. Literature is a study of books, a specifically library department, in the pursuit of which the largest possible facilities should be offered for the consulting of authors and for research. It is preeminently a Reading Course, by which, as Bacon suggests, one becomes a "full man." The awakened interest in the establishment of Libraries is a most encouraging feature of modern times. Men of wealth are contributing in this direction as never before. Governments are devoting revenue thereto, while our higher institutions are quicker than ever to make these bibliographical needs known to the public.

A further suggestion arises as To the Place of Literature in Schools of Science, in Technical and Professional Schools, one of whose leading features is, that they have little to do with the Humanities, and are thus non-literary. The old discussion as to the relative importance of Words and Things is here revived, and partly settled by the way of mutual concession. Schools of Letters and of Science are often established on the same ground, by the same benefactions and with the idea of reciprocal interests. In a few of our colleges, many of the courses in each of these Schools are open to members of each. Tho Literature is untechnical and, to this degree, non-scientific, there is a tendency to lessen the distance between these two sections of educational work, in order that Science may be liberalized and Literature enriched. Students of Humanism need some scientific instruction, while students of nature are also in need of the culturing courses. It may thus be urged that while Literature as a Liberal Study should find some place in technical instruction, such place should be manifestly limited and subordinate, just enough indeed to secure the cultivation and expression of good taste.

A final suggestion has reference to The Place of English Literature in English Institutions. Collin's plea for the study of Literature is, first and last, a plea for English, occasioned by the conspicuous absence hitherto of English studies at Oxford and Cambridge, and the sacrifice of Literature to Linguistics. He shows how such a study is to be applied; explains existing failure, and refutes the current idea that English Literature is to be read only and can not be taught as an educational subject. To this end, he adduces the opinion of Huxley, Cardinal Manning, Jowett, Farrar, Craik, Pater, Gladstone, Matthew Arnold and others.

Such a plea has force, this side the ocean, in that till recently English has been held in abeyance, so that the average student has known foreign literature, classical and continental, better than his own, and has been able to do almost anything else better than to use his vernacular with correctness and cogency. No department of collegiate work has so suffered at the hands of novices, even tho it is true, in the words of President Eliot, "that there is no subject in which competent guidance and systematic instruction are of greater value." If we inquire, therefore, as to its Rightful Place, we answer, as with regard to Literature in general, that it should have "equal academic value with any subject now most honored," equal as to the time allotted it, as to the facilities afforded it, as to the character of the instruction given, and the academic honors assigned it. Such a claim is eminently reasonable in the light of what our English Literature is in its scope and quality, and because we are living in an era when the vernacular is in evidence as never before. General literary culture, strange to say, and even special classical culture, strange to say, is too often found where a decided English culture is lacking. English literary culture must have the home flavor and savor. Every English educational center should be instinct with English literary life and its influence be quickening and chastening.

Hence—a closing question—What are our American Liberal Institutions doing for English Literature in America? We are told that our Literature is declining; that the heroic age of our Letters is in the past; that our literary product is still provincial; and that, in the main, it is confined to fiction and poetry and the lighter miscellany; that it is too journalistic. These reflections are worth heeding. It is answered by those heeding them that the mission of America is industrial, and that the nation is too young as yet to compete with the older peoples; too young, indeed, for a national literature. The difficulty lies deeper and, in part, at least, in the want of a more decided literary spirit and training in our Schools and Colleges. Students are not kept long enough in contact with the inner life of English Letters to take in something of that spirit that pervades them. It is not too much to say that in every graduating class there should be a goodly number of English literary specialists, men who would be willing to survey, at least, the literary outlook in America, and make the attempt to do something in the sphere of national authorship.

Motley, Prescott, Everett and Ticknor, at Harvard; Hawthorne and Longfellow, at Bowdoin; Willis, at Yale; and Bryant, at Williams, may be said to have opened their literary careers in college and to have graduated, in a sense, as American authors, bent on literary work, and who, in the early years of their graduate life, set the form for all later effort and opened the way for the

Golden Age of our authorship. Literary culture should be more and more a scholarly culture, as scholarship should be, more and more, inspired with a literary spirit.

Thus will scholarship and literature alike commend themselves to the intelligent world at large and the unity and catholicity of liberal studies be evinced.

Men of Letters and Men of Learning should labor together on common ground and for common interests

BIBLIOGRAPHY

(General Discussions)

Arnold's American Addresses (Literature and Science).
Arnold's Culture and Anarchy.
Arnold's Essays in Criticism (Literary Influence of Academies).
Azarius' Philosophy of Literature.
Bacon's Essays. (Studies.)
Bagehot's Literary Studies.
Bascom's Philosophy of English Literature.
Begg's Development of Taste.
Beers' English Romanticism in the Eighteenth Century.
Birrell's Obiter Dicta (I, II).
Brooke's Early English Literature.
Carlyle's Essays and Reviews.
Collins' Study of English Literature.
Cook's English Prose and English Bible.
Cooke's Poets and Problems.
Coppee's English Literature.
Corson's Aims of Literary Study.
Corson's Primer of English Verse.
Corson's Introduction to Shakespeare.
Corson's Introduction to Browning.
Courthope's Liberal Movement in English Literature.
Courthope's Life in Poetry.
Crashaw's Interpretation of Literature.
Crashaw's Literary Interpretation of Life.
Crawford's The Novel—What It Is?
Cross' Development of the English Novel.
De Quincey's Essays. (Rhetoric and Style.)
Devey's Modern English Poets (chapters 1–6).
Dowden's Transcripts and Studies.
Dowden's Studies in Literature.

Dowden's English Literature and The French Revolution.
Dunlop's History of Fiction.
Earle's English Prose (chapters 10–13).
Ellis' The New Spirit.
Emerson's Essays. (Sovereignty of Ethics, Literature, Culture.)
Everett's Poetry, Comedy and Duty.
Gayley's Literary Criticism.
Gummere's Old English Ballads.
Gummere's Handbook of Poetics.
Gummere's Beginnings of Poetry.
Hallam's Literary History.
Harrison's Choice of Books.
Hugo's Literature and Philosophy.
Hunt's Studies in Literature and Style.
Huxley's Science and Culture.
Jusserand's English Novel in time of Shakespeare.
Kerr's Epic and Romance.
Knight's Studies in Philosophy and Literature.
Lamb's Essays in Literature.
Lanier's English Novel
Lewes' Principles of Success in Literature.
Locke's Essay on Human Understanding.
Lowell's Essays. (Books and Libraries, Harvard Anniversary Address.)
Mabie's Essays on Literary Interpretation.
Mabie's Studies in Literature.
Maurice's Friendship of Books,
Morley's (H.) Illustrations of English Religion.
Morley's (J.) Studies in Literature.
Moulton's Shakespeare as a Dramatic Artist.
Morris' Art and Socialism.
Müller's Science of Thought.
Newman's Idea of a University.
Phelp's English Romantic Movement.
Phelp's (Austin) Men and Books.
Possnett's Comparative Literature.
Raleigh's English Novel.
Raymond's Poetry as a Representative Art.

Richardson's American Literature.
Saintsbury's English Prose Specimens (Introduction).
Saintsbury's The Flourishing of Allegory.
Saintsbury's History of Literary Criticism.
Sanford's Rise and Progress of Literature.
Santayana's Poetry and Religion.
Schlegel's Dramatic Literature.
Schiller's Æsthetic Letters.
Schopenhauer's Art of Literature.
Scudder's Social Ideals in English Letters.
Scudder's Life of the Spirit in Modern English Letters.
Selkirk's Ethics and Æsthetics of Modern Poetry.
Shairp's Culture and Religion.
Shairp's Poetry and Philosophy.
Shairp's Aspects of Poetry.
Shairp's Poetic Interpretation of Nature.
Shepherd's Authors and Authorship.
Sherman's Analytics of Literature.
Sismondi's Literature of Europe.
Spencer's Philosophy of Style.
Spingarn's Literary Criticism of the Renaissance.
Stanley's Essays on Literary Art.
Stedman's Nature of Poetry.
Stephens' Hours in a Library.
Stephens' History of English Thought in the Eighteenth Century.
Stoddard's Evolution of the English Novel.
Taine's English Literature.
Taylor's Studies in German Literature.
Thompson's Ethics of Literature.
Tuckerman's Prose Fiction.
Vinet's Outlines of Philosophy and Literature.
Ward's History of the English Drama.
Warner's Literature and Life.
Whipple's Literature and Life.
Wilson's Theology of Modern Literature.
Winchester's Principles of Literary Criticism.
Worsfold's Principles of Criticism.

INDEX

Academic prose, 255.
Aims of literary reading, 203.
Alfred, King, 217, 219.
Allegorical epic, 267.
American literature, 153.
American men of letters, 36.
Arcadia, 321.
Aristotle, 255.
Arnold, Edwin, 83.
Arnold, Matthew, 9, 22, 28, 29, 232, 234, 239.
Art epic, 269.
Artistic method and spirit, 177.
Aryan, 143.
Attic drama, 226.
Authors and statesmen, 87.
  first and second orders, 48.
  undergraduate, 393.
  uneducated, 171.
Authorship and scholarship, 171.
  average, 10.
  expression of thought, 26.
  literary or not, 30, 31.
  ideal, impassioned, untechnical, 25.
  written, 24.
Autobiography, 248.

Bacon, 26, 32, 78.
Bacon on studies, 204.
Balfour, 383
Ballads, epic, 269, 275.
Bascom, 3, 23.
Beauty, theories of, 289.
Beowulf, 13, 221.
Berkeley, 78.
Bibliography, critical, 123.
Biographies, literary, political, 94, 210.
Biography, 248.
Books, disciplinary, 210.
  helpful and wholesome, 212.
Brooke, 21.
Browning, Mrs., 241.
Bryant, 241.
Buckle, 249.
Burke, 26, 32.
Byron, 169.

Caedmon, 13.
Canterbury tales, 224, 240.
Caprice, 13.
Carlyle, 219.
Catholicity of view, 11.
Celtic literature, 78.
Chaucer, 47, 221, 228, 240, 244.
Chronicles, old English, 217, 221.
Civic questions discussed, 36.
Clarendon press series, 38.
Classical teaching, 117.
Clerical authors, 161.
Clough, 158, 166.
Coleridge, 41, 53.
Collins, 107, 381, 384.
Commercialism in literature, 153.
Complexity, 12.
Composition, poetic, 314.
Conservatism in literature, 214.
Constructive criticism, 128.
Courses, library, 390.
Courthope, 139, 141, 214, 281.
Courtly epic, 209.
Cousin, on taste, 288.
Craik, 38.
Crawford, 319, 323, 324.
Criticism, esthetic, 133.
  historical, 132.
  literary, 135.
  philosophic, 134.
  textual, 133.

Dante, 187.
Decadence in literature, 227,

Definition of literature, 30.
consequent suggestion, 30.
facts included, 24.
history of opinion, 26.
statement of, 24.
suggestions, 23.
Development in literature. 225.
Devey on poetry, 230.
Dialect poetry, 203.
Disciplinary literature, 119, 120.
Diversity of literary forms, 32.
Dogmatism, 13.
Dowden, 3, 239.
Drama and stage, 340.
and novel, 342.
as interpreting life. 150.
Drummond, 64.

Edinburgh review, 260.
Education and literature, 175.
Eliot, President, 383.
Elton, 8.
Emerson, 28, 184.
England and the continent, 441.
English literature in America, 393.
English men of letters series, 36.
English, old, modern, etc., 214.
Environment and literature, 144.
of authors and statesmen, 86.
Epics, medieval, 8.
Epoch and literature, 145.
Esthetics, 313.
Ethics and history, 159.
and fiction, 159, 160.
and poetry, 159, 160, 161.
Euphues, 321.
Exceptions, law of, 13.

Feeling in Poetry, 287.
Fiction as interpreting life, 149.
historical, etc., 325.
First English, 42.
Folk-epic, 269–272.
lore, 8.
Formalism, 179.
Forms, literary, 213.
general and special, 215.
Freeman's Norman conquest, 206.
French school of letter, 115.

Generalization in literature, 345.
German literature, 214.
school of letters, 114.
Gibbon, 47, 237.
Goethe in poetry, 231.
Greek literature and philosophy, 73.
Guiding principles of literature, 3.
absence of pre-judgments, 14.
constructive criticism, 16.
genuine contrasts, 9.
importance of beginnings, 6.
inner spirit, 17.
proper point of view, 4.
the primary and secondary, 6.
the unknown quantity, 11.
Guizot, 249.
Gummere, 281.

Hallam, 21.
Hebraism and hellenism in literature, 367.
statement of Arnold's view, 367, 369.
examination of his theory, 369, 370.
correct view, 370..
illustrations of it, 379.
Hegelian philosophy, 74.
Historical prose, 247.
History and literature, 140, 141, 142.
History, political, 88.
Hobbes on books, 204.
Hooker, 26, 32.
Hudibras, 219.
Hudson, 38.
Humanism, 386.
Hume. 47, 76, 247.
Huxley, 3, 22, 65.

Idealism in fiction, 321.
Imagination in poetry, 284, 285.
scientific, 61, 77.
Influence of France in English literature, 44.
of Germany in English literature, 44.
of Italy in English literature, 44.
Intellectual verse, 237.
Institutions, literary, 176.
Irving, Henry, 340.

Jebb, 22.
Journalism, 260.
  and literature, 175.
Jusserand on his novel, 321.

Language and literature, 106.
Lanier's theory of fiction, 219.
Leckey's European morals, 206, 251.
Leibnitz, 74, 76.
Lessing, 299.
Lewes, 3.
Liberal professions and literature, 169.
Liberal studies and literature, 381.
Library, functions of, 205.
Linguistic criticism, 111.
  study, 107, 108.
Literature, definition of, 20.
  guiding principles of, 3.
  methods of study, 36.
  scope of, 52.
Literature and arts, 168.
  classification of arts, 168.
  fine arts, 176.
  liberal arts, 168.
Literature and criticism, 127.
  definition of criticism, 127.
  methods of criticism, 132.
  primary purpose of, 131.
  results of, 135.
  species of, 126.
  suggestions, 138.
Literature and ethics, 156.
  history of opinion, Selkirk, etc., 156.
  illustration of relation, 159.
  influence of unbelief, 164.
  ultra moralism, 161.
Literature and language, 106.
  a natural relation, 107.
  dangerous extreme, 111.
Literature and life, 139.
  illustrative literary forms, 149.
  Taine's theory, 143.
Literature and philosophy, 69.
  mutual interaction, 73.
  presence of imagination, 76.
  philosophic method, 72.
  use of terms, 69.
Literature and politics, 85.
  reasons of relation, 86.
  specific forms, 88.
Literature and science, 56.
  scientific forms, 59.
  scientific material, 60.
  scientific method, 58.
Lowell on libraries, 210, 211.
Lyric verse, 356.

Macaulay, 287.
Macready, 343.
Manuals, literary, 112.
Masson, 48.
Medievalism, 231.
Melodrama, 341.
Metaphysical school, 82.
Methods of literary study, 36.
  comparative, 43.
  historical, 46.
  impartial, 48.
  literary, 37.
  logical, 41.
  suggestive, 39.
Middle English, 42.
Mill, 287.
Milton, meters of, 309-10.
Miracle plays, 221-222.
Miscellany, political, 75.
Mission of literature, 184.
  conception of great ideas, 186.
  interpretation of the age, 189.
  interpretation of human nature, 193.
  presentation of high ideals, 195.
Moore, 231.
Moralities, 221.
Morley, John, 382.
Moulton, 114.
Movements in literature, 214.
Mysteries, 221.
Mystical school, 82.

Napoleon, 52.
Newman, Cardinal, 59.
Novel, the ideal, 333.
  and drama, 342, 356.
  and romance, 325.
  development of English novel, 321.

Oration, as a written form, 353.
Oratorical prose, 252.
Orosius, 217,
Outlook in literature, 389.
    in poetry, 316.

Parochial literature, 161, 162.
Pater, 57.
Periods overlap, 42.
Personality in literature, 146.
Philology and literature, 106, 107, 115.
Philosophers, German and French, 86.
Philosophic spirit, 72.
Philosophy and literature, 69.
Piers the plowman, 148.
Pietism and Puritanism, 162.
Poetics, 300.
    diction, antique, figurative, 301, 302.
    structure, metrical, textual, verbal, 300, 303.
    terms, rhyme, rhythm, versification, etc., 305, 307.
Poetry, 206.
    affinities, 24.
    Characteristics, scope, rhythm, 271, 272.
    definition of, 238.
    essentials of, thought, etc., 282, 283.
    purpose of, 239.
    schools of, ethical, critical, etc., 231, 235.
    specific kinds of, 235.
    source of, 240.
    types of Oriental, Greek, etc., 230, 231.
    Uses of, pleasure, refinement, etc., 294, 297.
Points of view, one or more, 4.
    external and internal, 5.
Politics and literature, 85.
Politics defined, political poetry, 85, 100.
Possnett, 21, 23, 53, 64, 146.
Prejudices, literary, 14.
    inherited opinions, 15.
    undue estimate of vernacular, 14.
Prescott, 32.
Problems in criticism, 138.
Prose fiction, 219, 318.
    characteristics of, 325, 327.
    essentials to success, 329.
    forms of, critical, etc., 246.
    origin and purpose, 318, 319
    probable permanence, 333.
    types of, 325.
Prose writers as scholars, 169.

Questions, open, in literature, 335.
    generalization and specialization, 345.
    literary standards, 348.
    relations of drama and novel, 342.
    relation of drama to the stage, 340.
    relation of literature and style, 357.
    relation of literature as written and oral, 351.
    relation of prose and verse, 335.
    relative rank of epic and other verse, 338.
    the literary spirit, 360.

Race factors in literature, 143.
Raleigh, 217, 321.
Reading, literary, 203.
Realism, 10.
    in fiction, 322.
Realistic verse, 282.
Relations of literature, 56.
Renaissance, 227.
Results of literary criticism, 135.
    appreciation of literature, 135.
    education of taste, 136.
    enlargement of province, 136.
Revival of learning, 139, 227.
Romances, cycles of, 320.
    metrical, 268.
Romanticism, 10–11.
Romantic school of verse, 352, 282.

Saint-Beuve, 298.
Satire, 218.
    political, 101.
Schlegel, on drama, 221.
Science and literature, 56, 59, 361.
Scope of literature, 52.
Secrecy in literature, 12.

Shairp, 43.
Shakespeare, 38, 40, 228, 244.
Shelley, on verse, 218.
Sidney, on verse, 208, 217.
Skepticism in literature, 164–167.
Songs, 356.
Specialization in literature, 345.
Spencer, Herbert, 3.
Spirit, literary—elements, expression, etc., 361–365.
Stage and drama, 340.
Standards, literary, 348.
Stedman, 234.
Stephens, 83.
Stevenson, 267.
Study, literary, 209.
Style and literature, 357.
Subjective element in literature, 5.
Subject-matter, 10.
Sublimity, 62.

Tacitus, 266.
Tales, 322.
Taste in poetry, 288.
    cultivation of, 289.
    theories of, 288.
Teutonic literature, 213.
Tennyson, 9.
Thought and language, 357.
Tolstoi, 328.
Transcendental school, 82.
Transitions, 214.
Trouveres and Troubadours, 215.
Tyler's American literature, 216.
Tyler's Primitive Culture, 266.
Types of fiction, 325.

Unity of literary forms, 32.

Verse, 220, 235.
    epic, characteristics, etc., 265–9, 273–5.
    dramatic, 221–2. 338.
    lyric, rank, etc, 221–3.
Victorian age, 225.
Vinet, 22, 52, 64.

Webster, Daniel, 353.
Whitman, 7.
Worcester, 21.
World literature, 8, 197.
Writers, great, 323.

Zola, 328.